The Internet of Products

Robert Neumann

The Internet of Products

An Approach to Establishing Total Transparency in Electronic Markets

Robert Neumann
Magdeburg, Germany

Dissertation Otto-von-Guericke-Universität Magdeburg, 2012

ISBN 978-3-658-00904-5   ISBN 978-3-658-00905-2 (eBook)
DOI 10.1007/978-3-658-00905-2

The Deutsche Nationalbibliothek lists this publication in the Deutsche Nationalbibliografie; detailed bibliographic data are available in the Internet at http://dnb.d-nb.de.

Library of Congress Control Number: 2012953089

Springer Vieweg
© Springer Fachmedien Wiesbaden 2013

Printed on acid-free paper

Springer Vieweg is a brand of Springer DE.
Springer DE is part of Springer Science+Business Media.
www.springer-vieweg.de

Abstract

In April 2011, the European Commission in their Single Market Act announced that they would try to raise the percentage of inner-European, e-commerce-based trade from 3.4% to 6.8% until the year 2015. The rationale behind this plan is to foster a European electronic commerce infrastructure that enables enterprises to claim new markets and increase sales. At the same time, the EC hopes that their initiative would be the kick-off for an Information Systems-based European growth facilitator.

This thesis proposes the Internet of Products as a concept that aims to support the EC initiative from an information systems perspective. It approaches the difficult problem of providing Internet users with a completely transparent view of the inner-European market from a product information accessibility point of view. Furthermore, it analyzes economic, ecological, and societal gains of openly accessible product information in the form of theoretical models, and thereby underlines the EC's growth hypothesis. Though many aspects of very different research disciplines have to be investigated to gain a holistic view of the IoP, this thesis reduces the range of involved research topics to product information discoverability related questions.

When users employ online search engines for product search, the quality of the search results –to a vast extent– is determined by the product search engine itself. Among the list of insufficiencies of product search engines are potentially biased rankings (due to economic interests), a distorted view (due to weaknesses in search capabilities), as well as the inability to match queries and product descriptions among different languages and cultures.

This thesis introduces the concept of a Semantic Product Server (SPS) that aims to provide users with a highly effective tool for Internet-based product information discovery. The SPS is based upon a Semantic Product Description Language (S-PDL) that can be used to author attribute-based product descriptions. The product descriptions are hosted and interpreted by the SPS. The SPS, on the other hand, provides client applications with an interface to browse and search for particular goods, and –due to its integration into a wide network of SPS instances– allows suppliers for sharing their product descriptions among the world.

One of the major challenges of the SPS lies in ensuring real-time search performance. This thesis analyzes and provides insights from a reference application of the SPS, the so called ArbiterOne system. Based on measurement data that was collected from the ArbiterOne system, in its core this thesis engineers and shares an SPS reference architecture and a formal definition of the S-PDL.

Table of Contents

Acronyms

3BL	Triple Bottom Line
AOSE	Agent-oriented Software Engineering
B2B	Business to Business
B2C	Business to Consumer
BNF	Backus-Naur Form
BPD	Business Process Diagram
BPMN	Business Process Modeling Notation
C2C	Consumer to Consumer
CAD	Computer-aided Design
CAM	Computer-aided Manufacturing
CASE	Computer-aided Software Engineering
COTS	Commercials off the shelf
DNS	Domain Name System
EC	European Commission
HCSF	Hybrid Cloud Storage Framework
ICT	Internet and Communication Technology
IoP	Internet of Products
IoT	Internet of Things
IP	Internet Protocol
ISBSG	International Software Benchmarking Standards Group
ISO	International Organization for Standardization
JSON	JavaScript Object Notation
LSP	Logistics Service Provider
MSMEs	Micro, small, and medium enterprises

OASIS	Advanced Open Standards for the Information Society
OOSE	Object-oriented Software Engineering
OPC	Organic Product Catalog
OWL	Web Ontology Language
PBSE	Procedure-based Software Engineering
PD	Product Description
PNS	Product Name Server
QoS	Quality of Service
RDF	Resource Description Framework
S-PDL	Semantic Product Description Language
SOAP	Simple Object Access Protocol
SOSE	Service-oriented Software Engineering
SPQS	Semantic Product Query System
SPS	Semantic Product Server
STEP	Standard for the Exchange of Product Model Data
TCO	Total Cost of Ownership
TMSP	Technology-mediated Social Participation
UDDI	Universal Description, Discovery, and Integration
URI	Uniform Resource Identifier
URL	Uniform Resource Locator
W3C	World Wide Web Consortium
WSDL	Web Service Description Language
WWW	World Wide Web
XSD	XML Schema Definition
XML	Extensible Markup Language
YAML	Yet Another Markup Language

List of Figures

List of Tables

Listings

1 Introduction

"The Merchant has no country." (Thomas Jefferson)

1.1 Motivation

On April, 13th 2011, the European Commission (EC) launched an agenda to boost economic growth and strengthen confidence with respect to the inner-European trade in a document referred to as "Single Market Act – Working together to create new growth" [EC 2011]. The main goal of the Single Market Act is to increase the portion of electronic commerce measured by the totality of inner-European trade from 3.4% to 6.8% until the year 2015. Part of the agenda is to ease access to inner-European but international products and services on the internet, by establishing a single digital market ([EC 2011], pp.12-14).

The Single Market Act of the EC is driven by the perception that economic welfare correlates with economic growth. Inner-European economic growth can only be fostered, when parties from different countries are capable of doing business with another. To overcome lingual and cultural boundaries on a large scale, it requires information technology that radically changes the way Internet-based product search is conducted today.

This thesis elaborates upon the fundamental objectives of the Single Market Act and proposes a concept that is referred to as the "Internet of Products". The idea of having an Internet of Products is inspired by Kevin Ashton's "Internet of Things" [Ashton 2009], where objects (in this case product descriptions) are connected to the Internet and globally discoverable through a unique identifier. Another recent flavor of Ashton's vision is called the "Internet of Services", a THESEUS/BMWi research platform that allows for buying and consuming Internet services [url1]. The Internet of Products represents another but yet different kind of Ashton's Internet of Things that aims to provide an open information infrastructure that facilitates the retrieval of product information across cultural and lingual boundaries.

When product information is available in a language L and in a unit system U, then queries that were authored in a language L' and a unit system U' require automatic translation into L and U, in order to be able to perform a matching. If this process of matching does not occur completely transparently to the user and without any user involvement, users will struggle either with finding the products they are searching for or with obtaining a detailed-enough overview of the supply available in the market. As it will be shown throughout this thesis, especially the latter outcome is undesirable, since an increase in market transparency lowers transaction cost as well as the prices for goods.

In order for the EC to achieve the Single Market Act's goals, individuals and enterprises from different countries need to be able to discover and understand product descriptions that were originally authored in a different language and that are based on a different unit system. The Internet of Products provides a solution that is based on language- and culture-independent product descriptions. This implies that strings and units are automatically translated between product descriptions and product queries. Both language and culture independence are achieved through a special form of product data representation, the Semantic Product Description Language (S-PDL). Together with application logic that will be referred to as Semantic Product Server (SPS), the S-PDL represents the technological backbone of the Internet of Products. Hence, the Internet of Products implements a concept that aims to support the goals of the Single Market Act on a technological level.

1.2 Research Objectives

The development of an openly accessible Internet of Products is inspired by the Single Market Act's vision to ease transnational trade and thus boost inner-European economic growth. Since the Internet of Products is not only an information-technological challenge but as well touches economic, ecological, societal, infrastructural, and governmental topics, providing a holistic solution that covers every aspect is out of scope of this dissertation. Instead, this thesis attempts to provide a general motivation of the economic, ecological, and societal gains of a European openly accessible Internet of Products and accordingly derives requirements for the technological backbone, which the Internet of Products can be built upon. Based on the requirements, a technical solution is engineered and later implemented in the form of a number of application prototypes.

Due to the vision of the Internet of Products involving a variety of orthogonal aspects, this thesis covers four different academic disciplines that try to provide answers to the following questions:

▪ Economics & Electronic Markets:

▪ "What does the Internet of Products bring?"

▪ Semantic Web & Product Modeling:

▪ "Which technological problems have already been solved?"

▪ Distributed Systems Development:

▪ "How can the technology, which the Internet of Products is based upon, be engineered?"

▪ Software Quality & Measurement:

▪ "Which quality-related aspects exist that are of particular importance to the Internet of Products in order to gain wide acceptance?"

Research question that will be investigated throughout this thesis are [RQ1] – [RQ8]:

[RQ1] How can information technology help with increasing the transparency of markets and which effects does transparency have with respect to the macroeconomic situation of a nation or a society (chapter 2)?

[RQ2] How can the Internet of Products establish an information infrastructure that guarantees for openly accessible product information (chapter 2 and 3)?

[RQ3] Which impacts would openly accessible product information have in addition to macroeconomic benefits and which gains could the Internet of Products bring with respect to societal, ecological, and productivity-related factors (e.g., "The Triple Bottom Line (3BL)" (chapter 3)?

[RQ4] Which special technology is required for the Internet of Products to properly function and which product modeling approaches exist already (chapter 4)?

[RQ5] Which semantics are required from a product description in order for users to easily express their demand and for a computer to efficiently perform matching operations (chapter 5)?

[RQ6] How are product descriptions to be structured in order to be general enough to be applicable to every kind of good and yet contain enough structure to perform semantic search operations on them (chapter 5)?

[RQ7]   Which requirements exist with respect to a hosting environment for semantic product descriptions, which functional components would be involved, and how could this environment be deployed and distributed (chapter 6)?

[RQ8]   Which architectural and software quality-related aspects are of particular relevance to the hosting environment in order to be highly scalable and responsive (chapter 7)?

Questions that are not investigated but that might also be of particular interest with respect to the Internet of Products are:

[NQ1]   How can trust and reliability among suppliers and consumers from different countries be established in order to gain wide user acceptance and how does the current inner-European legal situation support this?

[NQ2]   Which new forms of logistics are required in order to guarantee for an agile logistics facility that allows for a timely delivery of goods (e.g., perishable goods) ordered from local suppliers (e.g., micro, small, and medium enterprises)?

[NQ3]   How could the Internet of Products help local micro, small, and medium businesses to increase their competitiveness as compared to large businesses and business chains, and how would this influence the economic infrastructure of urban areas and cities?

[NQ4]   What would be the Total Cost of Ownership (TCO) of a European Internet of Products and how could the cost be fairly distributed among its participants (e.g., multi-tenancy)?

[NQ5]   What is the average learning effort for suppliers in order to get accustomed with the technology of the Internet of Products and how does this influence the acceptance of the Internet of Products?

[NQ6]   Which ecological benefits does the Internet of Products bear in combination with an efficient logistics facility and how could savings in CO_2 emissions and petrol be quantified?

[NQ7]   How could artificial intelligence assist with monitoring, mining, and merging similar product descriptions of different suppliers to resolve ambiguity?

[NQ8] How can automated translation techniques be applied to provide product descriptions in a variety of languages, in order to increase market range and visibility?

Though the above eight questions ([NQ1] – [NQ8]) cannot be addressed throughout this thesis, they demand answers that might substantially influence future developments of the Internet of Products and its success. Albeit macroeconomic and technological aspects of the Internet of Products are covered, future work that –among others– investigates the above eight open questions is necessary, if not indispensable.

1.3 Chapter Overview

This thesis is divided into three parts and eight chapters. Every part represents a wrapper around a number of chapters that are logically related. Every chapter concludes with a chapter summary, which reviews the contents that were elaborated upon.

Part I covers the economics of electronic markets and the Internet of Products, and includes chapters two and three. It addresses the research question "What does the Internet of Products bring?" from an economics point of view.

Chapter two provides an introduction to the fundamental economics of electronic commerce and electronic markets. It covers which macroeconomic, microeconomic, and production-related principles exist and how they relate to market theory. Furthermore, it is discussed how electronic markets facilitate higher market transparency and hence provide for lower transaction cost. Transaction cost, on the other hand, is an important part of the price of a good. It is shown that if it was possible to further lower transaction cost through enhancements in Internet and Communication Technology (ICT), this would imply an increase in welfare.

Chapter three introduces the Internet of Products and distinguishes it from contemporary electronic markets. The elaborations in chapter three are based upon a category-theoretical market model that serves as foundation for revealing the potential for improvement of the Internet of Products. The prospective gains of the Internet of Products are captured through the three dimensions of the Triple Bottom Line (3BL), a public sector full cost accounting measure that was ratified by the United Nations and ICLEI TBL in 2007. Novel concepts of market coordination, such as Reverse Commerce/Total Commerce, and the results of a semantic product retrieval benchmark indicate that it would require a new form of product data representation that allows for highly detailed product search operations on the Internet.

Part II covers the technological foundations of the Internet of Products in form of a comprehensive literature review, and comprises chapter four. The theory that is covered in Part II is applied in chapters five and six, where the concepts of a Semantic Product Description (S-PDL) and a Semantic Product Server (SPS) are engineered from scratch.

Chapter four starts with an overview of the Semantic Web and Web 2.0 technologies, and analyzes structures for knowledge and data representation with respect to their suitability for forming the basis of the S-PDL. It is shown that due to their simplicity, taxonomies potentially provide for real-time query processing capabilities, while still being able to express any kind of product or service. Section two of chapter four reviews the state of the art of semantic product modeling and classification, and investigates to which extent existing technologies and concepts could be reused for the development of an S-PDL in chapter five. Section three addresses the basics of large-scale systems development, which will be of particular importance with respect to the design of a Semantic Product Server in chapter six. Section four covers software quality-related aspects that serve as a foundation for assuring that the SPS (in combination with the S-PDL) is capable of providing for real-time search performance.

Part III consists of chapters five and six and covers the design of the S-PDL and the implementation of the SPS.

Chapter five designs a model of an S-PDL that uses taxonomies. The model that is designed throughout this chapter is again based upon category theory. The development of the model is distinguished into multiple sections, where structure, internationalization, localization, automated matching, and dynamic behavior of product descriptions are detailed. The formal model is then translated into its Backus-Naur Form, which contains the syntactical rules of every document-oriented technology, which might potentially implement the S-PDL. A sample implementation of the S-PDL is provided as an XML Schema Definition (XSD).

Chapter six provides a concept for an SPS that serves as hosting environment for semantic product descriptions. In particular, a reference architecture of such a system that provides for real-time search performance is proposed. Furthermore, it is shown how the functors of the category-based model of the S-PDL seamlessly translate into functors in programming languages. The deployment of the SPS, either on premise or in the Cloud, is another aspect that is briefly reviewed throughout this chapter.

Chapter seven contains an overview of the prototypes that were developed based on the S-PDL and the SPS, and thereby discusses quality-related insights that were gained from software measurements with the goal to assure real-time search query processing and scalability.

Chapter eight concludes this thesis with a summary of the contributions that were made and an assessment of the solutions that were provided in correspondence with the initially stated research objectives.

1.4 A Word on Category Theory

The notion of functions is fundamental to most scientific disciplines, such as mathematics or science (including computer science). Functions express variability (e.g., the variation of a state of a system over time) [Walters 1991]. Category theory describes the "algebra of functions with composition being the main operation" ([Walters 1991], p. 1).

Categories are abstract structures that consist of a "collection of objects" and a "collection of arrows" between them ([Walters 1991], p. 1). The objects might, for example, be data types and the arrows might be programs ([Walters 1991], p. 1). In 1945, Eilenberg and Mac Lane published their original paper on "General theory of natural equivalences", in which the theory was first formulated ([Eilenberg 1945], p. 231). Since then, category theory had a great impact on major areas of mathematics (e.g., algebraic geometry, logic).

Walters summarizes three ways of how category theory is related to computer science ([Walters 1991], p. 1):

■ "An important aspect of computer science is the construction of functions out of a given set of simple functions, using various operations on functions like composition and repeated composition. Category theory is exactly the appropriate algebra for such constructions",

■ "Computing is concerned with machines –that is, dynamical systems, which have sets of states which vary over time. They are built up out of functions or elementary machines by an essentially algebraic process. Again underlying this is the theory of functions and composition",

■ "Sine category theory is an algebra of functions we can consider categories which are purely formal, and which don't really consist of functions. This is the syntactical side of computer science. Programs and languages are formal things which are intended to describe or specify actual functions. Category theory is well adapted to deal with the relation between syntax and semantics".

This thesis makes intensive use of category theory for the description of the contained formal models and software algorithms. Category theory was chosen, since one of its strengths lies in its capability to reveal how different kinds of structures are related to one another [Marquis 2011]. Many concepts elaborated upon within this thesis are orthogonal and yet category theory provides a unified and consistent way of describing and modeling these concepts. As will be shown later, the concept of functors, which is so representative for category theory, easily translates into functions or functional objects in software algorithms.

Last but not least, this thesis is based upon category theory since it represents "a revolutionary and infectiously attractive way of comprehending mathematics" ([Walters 1991], p. 1).

Part I:
Electronic Commerce and
the Internet of Products

Electronic commerce and in particular electronic markets –due to their character-istic of significantly reducing transaction cost– have facilitated welfare and eco-nomic growth.

The first part of this thesis consists of two chapters. Chapter two provides an overview of the economies of electronic markets and shows how an increase in market transparency causes an increase in economic welfare. Moreover, it ap-proaches the importance of electronic markets from a macroeconomic, microe-conomic, and production-oriented perspective.

Chapter three introduces the abstract concept of the Internet of Products and details how its targeted perfect transparency incorporates its major advantage over the current state of the art. Thereby, the benefits of the Internet of Products are described through a three-dimensional measure for public sector full cost accounting that is referred to as the Triple Bottom Line (3BL). The elaborations are based upon an integrated formal model that uses category theory for high-lighting the interrelations that exist between certain market components and the 3BL. New concepts of market coordination, such as Reverse Commerce/Total Commerce, as well as the results of a semantic product retrieval benchmark imply that it would require a new form of product data representation and pro-cessing, in order to overcome the limited transparency of today's electronic mar-kets and product search engines.

2 The Economics of E-Economies

"There are three stages of scientific discovery: first people deny it is true; then they deny it is important; finally they credit the wrong person." (Alexander von Humboldt)

2.1 Fundamentals

The Internet of Products aims to improve the discoverability of product information across lingual and cultural boundaries. This chapter lays the fundamental economic foundations of commerce in general and electronic commerce in particular. It is shown how electronic markets create value and which impact they have on the welfare of a society. The economic concept of welfare, thereby, plays an important role, as it serves as key metric and motivation for determining the economic outcomes of an openly accessible Internet of Products.

The terms and concepts are introduced in the form of so called Galleries; that is listings of substantial literature that assign every term or concept a definition and that were authored by distinguished international researchers.

2.1.1   Gallery of Economics

This section describes the fundamental economic basics of electronic markets, including their components, structures, and characteristics. A profound overview of relevant economic concepts is provided, which will later be used to argue for the need of an open exchange of product information in the Internet of Products. The introduced economic terms and concepts are distinguished into (general) macroeconomic, production and cost-related, and (market-specific) microeconomic (as (Samuelson's) Gallery of Economics):

Macroeconomics:

[EcoMac01]   "Economics is the study of how societies use scarce resources to produce valuable commodities and distribute them among different people" ([Samuelson 2005], p. 4),

[EcoMac02]   Macroeconomics "is concerned with the overall performance of the economy" ([Samuelson 2005], p. 5). "Macroeconomics is the study of the economy as a whole. The goal of macroeconomics is to explain the economic changes that affect many households, firms, and markets simultaneously" ([Mankiw 2011], p. 196),

[EcoMac03] "A modern economy depends upon special features to become highly productive. Specialization creates enormous efficiencies; overproduction makes trade possible; money allows trade to take place quickly and efficiently; and a sophisticated financial system is crucial for transforming some people's savings into other people's capital" ([Samuelson 2005], p. 35),

[EcoMac04] "Public goods are ones whose benefits are indivisibly spread among the entire community, whether or not individuals desire to purchase the public good. Private goods, by contrast, are ones that can be divided up and provided separately to different individuals, with no external benefits or costs to others. Efficient provision of public goods often requires government action, while private goods can be efficiently allocated by markets" ([Samuelson 2005], p. 370),

[EcoMac05] "Economic activity involves forgoing current consumption to increase our capital. Every time we invest –building a new factory or road, increasing the years of quality of education, or increasing the stock of useful technical knowledge– we are enhancing the future productivity of our economy and increasing future consumption" ([Samuelson 2005], p. 34),

[EcoMac06] "Economic growth involves the growth of potential output over the long run. The growth in output per capita is an important objective of government because it is associated with rising average real incomes and living standards" ([Samuelson 2005], p. 557),

[EcoMac07] "Modern theories of endogenous growth attempt to explain the rate of technology progress [...]. These models try to explain the decisions that determine the creation of knowledge through research and development" ([Mankiw 2007, p. 241),

[EcoMac08] "A nation has two major kinds of policies that can be used to pursue its macroeconomic goals –fiscal policy and monetary policy" ([Samuelson 2005], p. 413),

[EcoMac09] "Macroeconomic policies for stabilization and economic growth include fiscal policies (of taxing and spending) along with monetary policies (which affect interest rates and credit conditions)" ([Samuelson 2005], p. 40),

[EcoMac10] "An efficient system of fiscal federalism takes into account the way the benefits of public programs spill over political boundaries. The most efficient arrangement is to locate the tax and spending decisions so that the beneficiaries of programs pay the taxes can weigh the tradeoffs" ([Samuelson 2005], p. 325),

[EcoMac11] "The incidence of a tax denotes the impact of the tax on the incomes of producers and consumers. In general, the incidence depends upon the relative elasticities of demand and supply" ([Samuelson 2005], p. 77),

[EcoMac12] "Regulation consists of government rules or market incentives designed to control the price, sale, or production decisions of firms" ([Samuelson 2005], p. 342),

[EcoMac13] "The international economy is an intricate web of trading financial connections among countries. When the international economy system runs smoothly, it contributes to rapid economic growth; when trading systems break down, production and incomes suffer throughout the world. Countries therefore consider the impacts of trade policies and international financial policies on their domestic objectives of output, employment and price stability" ([Samuelson 2005], p. 414),

[EcoMac14] "The model of the large open economy makes a different assumption about international capital flows. To understand this assumption, keep in mind that the net capital outflow is the amount that domestic investors lend abroad minus the amount that foreign investors lend here" ([Mankiw 2007, p. 149),

[EcoMac15] "When countries concentrate on their areas of comparative advantage under free trade, each country is better off. Compared to a no-trade situation, workers in each region can obtain a larger quantity of consumer goods for the same amount of work when they specialize in their areas of comparative advantage and trade their own production for goods in which they have a relative disadvantage" ([Samuelson 2005], p. 297). "Trade between two countries can benefit both countries if each country exports the goods in which it has a comparative advantage" ([Krugman 2011], p. 56),

[EcoMac16] "The theory of real business cycles is an explanation of short-run economic fluctuations built on the assumptions of the classical model, including the classical dichotomy and the flexibility of wages and prices. According to this theory, economic fluctuations are the neutral and efficient response of the economy to changing economic circumstances, especially changes in technology" ([Mankiw 2007], p. 545),

[EcoMac17] "Business fluctuations in output, employments, and prices are often caused by shifts in aggregate demand. These occur as consumers, businesses, or governments change total spending relative to the economy's productive capacity. When these shifts in aggregate demand lead to sharp business downturns, the economy suffers recession or even depression. A sharp upturn in economic activity can lead to inflation" ([Samuelson 2005], p. 471),

[EcoMac18] "Technological change –which increases output produced for a given bundle of inputs– is a crucial ingredient in the growth of nations. The new growth theory seeks to uncover the processes which generate technological change. This approach emphasizes that technological change is an output that is subject to severe market failures because technology is a public good that is expensive to produce but cheap to reproduce. Governments increasingly seek to provide strong intellectual property rights for those who develop new technologies" ([Samuelson 2005], p. 567),

[EcoMac19] "GDP measures the total value of all goods and services produced in an economy" ([Krugman 2011], p. 41). GDP can be measured in two different ways: (1) as the flow of final products, or (2) as the total costs or earnings of inputs producing output. Because profit is a residual, both approaches will yield exactly the same total GDP" ([Samuelson 2005], p. 424-426),

[EcoMac20] "Net domestic product (NDP) equals the total final output produced within a nation during a year, where output includes net investment, or gross investment less depreciation" ([Samuelson 2005], p. 434),

[EcoMac21] "Gross national product (GNP) is the total final output produced with inputs owned by the residents of a country during a year" ([Samuelson 2005], p. 434),

[EcoMac22] Welfare is the "aggregation of utility of single individuals or groups" ([Varian, 1992], p. 556)."

The fundamental assumption, which the study of Macroeconomics underlies, assumes that resources are scarce [EcoMac01]. It studies how people use scarce resources to produce commodities that are then distributed among other people [EcoMac01]. The way resources are used depends on the willingness of individuals to invest [EcoMac02], [EcoMac14], [EcoMac20], on the availability of technology [EcoMac18], and on economic activities [EcoMac05]. The outcome of all economic activities within one country is quantified as GDP [EcoMac19], NDP [EcoMac20], or GNP [EcoMac21]. If the three before mentioned economic output measures increase over time, the economy is said to grow [EcoMac06]. The wellbeing of the individuals within one economy is measured as welfare [EcoMac22].

Production and Cost:

[EcoProd01] "Business firms are specialized organizations devoted to managing the process of production. Production is organized in firms because efficiency generally requires large-scale production, the raising of significant financial resources, and careful management and monitoring of ongoing activities" ([Samuelson 2005], p. 118),

[EcoProd02] "Efficient production requires time as well as conventional inputs like labor. It is therefore distinguished between two different time periods in production and cost analysis" ([Samuelson 2005], p. 112):

"The short run is the period of time in which only some inputs, the variable inputs, can be adjusted. In the short run, fixed factors, such as plant and equipment, cannot be fully modified or adjusted" ([Samuelson 2005], p. 112),

"The long run is the period in which all factors employed by the firm, including capital, can be changed" ([Samuelson 2005], p. 112),

[EcoProd03]   "The production function specifies the maximum output that can be produced with a given quantity of inputs: It is defined for a given state of engineering and technical knowledge" ([Samuelson 2005], p. 108),

[EcoProd04]   "The law of diminishing returns holds that we will get less and less extra output when we add additional doses of an input while holding other inputs fixed. In other words, the marginal product of each unit of input will decline as the amount of that input increases, holding all other inputs constant" ([Samuelson 2005], p. 109),

[EcoProd05]   "Because any economy has limited resources, there are limits on what it can produce, and there are always trade-offs; to produce more of one good, the economy must sacrifice some production of another good. These trade-offs are illustrated graphically by a PPF" ([Samuelson 2005], p. 11). "The PPF (Production Possibility Frontier) represents the menu of goods and services available to society" ([Krugman 2011], p. 57),

[EcoProd06]   "Productive efficiency occurs when an economy cannot produce more of one good without producing less of another good; this implies that the economy is on its production-possibility frontier" ([Samuelson 2005], p. 13),

[EcoProd07]   Economic analysis is based on total costs (represents the lowest total dollar expense needed to produce each level of output) that summarizes the fixed costs (represents the total dollar expense that is paid out even when no output is produced) and the variable costs (represents expenses that vary with the level of output and include all costs that are not fixed" ([Samuelson 2005], p. 125). "The opportunity cost is the value of the most valuable good or service forgone" ([Samuelson 2005], p. 137),

[EcoProd08] "Least-cost rule: To produce a given level of output at least cost, a firm should buy inputs until it has equalized the marginal product per dollar spent on each input" ([Samuelson 2005], p. 133),

[EcoProd09] "Substitution rule: If the price of one factor falls while all other factor prices remain the same, firms will profit by substituting the now-cheaper factor for the other factors until the marginal products per dollar are equal for all inputs" ([Samuelson 2005], p. 133),

[EcoProd10] "Rule for a firm's supply under perfect competition: A firm will maximize profits when it produces at that level where marginal cost equals price" ([Samuelson 2005], p. 149),

[EcoProd11] Shutdown rule: "The firm is better off going out of business [...] when the profits from producing nothing, and just paying the fixed costs, exceed the profits from producing where price equals marginal cost. [...] If average variable costs are greater than p (selling price), the firm would be better off producing zero units of output" ([Varian], p. 380),

[EcoProd12] "Externalities (or spillover effects) occur when firms or people impose costs or benefits on others outside the marketplace" ([Samuelson 2005], p. 36).

Production takes place in firms, because efficiency generally requires large-scale production [EcoProd01]. Production is furthermore distinguished into short-run and long-run [EcoProd02], which differ in their variability of factor input. Functions of factor input adhere to the law of diminishing returns [EcoProd04]. Moreover, the production possibility frontier determines the maximum output that can be achieved with a given technology and the available inputs. When considering which inputs to use for the production of which outputs, the opportunity cost is the value that determines the most profitable option [EcoProd07].

Microeconomics:

[EcoMic01] Microeconomics is "the branch of economics which today is concerned with the behavior of individual entities, such as markets, firms, and households" ([Samuelson 2005], p. 5),

[EcoMic02] "A market is a mechanism through which buyers and sellers interact to determine prices and exchange goods and services" ([Samu-
elson 2005], p. 26),

[EcoMic03] "Money is the medium of exchange. Proper management of the
money supply is one of the major issues for government macroeconomic policy in all countries" ([Samuelson 2005], p. 33),

[EcoMic04] "Prices coordinate the decisions of producers and consumers in a
market. Higher prices tend to reduce consumer purchases and encourage production. Lower prices encourage consumption and dis-
courage production. Prices are the balance wheel of the market
mechanism" ([Samuelson 2005], p. 27),

[EcoMic05] "The equilibrium price and quantity come where the amount willingly supplied equals the amount willingly demanded. In a competitive market, this equilibrium is found at the intersection of the
supply and demand curves. There are no shortages or surpluses at
the equilibrium price" ([Samuelson 2005], p. 55),

[EcoMic06] The theory of supply and demand "shows how consumer preferences determine consumer demand for commodities, while business costs are the foundation of the supply of commodities"
([Samuelson 2005], p. 45),

[EcoMic07] "There exists a definite relationship between the market price of a
good and the quantity demanded of that good, other things held
constant. This relationship between price and quantity bought is
called the demand schedule, or the demand curve" ([Samuelson
2005], p. 46),

[EcoMic08] "Law of downward-sloping demand: When the price of a commodity is raised (and other things are held constant), buyers tend
to buy less of the commodity. Similarly, when the price is lowered,
other things being constant, quantity demanded increases" ([Sam-
uelson 2005], p. 47),

[EcoMic09] "Demand rule: (a) generally, an increase in demand for a commodity (the supply curve being unchanged) will raise the price of the
commodity. (b) For most commodities, an increase in demand will

also increase the quantity demanded. A decrease in demand will have opposite effects" ([Samuelson 2005], p. 155),

[EcoMic10] "The market demand curve is the sum of individual demands at each price" ([Samuelson 2005], p. 91),

[EcoMic11] In microeconomics the "price elasticity of demand (sometimes simply called price elasticity) measures how much the quantity demanded of a good changes when its price changes. The precise definition of price elasticity is the percentage change in quantity demanded divided by the percentage change in price" ([Samuelson 2005], p. 66),

[EcoMic12] "Marginal revenue is positive when demand is elastic, zero when demand is unit-elastic, and negative when demand is inelastic" ([Samuelson 2005], p. 176),

[EcoMic13] "The supply schedule (or supply curve) from a commodity shows the relationship between its market price and the amount of that commodity that producers are willing to produce and sell, other things held constant" ([Samuelson 2005], p. 51),

[EcoMic14] "Supply rule: An increase in supply of a commodity (the demand curve being constant) will generally lower the price and increase the quantity bought and sold. A decrease in supply has the opposite effects" ([Samuelson 2005], p. 155),

[EcoMic15] In microeconomics, "the price elasticity of supply is the percentage change in quantity supplied divided by the percentage change in price" ([Samuelson 2005], p. 72),

[EcoMic16] "The theory of efficient markets holds that market prices contain all available information. It is not possible to make profits by acting on old information or at patterns of past price changes. Returns on stocks will be primarily determined by their riskiness relative to the market" ([Samuelson 2005], p. 525),

[EcoMic17] "Markets do not necessarily produce a fair distribution of income. A market economy may produce inequalities in income and consumption that are not acceptable to the electorate" ([Samuelson 2005], p. 38),

[EcoMic18]   "In the world of scarcity one thing means giving up something
             else. The opportunity cost of a decision is the value of the good or
             service forgone" ([Samuelson 2005], p. 13),

[EcoMic19]   "Allocative efficiency (or efficiency) occurs when no possible
             reorganization of production can make anyone better off without
             making someone else worse off. Under conditions of allocative ef-
             ficiency, one person's satisfaction or utility can be increased only
             by lowering someone else's utility" ([Samuelson 2005], p. 158).
             Allocative efficiency is sometimes also referred to as Pareto effi-
             ciency ([Varian 1999], p. 15),

[EcoMic20]   "The earnings in market economy are distributed to the owners of
             the economy's factor of production in the form of wages, profits,
             rent, and interest" ([Samuelson 2005], p. 226),

[EcoMic21]   "Zero-profit long-run equilibrium: In a competitive industry popu-
             lated by identical firms with free entry and exit, long-run equilibri-
             um condition is that price equals marginal cost equals the mini-
             mum long-run average cost for each identical firm. This is the
             long-run zero-economic-profit condition" ([Samuelson 2005], p.
             155),

[EcoMic22]   "The relationship between innovation and market is complex.
             Because large firms have made a major contribution to research
             and innovation, we should be cautious about claims that bigness is
             unmitigated badness" ([Samuelson 2005], p. 197),

[EcoMic23]   In financial markets, the "interest rate is the price paid for borrow-
             ing money. We usually calculate interest as percent per year on the
             amount of borrowed funds. There are many interest rates depend-
             ing upon the maturity, risk, tax status, and other attributes of the
             borrower" ([Samuelson 2005], p. 505),

[EcoMic24]   "In a competitive economy without risk and inflation, the competi-
             tive rate of return in capita would be equal to the market interest
             rate. The market interest rate serves two functions: It rations out
             society's scarce supply of capital goods or the uses that have the
             highest rates of return, and it induces people to sacrifice current

consumption in order to increase the stock of capital" ([Samuelson 2005], p. 275).

Demand is downward-sloped, which means that the demanded price and quantity are positively proportional [EcoMic07], [EcoMic08], and a lower price implies a higher quantity. Supply is upward-sloped, which means that the supplied price and quantity are negatively proportional [EcoMic13], [EcoMic14], and a higher price yields a higher quantity. The market equilibrium is the point where the supply curve hits the demand curve [EcoMic05], [EcoMic21]. Markets are hence virtual places where demand meets supply [EcoMic02]. The theory of efficient markets says that market prices are formed out of all available information [EcoMic16].

When all of the above three parts of the gallery (Macroeconomics, Production, and Microeconomics) are considered together, the result is the following:

- Resources are scarce, but are used as inputs and transformed into outputs,

- When outputs or inputs are demanded, they can be procured from suppliers in markets,

- When inputs are chosen for output transformation, the opportunity cost of an alternative determines whether the alternative is efficient or not, and

- When production possibility frontiers are hit, additional productivity can be achieved by procuring inputs from markets and engaging in trade.

According to the above four points, trade fosters an ongoing economic growth. The relation R between macroeconomic aspects (A), production (Π), microeconomic aspects (I), and trade (T) can be expressed as in (2.1.1.1). [Smith 1776] furthermore implies that trade translates into welfare (Ω):

$$R: (A, I, \Pi) \rightarrow T \rightarrow \Omega \qquad (2.1.1.1)$$

Two different types of trade are distinguished: traditional commerce (T_{Com}) and e-commerce (T_{Ecom}):

$$T = \{T_{Com}, T_{Ecom}\} \qquad (2.1.1.2)$$

with

$$T_{Com} = \Sigma \times \Gamma \rightarrow M,$$

$$T_{Ecom} = \Sigma \times \Gamma \rightarrow \Xi \times M \qquad (2.1.1.3)$$

whereby Σ represents the supply, Γ represents the demand, M represents the market, and Ξ represents the technology.

The fundamental motivation of this thesis underlies the assumption that electronic commerce (based on advantages in technology) can boost welfare; that is that the following holds true:

$$\Omega(T_{Ecom}) > \Omega(T_{Com}) \leftrightarrow \Omega(\Xi \times M) > \Omega(M) \qquad (2.1.1.4)$$

A model that provides evidence for this assumption and that is based on the Gallery of Economics is introduced in 2.1.8.

Figure 1 summarizes the core concepts of this section and emphasizes the importance of trade.

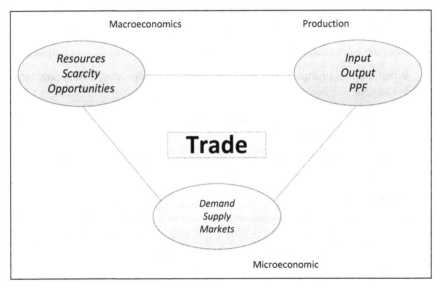

Figure 1: Macroeconomics, production, microeconomics, and trade.

2.1.2   From Economy to E-Economy

The manifestation of the Internet as global basis for information exchange has begun in the mid-90s and lasts until today. Information has become the most important competitive advantage. It is not even possible to make profits by acting on old information [EcoMic16]. While the worldwide total penetration of the Internet lies at around 30% [url2], in industry nations this value reaches even higher. In Europe, for example, 58% of the population has access to the Internet. With 78% for North America, this value lies even higher [url2]. Only the Scandinavian countries, including Sweden (93%), Norway (95%), and Iceland (98%) show rates of Internet penetration beyond the 90% mark [url2].

In the course of the wide-spread distribution of the Internet, societies have turned into information societies and economies into Electronic Economies, so called E-Economies. The word "E-Economy" refers to the "behavior of economic agents and citizens resulting from the possibilities offered by the [...] development and reduction in price of ICT[1] and, in particular, from the development of the Internet" (EC 2001, p. 4). Especially the price reduction of ICT has led to progress in opening up markets and facilitating structural reforms. The term e-business (electronic business) summarizes a variety of electronic business models and technologies. Laudon's Gallery of Electronic Business summarizes electronic business functions and their related information systems.

Gallery of Electronic Business:

[BusProc01]   "Electronic business, or e-business, designates the use of Internet and digital technology to execute all of the activities in the enterprise. E-business includes activities for the internal management of the firm and for coordination with suppliers and other business partners" ([Laudon 2006], p. 9),

[BusProc02]   Major business functions are sales and marketing (selling the organization's products and services), manufacturing and production (producing products and services), and finance and accounting (managing the organization's financial assets and maintaining the organization's financial records) ([Laudon 2006], p. 21),

[BusProc03]   Major types of business information systems are "Executive Support Systems (ESS) at the strategic level, Management Information Systems (MIS) and Decision Support Systems (DSS) at the management level, and Transaction Processing Systems (TPS) at the operational level" ([Laudon 2006], p. 41),

---

[1]   Information and Communication Technology

[BusProc04]   Enterprise Resource Planning (ERP): "One of the most important
               issues in planning and controlling operations is managing the
               sometimes vast amounts of information generated by the activity.
               [...] It is important that all relevant information that is spread
               throughout the organization is brought together. Then it can in-
               form planning and control decisions such as when activities
               should take place, where they should happen, who should be do-
               ing them, how much capacity will be needed, and so on. This is
               what enterprise resource planning (ERP) does" [Slack 2011] (al-
               so compare [Hart 2002]). ERP is described as software system
               that integrates application programs in manufacturing, logistics,
               sales, etc. ([Vollmann 2005], p.109),

[BusProc05]   Customer Relationship Management (CRM) is a "business and
               technology discipline that uses information systems to coordinate
               all of the business processes surrounding the firm's interactions
               with its customers in sales, marketing, and service" ([Laudon
               2006], p. G3),

[BusProc06]   "Supply chain management involves the management of flows
               between and among stages in a supply chain to maximize total
               profitability" ([Chopra 2001], p. 6),

[BusProc07]   Procurement is the process of "sourcing goods and materials,
               negotiating with suppliers, paying for goods, and making deliv-
               ery arrangements" ([Laudon 2006], p. G10).

When enterprises started to embrace ICT on a wide scale, they were able to leverage significant gains in productivity (cp. [EcoProd01] - [EcoProd11]). Along
with rapid changes in markets and competitive advantage (Figure 2) were changes in the firms themselves ([Laudon 2006], p. 9). This was because "the Internet
and the new markets were changing the cost and revenue structure of traditional
firms and were hastening the demise of traditional business models" ([Laudon
2006], p. 9).

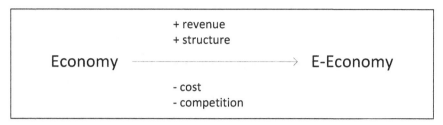

Figure 2: Transition from Economy to E-Economy.

2.1.3 From Commerce to E-Commerce

Based on an OECD definition, electronic commerce is defined as "commercial transactions occurring over open networks, such as the Internet" ([OECD, 1997], p. 3). Bichler adds that new information technologies "provide new opportunities and mechanisms to cooperate or to compete" ([Bichler, 2001], p. 1), thereby taking advantage of computer power, the enhanced communication options over the internet and the fact that millions of people can be simultaneously online. An attempt toward a definition of the terminology "e-commerce" is given by Laudon as:

Definition "E-Commerce":

"E-Commerce is the part of e-business that deals with the buying and selling of goods and services electronically with computerized business transactions using the Internet, networks, and other digital technologies. It also encompasses activities supporting those market transactions, such as advertising, marketing, customer support, delivery, and payment" ([Laudon 2006], p. 9).

Analogously to the Gallery of Electronic Business, the Gallery of E-Commerce summarizes the major characteristics of E-Commerce:

Gallery of E-Commerce:

[ECom01] "E-Commerce facilitates the means to enable external consumers to conduct various e-commerce services in ways that suit their life styles and are not driven by technology" ([Rajput 2000], pp. 22-23),

[ECom02] "E-Commerce provides ingenious means to collaborate with supplies and partners that in turn minimize the overhead of delivering products and services to customers" ([Rajput 2000], pp. 22-23),

[ECom03] Products traded via E-Commerce distribution channels are:

[ECom03a] tangible goods: goods that have a real/physical appearance,

[ECom03b] intangible goods: goods that have no real/physical appearance and depend upon a media in order to be accessible. All Information and information services, for example, are intangible goods [Günter 2000],

[ECom03c] digital goods: represent a special form of intangible goods that require electro-technological devices in order to be accessed. Examples of digital goods are e-books, websites, videos, music files, computer games, etc.

[ECom04] E-Commerce can be distinguished into ([Laudon 2006], p. 120),

[ECom04a] business-to-consumer (B2C): businesses provide goods and services on the Internet and offer sufficient information and convenient interfaces, in order to attract customers and eliminate channel intermediaries [Li 2007],

[ECom04b] business-to-business (B2B): commerce among businesses can be conducted over the Internet to integrate supply chains and logistics, in order to reduce cost and promote efficiency [Li 2007],

[ECom04c] consumer-to-consumer (C2C): website operators help gathering transaction data, but are not responsible for the logistics [Li 2007].

[ECom05] Examples of electronic payment systems for e-commerce are summarized by Laudon as follows: ([Laudon 2006], p. 130),

[ECom05a] digital credit card payment systems: secure services for credit card payments on the internet that protect information transmitted among users, merchant sites, and processing banks (e.g., eCharge),

[ECom05b] digital wallet: software that stores credit card and other information to facilitate payment for goods on the Web (e.g., MSN Wallet, MasterCard Wallet),

[Ecom05c]   accumulated balance payment systems: accumulates micro-payment purchase as a debit balance that must be paid periodically on credit card of telephone bills (e.g., PaymentOne),

[ECom05d]   stored value payment systems: enables consumers to make instant payments to merchants based on value stored in a digital account (e.g., Ecount, smart card),

[ECom05e]   digital cash: digital currency that can be used for micro-payments or larger purchases (e.g., eCoin.net),

[ECom05f]   peer-to-peer payment systems: sends money using the Web to individuals or vendors who are not set up to accept credit card payments (e.g., PayPal),

[ECom05g]   digital checking: electronic check with a secure signature (e.g., Echeck),

[ECom05h]   electronic billing presentment and payment system: supports electronic payment for online and physical store purchases of goods or services after the purchase has taken place (e.g., CheckFree, MSN Bill Pay).

2.1.4   *Electronic Commerce Busines Models*

A variety of e-commerce business models exist. E-commerce business models are described by Laudon [Laudon 2006] and Menasce [Menasce 2000] in Menasce's Gallery of E-Commerce Business Models:

Gallery of E-Commerce Business Models:

[BusMod01]   Virtual storefront: sells physical products directly to consumers or to individual business (e.g., Amazon.com, EPM.com),

[BusMod02]   Online marketplace: provides a digital environment where buyers and sellers can meet, search for products, display products, and establish prices for those products (e.g., eBay.com, Priceline.com). The general components of an electronic market service are described in Figure 3,

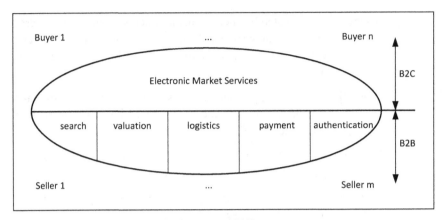

Figure 3: Electronic market model [Menasce 2000].

[BusMod03] Information broker: provides product, pricing, and availability information to individuals and business; generates revenue from advertising or from directing buyers to sellers (e.g., edmunds.com, insweb.com),

[BusMOD04] Transaction broker: saves users money and time by processing online sales transactions, generating a fee each time a transaction occurs; also provides information on rates and terms (e.g., expedia.com),

[BusMod05] Content provider: creates revenue by providing digital content, such as digital news, music, photos, or video, over the Web; the customer may pay to access the content, or revenue may be generated by selling advertising space (e.g., CNN.com, MP3.com),

[BusMod06] Online service provider: Provides online service for individuals and business; generates revenue from subscription or transaction fees, from advertising or from collecting marketing information from users (e.g., Xdrive.com, Salesforce.com).

Furthermore, Rappa adds the following kinds of electronic commerce business models [url6]:

[BusMod07] Brokerage model: "Brokers are market-makers: they bring buyers and sellers together and facilitate transactions. Brokers play a frequent role in business-to-business (B2B), business-to-consumer

(B2C), or consumer-to-consumer (C2C) markets. Usually a broker charges a fee or commission for each transaction it enables. The formula for fees can vary" [url6]. Brokerage models include marketplace exchange, buy/sell fulfillment, demand collection system, auction broker, transaction broker, distributer, and search agent. An online auction model is depicted Figure 4,

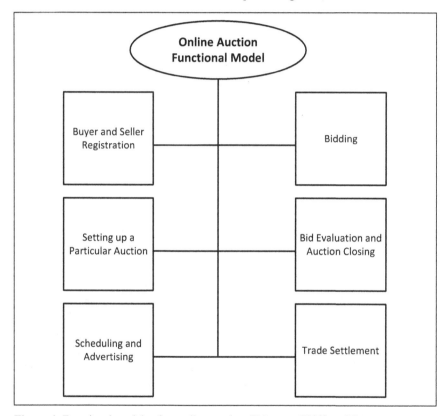

Figure 4: Functional models of an online auction ([Menasce 2000], p. 29).

[BusMod08] Merchant model (wholesalers and retailers of goods and services). Sales may be made based on list prices or through auction [url6]. Components of this model are virtual merchant, catalog merchant, click and mortar, and bit vendor. A general e-commerce system architecture is described by Menasce as:

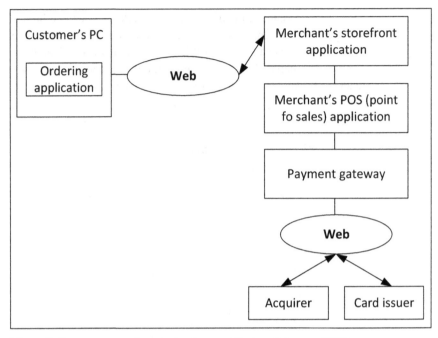

Figure 5: E-commerce systems technology architecture [Menasce 2000].

[BusMod09]   Manufacturer model: "The manufacturer or 'direct model', it is
              predicated on the power of the web to allow a manufacturer (i.e.,
              a company that creates a product or service) to reach buyers di-
              rectly and thereby compress the distribution channel. The manu-
              facturer model can be based on efficiency, improved customer
              service, and a better understanding of customer preferences"
              [url6]. This business model includes purchase, lease, license, and
              brand integrated content.

2.1.5   Electronic Commerce Pricing Models

Traditional commerce has been dominated by fixed pricing mechanisms, where
the prices are set by the suppliers and are mostly non-negotiable. Electronic
commerce facilitates so called dynamic pricing models. Special models of dynamic pricing are described in Scharl's Gallery of Dynamic Pricing Models
[Scharl 2000]:

Gallery of Dynamic Pricing Models:

[PricMod01]   Name-your-price model: empowers customers by allowing them to state the price they want to pay for products and services [Scharl 2000],

[PricMod02]   Comparison pricing model: compares desired products and services and finds the lowest price [Scharl 2000],

[PricMod03]   Demand sensitive pricing model: assumes that for the increasing number of items per purchase the cost per person decreases [Scharl 2000],

[PricMod04]   Bartering model: conducts transactions based on the exchange of goods [Scharl 2000],

[PricMod05]   Discounts model: focuses on the reduction of prices on special goods and/or for limited time only [Scharl 2000].

2.1.6   *Markets vs. Electronic Markets*

[BusMod01] – [BusMod09] gave an overview of the different types of e-commerce business models. The remainder of this thesis focuses upon electronic markets. Electronic markets are not restricted to any particular kind of pricing model, which is why [PricMod01] – [PricMod05] might be implemented by any real electronic market platform. In economics, markets are usually referred to as "virtual places where demand meets supply" ([Siebert 1992], p. 134). Even though a market can have a physical appearance, the term "virtual" encompasses even more than the traditional perception of a market being of a physical location where customers and suppliers come together to make business. The pervasiveness of trading platforms has proven that markets are not necessarily restricted to physical places anymore. Instead, electronic commerce has put the focus of the term market back on its original meaning: bringing buyers and sellers together and matching demand with supply [Rensmann 2007].

Four important functions of a market (or intermediary) are identified in [Spulber 1999] as:

- Price setting,

- Providing liquidity and immediacy,

- Searching and investigating, and

■ Guaranteeing and monitoring.

Bailey and Bakos derived four related roles from the above mentioned functions ([Bailey 1997], p. 9):

■ Aggregation of buyer demand or seller products to achieve economies of scale, in order to reduce "bargaining asymmetry",

■ Protection of buyers and sellers from opportunistic behavior of other market participants, thereby becoming an "agent of trust",

■ Facilitation of business by reducing operating (e.g., transaction) cost, and

■ Matching of buyers and sellers.

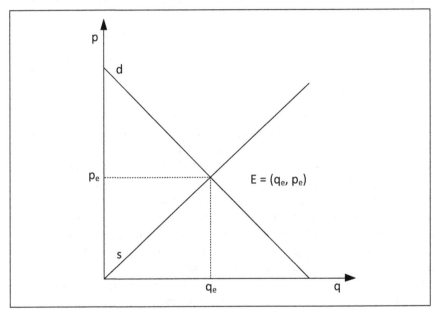

Figure 6: Market equilibrium in competition.

In markets, products are offered by suppliers to buyers, whereby the price of the offered goods determines the quantity at which the goods are bought ([Neumann 2010a], p. 16). So called "market determining forces" determine the design of the market (e.g., competition, oligopoly, monopoly) and have an impact on the price and quantity at which goods are traded ([Benjamin 1987], p. 485). Independently of those forces, buyers compare the available offers in the market with another and choose the best one. Figure 6 visualizes how in competition the buyers' demand and the sellers' supply meet in a so called "equilibrium", which is the price-quantity combination that clears the market [Brickley 2006].

Thereby, the following (linear) equations describe the supply s and the demand d:

$$s = \frac{p_e}{q_e} q$$

$$d = p_0 - \frac{p_e - p_0}{q_e} q = p_0 - \frac{p_0}{q_0} q \qquad (2.1.6.1)$$

The matching in the equilibrium establishes a contract between buyer and seller [Bichler 2001]. Once both buyer and supplier have settled the contract, the bought goods need to be transported to the buyer and the funds need to be transferred to the seller. According to Bichler, logistics and payment require a certain level of trust that protects buyers and sellers [Bichler 2001]. Trust is often provided through market internal or external services, such as Paypal, who issue letters of credit or ratings of participants [Bichler 2001]. Other sources of trust are general institutional infrastructures that specify law, rules, and regulations to govern market transactions [Bichler 2001].

Though electronic markets serve the same purpose as traditional markets, one of their distinctive features is that they do so by employing information and communication technology [Merz 1999]. Bakos defines an electronic market system as "an inter-organizational information system that allows the participating buyers and sellers to exchange information about prices and product offerings" ([Bakos 1991], p. 296). Other fundamental differences of electronic markets to traditional markets are:

- Transparency: electronic markets can hypothetically be completely transparent, since the cost of search is marginal [Picot 1996]. Market transparency is defined as "the ability of market participants to observe the information in the trading process" ([Bichler 2001], p. 5),

- Size: electronic markets are conceptually not limited to regional borders, allowing for easy matching of global demand with global supply. This aspect of electronic markets significantly increases the number of potential trading partners. The complexity of interaction, however, might be heightened in global trading scenarios as partners might be located in different countries with different laws, cultures, languages, and trade customs [Bichler 2001],

■ Cost: transaction costs that evolve from advertising, searching for trade partners, and subsequent coordination are generally low in electronic markets due to their high degree of automation and their cheap connectivity to the internet [Benjamin 1995]. Based on [Bichler 2001], in the early days of the Internet switching costs for consumers were rather high due to significant setup costs for electronic transactions. This cost, however, has decreased significantly as the Internet and its related standards "homogenized the access channels" ([Bichler 2001], p. 6).

2.1.7   Macroeconomic Implications of Electronic Markets

As indicated previously, one feature of electronic markets is their reduced transaction cost due to more efficient forms of coordination. A reduction in transaction cost coherently reduces the prices of goods ([Neumann, 2010a], p. 18). The reason for this lies in the market price p_E actually being an aggregate $p_E = c_P + c_T + m$, with

■ c_P being the cost of production,

■ c_T being the transaction cost that is based on coordination inefficiencies, and

■ m being the margin the supplier makes with the transaction.

No matter where suppliers decide to sell their goods –whether on traditional or on electronic markets– their decision does not change the cost that is involved in producing the good. That is why electronic markets cannot alter the production cost c_P. With respect to the margin m, which the supplier makes with the transaction, it needs to be distinguished into short-run and long-run. The following formula summarizes the short run equilibrium price p_E^{Short} as consisting of a constant cost of production $\overline{c_P}$, the transaction cost c_T, and the short-run margin m^{Short} [Herschley 2009].

$$p^{Short} = \overline{c_P} + c_T + m^{Short} \tag{2.1.7.1}$$

In the short run, that is the number of competitors in the market is fixed, electronic markets do not exhibit a negative impact on the supplier's margin m. The assumption that underlies the short-run scenario is that the competitive situation in both the traditional and the electronic markets remains the same. In the short, no additional competitors will enter the market, neither the traditional nor the electronic one. The supplier does not have to fear that the margin is going to underlie an increased competitive pressure, once the supplier entered the electronic market. Instead, in the short run the supplier's margin could even increase, as long as $^Tc_T - {}^Ec_T \geq {}^Em^{Short} - {}^Tm^{Short}$. In this case, –due to the reduced transaction cost of the electronic market– the supplier can offer his goods at a lower price while still making a higher margin than in the traditional market. Formulas 2.1.7.2 distinguish the above formula of the short-run equilibrium price into traditional (T) and electronic markets (E) and summarize above constraints and conditions:

$$^Tp^{Short} = {}^T\overline{c_P} + {}^Tc_T + {}^Tm^{Short}$$

$$^Ep^{Short} = {}^E\overline{c_P} + {}^Ec_T + {}^Em^{Short}$$

with

$$^T\overline{c_P} = {}^E\overline{c_P}$$

$$^Tc_T > {}^Ec_T$$

$$^Tc_T - {}^Ec_T \geq {}^Em^{Short} - {}^Tm^{Short}$$

$$^Tm^{Short} \leq {}^Em^{Short}$$

$$^Tp^{Short} \geq {}^Ep^{Short} \tag{2.1.7.2}$$

The long-run scenario assumes that additional competitors will enter the market as long as other competitors generate profit ([Jehle 2011], p. 168). As competitors enter the market, the supply curve shifts out to the right, which causes prices to fall ([Frank 2008], p. 351). Existing firms react to the change in supply by adjusting their own prices downward ([Frank 2008], p. 351). In this case, the supplier's margin will get under additional competitive pressure and decreases. Compared to the right shift of the short-run supply curve, the right shift of the long-run supply curve will be even more significant, as the transaction cost as well as the long-run margin decrease. Consequentially, the long-run prices will also be lower than the short-run prices:

$$p^{Long} = \overline{c_P} + c_T + m^{Long}$$

with

$$p^{Long} < p^{Short} \tag{2.1.7.3}$$

Analogous to the short-run equilibrium price p^{Short}, p^{Long} is also distinguished into traditional and electronic markets:

$$^T p^{Long} = {}^T\overline{c_P} + {}^T c_T + {}^T m^{Long}$$

$$^E p^{Long} = {}^E\overline{c_P} + {}^E c_T + {}^E m^{Long}$$

with

$$^T\overline{c_P} = {}^E\overline{c_P}$$

$$^T c_T > {}^E c_T$$

$$^T m^{Long} = {}^E m^{Long} = 0$$

$$^T p^{Long} > {}^E p^{Long} \tag{2.1.7.4}$$

Both the short-run and the long-run scenarios show that the effects of electronic markets on the equilibrium price can be quite complex. Regardless of whether the short-run margin m^{Short} rises, falls, or remains constant, the transaction cost of an electronic market is lower than a traditional market's transaction cost. The expression $^T c_T - {}^E c_T \geq {}^E m^{Short} - {}^T m^{Short} \geq 0$ guarantees that the short-run equilibrium price of the electronic market is lower than or equal to the short-run equilibrium price of the traditional market. Furthermore, the long-run equilibrium price of the electronic market is lower than the long-run equilibrium price of the traditional market, since $^T c_T > {}^E c_T$ and $^T m^{Long} < {}^T m^{Short}$, $^E m^{Long} < {}^E m^{Short}$:

$$^T p^{Long} < {}^T p^{Short}$$

$$^E p^{Long} < {}^E p^{Short}$$

$$^E p^{Short} \leq {}^T p^{Short}$$

$$^E p^{Long} < {}^T p^{Long} \tag{2.1.7.5}$$

As the above discussion aimed to demonstrate, in electronic markets the equilibrium prices are always lower than or equal to the prices in traditional markets, regardless of whether short-run or long-run. This conclusion is important, as it substantially influences the welfare of an economy.

2.1.8   Implications on Welfare

The lower prices for goods in electronic markets solely result from the reduction in transaction cost. The (long-run) margin of the supplier per good remains the same, and yet more individuals are able to purchase goods. The supplier's total revenue increases as in the new market equilibrium (E_2) –though the suppliers' margin remains constant– more goods are sold. Figure 7 shows how lower prices result in the supply curve shifting to the right (from s_1 to s_2).

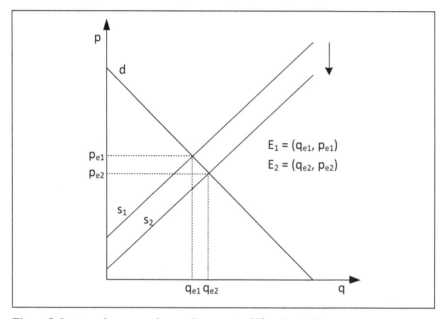

Figure 7: Lower prices cause the supply curve to shift to the right.

In order to comprehend the macroeconomic impact of electronic markets, the measure "welfare" is introduced. Welfare refers to the aggregation of utility of single individuals or groups ([Varian, 1992], p. 222). Individuals or groups are either suppliers or consumers. The utility of suppliers is measured as "supplier surplus" (or "producer surplus"). The utility of consumers is measured as "consumer surplus" ([Varian 1992], p. 224.). Both supplier surplus and consumer surplus measure how much of the equilibrium price the suppliers/consumers earned/saved compared to their minimum requested price or maximum willing-

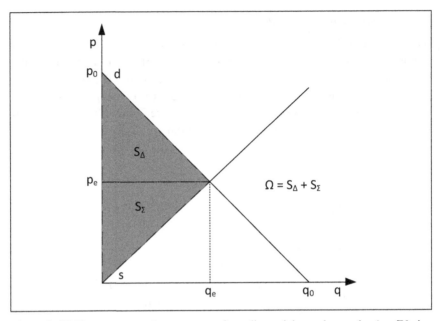

Figure 8: Welfare represents the aggregate of supplier and demander surplus (cp. [Varian 1992]).

ness to pay, respectively. Figure 8 visualizes the welfare concept and shows that both consumer surplus and supplier surplus can be comprehended as the areas of the triangles above or below the market equilibrium price (p_e).

The formula for welfare (Ω) results from [EcoMac22] as being the sum of S_Δ and S_Σ:

$$\Omega = S_\Delta + S_\Sigma \tag{2.1.8.1}$$

When due to lower transaction cost the equilibrium price falls, the supply shifts out to the right. The consumer surplus increases. So does the welfare (Figure 9).

Based on the above Figure 9, welfare can be characterized as inversely related to the equilibrium price p_e. A decrease in p_e unconditionally results in an increase in welfare (at least as long as $s(0) \geq 0$). An increase in p_e (the supply curve shifts to the left) results in a decrease in welfare. That is why electronic markets –since they lower the transaction cost and reduce the equilibrium price as com-

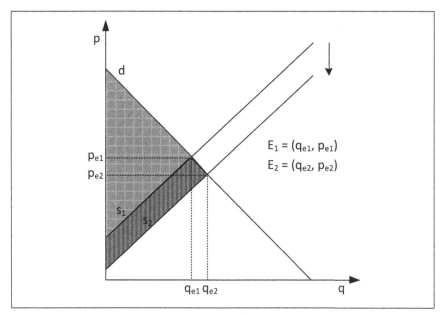

Figure 9: Lower prices cause an increase in welfare.

pared to traditional markets– can be thought of as a computer-based instrument to increase the welfare of an economy by enhancing the coordination efficiency of a market.

2.2 E-Commerce Process Modeling

This section covers business processes involved in electronic commerce systems. The proposed process model was originally developed in [Neumann 2010a].

2.2.1   BPMN-based E-Commerce Process Model

The business process modeling notation represents a unified way of modeling business processes and web services processes [Owen 2008]. The goal of BPMN is to provide a notation that is understandable by all business users [Owen 2008]. BPMN specifies a single business process diagram, called (BPD). The following BPD takes the e-commerce process model in [Neumann 2010a] and expresses its semantics in BPMN notation.

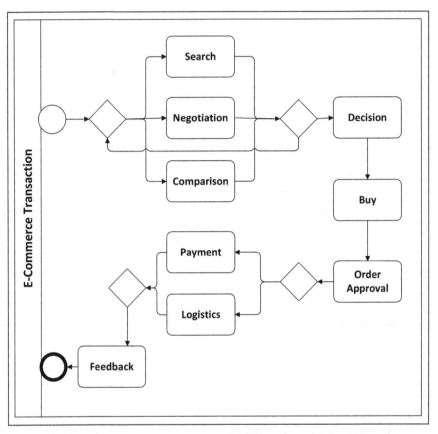

Figure 10: BPD of an e-commerce process model ([Neumann 2010a], p. 45).

The diagram is to be understood as follows. The first phase of the e-commerce process in Figure 10 contains an iterative selection and refinement of search, negotiation, and comparison activities of the consumer. One of these activities finally results in a decision of the consumer to buy a good. After the order was approved by the supplier, the payment and logistics activities will start (in this case in parallel). When the supplier obtained the funds and the consumer received the good, both will be able to provide credit to another in a feedback activity. The process concludes.

2.2.2 π Calculus-based E-Commerce Process Model

Though it can be considered as the basis for BPMN, the π calculus is a formal approach for process specification of communication that is based on process algebra and that belongs to the family of process calculi. The essential components of this algebra are communication ports, variables, data values and a set of agents. The basic definitions of this calculus include ([Masak 2009], [Parrow 2001]):

■ The empty agent 0 without any actions,

■ The output prefix $\bar{a}x.P$. The name x is sent along the name a. The agent continues as P. Essentially, $\bar{a}$ represents the output port and x the datum sent from the output port" ([Parrow 2001], p. 189),

■ The input prefix $a(x).P$, "meaning that a name is received along a name a, and x is a placeholder for the received name" ([Parrow 2001], p. 189). After having received the input the agent continue as P but with a new name that replaces x. Essentially, a represents the output port and x as a datum sent from the output port,

■ The silent prefix $\tau.P$, "which represents an agent that can evolve to P without interaction with the environment" ([Parrow 2001], p. 189). The symbols α, β are used to range over $a(x)$, $\bar{a}x$ and τ. They are called prefixes; that is that $\alpha.P$ is a prefix form,

■ The sum $P + Q$ "represents an agent that can enact either P or Q" ([Parrow 2001], p. 189),

■ The parallel composition $P \mid Q$, "which represents the combined behavior of P and Q executing in parallel" ([Parrow 2001], p. 189). Both P and Q can act independently, and may communicate if one acts an input for the other,

■ The match, if $x = y$ then P,

■ The mismatch, if $x \neq y$ then P,

■ The restriction $(vx)P$. with the agent behaving as P but with the local name x. x cannot immediately be used as a port for communication within P,

■ The identifier $A(x_1, ...,x_n) \overset{\text{def}}{=} P$, "where x_i must be pairwise distinct" ([Parrow 2001], p. 189). $A(y_1, ..., y_n)$ acts as P with y_i replacing x_i for each I, and

■ The replication $!P$, where a process term is described with P being repeatable based on a parallel composition.

Furthermore, the π calculus defines structural congruencies, such as:

■ $P \mid Q \equiv Q \mid P$,

■ $(P \mid Q) \mid R \equiv P \mid (Q \mid R)$, and

■ $(vx) \, (vy)P \equiv (vy) \, (vx)P$

The following example expresses the e-commerce process model (E) in Figure 10 in π calculus notation:

$$E = (vx) \, (vy) \, x(S). \bar{S}\langle x \rangle. x(T). \bar{T}\langle x \rangle. 0 \qquad (2.2.2.1)$$

with

$$S = (vx) \, (vy)! \, ([x \approx y]. x(B). \bar{B}\langle x \rangle. x(I). \bar{I}\langle x \rangle. x(N). \bar{N}\langle x \rangle. 0) \qquad (2.2.2.2)$$

and

$$T = (vx) \, (vy) \, (x(D). \bar{D}\langle x \rangle. (y(P). \bar{P}\langle y \rangle | x(L). \bar{L}\langle x \rangle). x(F). \bar{F}\langle x \rangle. 0) (2.2.2.3)$$

whereby x represents the supply, y the demand, E the e-commerce process, S the search phase, T the transaction phase, B the browsing process, I the investigation process, N the negotiation process, D the decision process, P the payment process, L the logistics process, and F the feedback process.

In the above example, S and T (and E, respectively) define two variables (or names) x, y at their beginning. The process S is defined as a repeatable sequence of B, I, and N, whereby x moves along all three processes as input and output, respectively, if and only if x matches y $([x \approx y])^2$. The process S is defined as non-repeatable sequence of D, $P|L$, and F, whereby $P|L$ characterizes the parallel execution of P and L. The only process in T that refers to y is P (payment). While L referring to x symbolizes the supply being shipped to the consumer, the intention behind P referring to y is that the payment for the demanded good is conducted by the consumer.

---

2 Extensions of the π calculus include the operator $=$ to test for name equality. The test in the model, however, rather aims at testing for a match between x and y, which is expressed by the operator $\approx$.

2.2.3 System Theoretical Market Model

The third and last theoretical model aims to express the mechanics of an (electronic) market in terms of systems theory. Systems theory defines systems as pairs of components and their relationships. Based on Skyttner's system theoretical foundations [Skyttner 2005], a market M, for instance, can be defined as [Neumann 2011c]:

$$M = (\Sigma \cup \Gamma \cup \Delta, R_E) \tag{2.2.3.1}$$

where $\Sigma = \{\sigma_1, \dots, \sigma_n\}$ represents the supply, $\Gamma = \{\gamma_1, \dots, \gamma_m\}$ represents the demand, $\Delta = \{\delta_1, \dots, \delta_k\}$ represents the goods, and R_E summarizes the relations between Σ, Γ, Δ.

According to the Gallery of Economics (cp. section 2.1.1), special characteristics of the market are defined as $r_e \in R_E$:

- The demand schedule (demand curve) ([EcoMic7]):

$$r_e{}^{demandCurve} \in R_E: quantity_\gamma \to price_\gamma \tag{2.2.3.2}$$

- The supply schedule (supply curve) ([EcoMic13]):

$$r_e{}^{supplyCurve} \in R_E: quantity_\sigma \to price_\sigma \tag{2.2.3.3}$$

- The demand rule ([EcoMic09]):

$$r_e{}^{demandRule} \in R_E: quantity_\gamma \to price_\sigma \tag{2.2.3.4}$$

- The supply rule ([EcoMic14]):

$$r_e{}^{supplyRule} \in R_E: quantity_\sigma \to price_\gamma \tag{2.2.3.5}$$

Similarly to M, an electronic market M^e can be defined as:

$$M^e = (\Sigma^e \cup \Gamma^e \cup \Delta^e, R_E{}^e) \tag{2.2.3.6}$$

where

$$\Sigma^e \subseteq \Sigma, \Gamma^e \subseteq \Gamma, \Delta^e \subseteq \Delta, R_E{}^e \subseteq R_E \tag{2.2.3.7}$$

The intuition behind (2.2.3.7) is that goods earlier exclusively traded on traditional markets are more and more traded via electronic markets ($\Sigma \to \Sigma^e$). Contrarily, an increasing number of consumers use electronic markets to procure goods from ($\Gamma \to \Gamma^e$). Moreover, it is observable that nowadays certain (mostly intangible) goods, such as MP3 music, etc., are exclusively traded on electronic markets ($|\Sigma \cap \Sigma^e| < |\Sigma|$ or $|\Sigma| < |\Sigma^e|$, respectively).

2.3 Chapter Summary

This chapter aimed to establish a fundamental understanding for the principles of economics in general (cp. Gallery of Economics) as well as the mechanics of e-commerce and electronic markets in particular (cp. Gallery of Electronic Business, Gallery of E-Commerce, and Gallery of E-Commerce Business Models). It was discussed how the transition from commerce to e-commerce and from economies to e-economies, respectively, enabled firms to realize certain competitive advantages, such as higher revenue, reduced cost, and better structure.

E-Commerce is based upon electronic markets, which were defined as virtual places, where supply meets demand. In contrast to traditional markets, electronic markets facilitate trade through higher transaction efficiency, which is a consequence of lower transaction cost (cp. section 2.1.7). An economic impact analysis revealed that electronic markets enhance welfare, since the lower prices result in more consumers being able to purchase goods (cp. section 2.1.8).

The process of discovering and purchasing goods on electronic markets was described in three separate models that differ in the detail and the perspective they provide (cp. sections 2.2.1, 2.2.2, and 2.2.3). Figure 11 summarizes the three subjects of electronic markets (supply, demand, and goods) and integrates them with the formerly mentioned process models.

The key finding of this chapter is that higher search efficiency and lower transaction cost increases economic welfare. These two aspects are thus beneficial to every individual within an economy, at least in average. Though the Internet has brought a dramatic increase in market transparency –under the aspect of economic welfare– it is desirable to keep increasing this transparency even further.

The next chapter details how an openly accessible Internet of Products promises to even further reduce transaction cost and hence increase market transparency. Certain aspects of the IoP are related to or stem from the initially mentioned Single Market Act of the European Commission [EC 2011]. The idea of using the concept of economic welfare as an indicator to measure the impact of the IoP on the wellbeing of a society is extended by a more sophisticated concept that adds two more dimensions. The so called "Triple Bottom Line" (3BL) represents a unified full cost accounting measure for public sector sustainability evaluation.

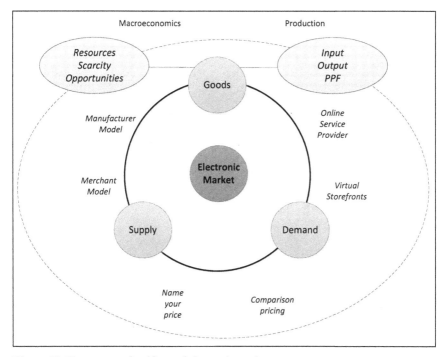

Figure 11: Processes and artifacts of electronic markets.

Together with an integrated model of electronic markets, 3BL is exposed as a category, whereby functors between the modeled categories indicate what kind of impact the IoP has on the 3BL.

3 The Internet of Products and The Triple Bottom Line

"We're all better off if we cooperate than if we try to compete on the basic descriptions of products. Better to share the descriptions and then compete on price, availability, service, etc." (Jay Myers)

The previous chapter outlined the importance of electronic markets with respect to an increased coordination efficiency and a reduced transaction cost. Moreover, it was shown that lower prices for goods as a result of lower transaction cost positively influence the economic welfare of a society. This chapter details why current electronic markets still lack transparency and how the Internet of Products aims at correcting this situation. Empirical evidence for the lack of transparency of three large electronic markets was gathered in a semantic product retrieval benchmark.

The second part of this chapter introduces a new measure for public sector full cost accounting, namely the Triple Bottom Line (3BL). 3BL thereby provides a means for measuring the sustainability of the potential outcomes of the Internet of Products and compares them with the status quo. In this sense, 3BL complements the welfare measure by introducing two additional dimensions.

The elaborations contained within this chapter are to a vast majority based on category theory. Category theory was chosen as a modeling approach, since it provides a powerful formal framework that allows for regarding the covered market objects under an isolated perspective and in their own complexity (cp. section1.4). Yet so called functors make it possible to express mappings and interrelations between individual market categories, and this way comprehend the entire complexity of the whole market system.

3.1 Market-based Categories

While a BPMN-based, a π calculus-based, and a system-theoretical model of electronic markets were covered throughout sections 2.2.1 – 2.2.3, a more sophisticated and more powerful model of electronic markets, which uses category theory, is covered throughout this section. Based on the system-theoretical model in section 2.2.3, the categories, which are developed throughout this chapter, are distinguished into the Category of Supply, the Category of Demand, the Category of Markets, as well as the Functor Category of Markets. These categories will then be used for extrapolating certain qualitative characteristics of the status quo and for demonstrating the essential consequences of the IoP.

3.1.1 Basics of Category Theory

Category theory provides a framework, which is independent of any particular algebra and which can be used to describe general principles and theorems about homomorphisms ([Fenton 1992, p. 221]). A category C consists of the following elements (see also [Ehrig 1999], p. 384) and ([Fiadeiro 2005], p. 20)):

A category C is defined as a quadruple $(O_C, M_C, \circ_C, I_C)$ with:

1. O_C being the objects of C,

2. M_C as morphisms (or arrows) between all O_i and O_j with $i, j \in \{1, 2, \ldots, n\}$,

3. $\circ_C$ as composition of the morphisms, and

4. I_C as identity morphisms of the objects.

A simple example of a category is given in the form of a poset $(S, \leq)$. The objects are the elements of S. For two objects $A, B \in S$, there exists an arrow $f: A \rightarrow B$, if and only if $A \leq B$. Composition of morphisms is associative.

Further characteristics of categories and their elements are:

■   The first element of a morphism is called the domain (or source). The second element is called the codomain (or target),

■   In the same way set-based relations are characterized as injective, surjective or bijective, morphisms are characterized as monomorphisms (or monic), epimorphism (or epic) and isomorphisms,

■   Sub categories can be derived from categories, which includes that $O_{C_{Sub}} \subseteq O_C$ and $M_{C_{Sub}} \subseteq M_C$,

■   A product category over C_1 and C_2 is defined as $C_1 \times C_2$, including the following characteristics ([Ehrig 1999], p. 396):

    1. $O_{C_1 \times C_2} = O_{C_1} \times O_{C_2}$,

2. $M_{C_1 \times C_2}\big((O_1, O_2), (O_1', O_2')\big) = M_{C_1}(O_1, O_1') \times M_{C_2}(O_2, O_2')$,   for $O_1, O_1' \in O_{C_1}$ and $O_2, O_2' \in O_{C_2}$, which means that the morphisms from (O_1, O_2) to (O_1', O_2') in $C_1 \times C_2$ are pairs of morphisms $O_1 \to O_1'$ in C_1 and $O_2 \to O_2'$ in C_2,

3. $(f_2, g_2) \circ^{C_1 \times C_2} (f_1, g_1) = (f_2 \circ^{C_1} f_1, g_2 \circ^{C_2} g_1)$, for all $f_1: O_1 \to O_1', f_2: O_1' \to O_1''$ in C_1 and all $g_1: O_2 \to O_2', g_2: O_2' \to O_2''$ in C_2,

4. $I_{C_1 \times C_2}^{(A,B)} = (I_A^{C_1}, I_B^{C_2})$.

▨ Objects can furthermore be initial or terminal. An object $x \in C$ is called initial, if for every object $y \in C$ there exists a unique morphism $f: x \to y$ ([Fiadeiro 2005], p. 58). An object $x \in C$ is terminal, if for every object $y \in C$ there exists a unique morphism $g: y \to x$ ([Fiadeiro 2005], p. 59),

▨ The sum or coproduct of objects: "let C be a category and x, y be objects of C. An object z is a sum (or coproduct) of x and y with injections $i_x: x \to z$ and $i_y: y \to z$, if for any object v and pair of morphisms $f_x: x \to v$ and $f_y: y \to v$ of C there is a unique morphism $k: z \to v$ in C such that $i_k: k \to f_y''$" ([Fiadeiro 2005], p. 62),

▨ The product of objects: "let C be a category and x, y be objects of C. An object z is a product of x and y with projections $\pi_x: z \to x$ and $\pi_y: z \to y$, if for any object v and pair of morphisms $f_x: v \to x$ and $f_y: v \to y$ of C there is a unique morphism $k: v \to z$ in C such that $k \circ i_x = f_x$ and $k \circ i_y = f_y''$" ([Fiadeiro 2005], p. 62),

▨ A functor F between the categories C and D is defined as ([Ehrig 1999], p. 396):

▨ $F = (F_O, F_M): C \to D$, with

1. the relation $F_O: O_C \to O_D$,

2. the characteristic that for any two objects $O_1, O_2 \in O_C$ follows,

3. $F_{M(O_1, O_2)}: M_C(O_1, O_2) \to M_D(F_O(O_1), F_O(O_2))$,

4. for all morphisms $f: O_1 \to O_2$ and $g: O_2 \to O_3$ holds $F_{M(O_1, O_3)}(g \circ^C f) = F_{M(O_2, O_3)}(g) \circ^D F_{M(O_1, O_2)}(f)$, and

5. for all $O_1 \in O_C$ implies $F_{M(O_1, O_1)}(I_{O_1}^C) = I_{F_O(O_1)}^D$.

Table 1: Overview of known categories [Marquis 2011].

Category name	Objects	Morphisms
Set	Sets	functions, partial functions, injective functions, surjective functions
Top	Topological spaces	Continuous functions, open continuous functions
hoTop	Topological spaces	Equivalence classes of homotopic functions
Vec	Vector spaces	Linear maps
Diff	Midderential manifolds	Smooth maps
Pord	Preorders	Monotone functions
PoSet	Posets	Monotone functions
Lat	Lattices	Structure preserving homomorphisms
Bool	Boolean algebras	$(\top, \bot, \land, \lor)$ homomorphisms
Heyt	Heyting algebras	$(\top, \bot, \land, \lor, \rightarrow)$ homomorphisms
AbGrp	Abelian groups	Group homomorphisms
Grp	Groups	Group homomorphisms
Rings	Rings	Rings homomorphisms
Fields	Fields	Fields homomorphisms
"Any deductive System T"	Formulae	Proofs

A special type of functor is the forgetful functor, which "forgets" certain relations by defining morphisms as partial relations. Forgetful functors are useful, when new categories are constructed out of old ones.

Several known categories exist, each of them with different properties and characteristics. Table 1 contains an overview of known categories together with a short characterization of their objects and morphisms.Out of the above known categories, this thesis solely concentrates upon Set and PoSet. Reasons for that will be provided later.

3.1.2   Category of Supply

This section introduces the category of supply C_Σ, based on the Gallery of E-Commerce as well as the characteristics [EcoMic13], [EcoMic14], [EcoMic15], defined in the Gallery of Economics. C_Σ consists of:

1. O_Σ or Σ as the supply $\sigma_1, \ldots, \sigma_n$ being available in the market. All objects $\sigma \in O_\Sigma$ are tuples of the form $(id, \delta_{id}, q, p)_\sigma$, with id being the id of the supply offer, δ_{id} being the id of the offered good, q being the offered quantity, and p being the offered price.

2. M_Σ as being the morphisms between the objects $\sigma \in O_\Sigma$. A non-exclusive list of morphisms of M_Σ could include:

    ▪ $M_{\Sigma, i \to j}^{trustful}$ or $M_{i \to j}^{trustful}$,   whereby $M_{i \to j}^{trustful}: O_\Sigma \times O_\Sigma \to$ $(true, false)$ is defined as "the supply offer σ_i is more trustful than σ_j" or $\sigma_i \sqsupset_{tustful} \sigma_j$, with respect to the suppliers' credibility and reliability,

    ▪ $M_\Sigma^{high\_trust}$ or M^{high_trust}, whereby $M^{high\_trust}: O_\Sigma \to \sigma^m$ is defined as "the m supply offers that are considered to be of particularly high trust" with respect to their suppliers' credibility and reliability,

    ▪ $M_{\Sigma, i \to j}^{quality}$ or $M_{i \to j}^{quality}$,   whereby $M_{i \to j}{}^{quality}: O_\Sigma \times O_\Sigma \to$ $(true, false)$ is defined as "the supply offer σ_i is of a higher quality than σ_j" or $\sigma_i \sqsupset_{quality} \sigma_j$, with respect to the innate quality of the supply offer,

    ▪ $M_\Sigma^{high\_quality}$ or $M^{high\_quality}$, whereby $M^{high\_quality}: O_\Sigma \to \sigma^m$ is defined as "the m supply offers that are considered to be of particularly high quality", with respect to the quality of the good being offered,

    ▪ $M_\Sigma^{quality\_leader}$ or $M^{quality\_leader}$, whereby $M^{quality\_leader}: O_\Sigma \to \sigma$ is defined as "the supply offer σ that has the highest quality in the market",

    ▪ $M_{\Sigma, i \to j}^{price}$ or $M_{i \to j}^{price}$, whereby $M_{i \to j}^{price}: O_\Sigma \times O_\Sigma \to (true, false)$ is defined as "the supply offer σ_i is cheaper than σ_j" or $\sigma_i \sqsubset_{price} \sigma_j$. It must be noted that $M_{i \to j}^{price}$ only yields a meaningful statement, when two supply offers $\sigma_i, \sigma_j \in O_\Sigma$ are compared with each other that refer to the same good δ_{id},

- $M_\Sigma^{low\_price}$ or M^{low_price}, whereby $M^{low\_price}: O_\Sigma \to \sigma^m$ is defined as "the m supply offers that have a particularly low price",

- $M_\Sigma^{price\_leader}$ or M^{price_leader}, whereby $M^{price\_leader}: O_\Sigma \to \sigma$ is defined as "the supply offer σ that has the lowest price in the market",

- $M_{\Sigma, i \to j}^{same\_domain}$ or $M_{i \to j}^{same\_domain}$, whereby $M_{i \to j}^{same\_domain}: O_\Sigma \times O_\Sigma \to (true, false)$ is defined as "the supply offers σ_i and σ_j are of the same product domain (e.g., computers, groceries, etc.)" or $\sigma_i \equiv_{same\_domain} \sigma_j$,

- $M_{\Sigma, i \to j}^{faster\_available}$ or $M_{i \to j}^{faster\_available}$, whereby $M_{i \to j}^{faster\_available}: O_\Sigma \times O_\Sigma \to (true, false)$ is defined as "the good in the supply offer σ_i is faster available than the good in σ_j" or $\sigma_i \sqsubset_{faster\_available} \sigma_j$,

- M_Σ^{deal} or M^{deal}, whereby $M^{deal}: \sigma \to (true, false)$ is defined as "the supply offer σ is a special deal (e.g., reduced price for a limited time.)",

3. $\circ_\Sigma$ as composition of above morphisms. Examples of compositions are not limited to but may include:

- $M_\Sigma^{low\_price\_quality\_leader}$ or $M^{low\_price\_quality\_leader}$, whereby $M^{low\_price\_quality\_leader}: M^{low\_price} \circ_\Sigma M^{quality\_leader}$ is defined as "the supply offer σ that out of all low-price supply offers has the highest quality in the market",

- $M_\Sigma^{high\_trust\_quality\_leader}$ or $M^{high\_trust\_quality\_leader}$, whereby $M^{high\_trust\_quality\_leader}: M^{high\_trust} \circ_\Sigma M^{quality\_leader}$ is defined as "the supply offer σ that out of all high-trust supply offers has the highest quality in the market",

4. I_Σ as the identity morphisms of O_Σ.

3.1.3 Category of Demand

This section introduces the category of demand C_Γ, based on the Gallery of E-Commerce as well as the characteristics [EcoMic8], [EcoMic9], [EcoMic10], [EcoMic11, [EcoMic12], which were defined in the Gallery of Economics. Analogously to C_Σ, C_Γ consists of:

1. O_Γ or shortly Γ as the demand $\gamma_1, ..., \gamma_m$ being available in the market. All objects $\gamma \in O_\Gamma$ are tuples of the form $(id, \delta_{id}, q, p)_\gamma$, with id being the identifier of the demand request, δ_{id} being the id of the demanded good, q being the demanded quantity, and p being the demanded price.

2. M_Γ as being the morphisms between the objects $\gamma \in O_\Gamma$. A non-exclusive list of morphisms of M_Γ could include:

   ▪ $M_{\Gamma,i \to j}^{credibility}$ or $M_{i \to j}^{credibility}$, whereby $M_{i \to j}^{credibility} : O_\Gamma \times O_\Gamma \to$ $(true, false)$ is defined as "the demand γ_i is more credible than γ_j" or $\sigma_i \sqsupseteq_{credible} \sigma_j$, with respect to the consumers' credibility and reliability,

   ▪ $M_\Gamma{}^{high\_credibility}$ $M_\Gamma^{high\_credibility}$ or $M^{high\_credibility}$, whereby $M^{high\_credibility} : O_\Gamma \to \gamma^m$ is defined as "the m demands that are considered to be of particularly high credibility",

   ▪ $M_{\Gamma,i \to j}^{wtp}$ or $M_{i \to j}^{wtp}$, whereby $M_{i \to j}^{wtp} : O_\Gamma \times O_\Gamma \to (true, false)$ is defined as "the demand γ_i has a higher willingness to pay (wtp) than γ_j" or $\gamma_i \sqsupseteq_{wtp} \gamma_j$. It should be noted that $M_{i \to j}^{wtp}$ only yields a meaningful statement, when two demands $\gamma_i, \gamma_j \in O_\Gamma$ are compared with each other that refer to the same good δ_{id},

   ▪ $M_\Gamma^{high\_wtp}$ or M^{high_wtp}, whereby $M^{high\_wtp} : O_\Gamma \to \gamma^m$ is defined as "the m demands that have a particularly high willingness to pay",

   ▪ $M_\Gamma^{wtp\_leader}$ or M^{wtp_leader}, whereby $M^{wtp\_leader} : O_\Gamma \to \gamma$ is defined as "the demand γ that has the highest willingness to pay in the market",

■ $M_{\Gamma,i\to j}^{same\_domain}$ or $M_{i\to j}^{same\_domain}$, whereby $M_{i\to j}^{same\_domain}: O_\Gamma \times O_\Gamma \to (true, false)$ is defined as "the demands γ_i and γ_j are of the same product domain (e.g., computers, groceries, etc.)", or $\gamma_i \equiv_{same\_domain} \gamma_j$,

■ $M_\Gamma^{fast\_delivery}$ or $M^{fast\_delivery}$, whereby $M^{fast\_delivery}: O_\Gamma \to \gamma^m$ is defined as "the m demands that require particularly fast delivery",

■ $M_{\Gamma,i\to j}^{faster\_delivery}$ or $M_{i\to j}^{faster\_delivery}$, whereby $M_{i\to j}^{faster\_delivery}: O_\Gamma \times O_\Gamma \to (true, false)$ is defined as "the demand γ_i needs to be faster fulfilled than γ_j, in terms of delivery times for the good in γ_j", or $\gamma_i \sqsubset_{faster\_delivery} \gamma_j$,

■ M_Γ^{deal} or M^{deal}, whereby $M^{deal}: \gamma \to (true, false)$ is defined as "the demand γ seeks special deals (e.g., bargains, price reductions, etc.)".

3. $\circ_\Gamma$ as composition of above morphisms. Examples of compositions are not limited to but may include:

■ $M_\Gamma^{high\_credibility\_wtp\_leader}$ or $M^{high\_credibility\_wtp\_leader}$, whereby $M^{high\_credibility\_wtp\_leader}: M^{high\_credibility} \circ_\Gamma M^{wtp\_leader}$ is defined as "the demand γ that out of all demands with a high credibility has the highest willingness to pay in the market",

■ $M_\Gamma^{high\,credibility\,fast\,delivery}$ or $M^{high\,credibility\,fast\,delivery}$, whereby $M^{high\,credibility\,fast\,delivery}: M^{high\_credibility} \circ_\Gamma M^{fast\_delivery}$ is defined as "the demands that have a high credibility and at the same time require fast delivery".

4. I_Γ as the identity morphisms of O_Γ.

3.1.4   Category of Markets

This section introduces the category of markets C_M. Based on the definition of markets as being "virtual places where demand meets supply" [EcoMic05], this section defines the category of markets as $C_\Sigma \times C_\Gamma \to C_M$; that is, there exists an arbitrary number of functors from the product category $C_\Sigma \times C_\Gamma$ to C_M that match the available demand with the available supply. It will later be shown how different functors create special types of markets (e.g., monopolies, competitions, etc.).

1. O_M or shortly M as the transactions $\mu_1, \ldots, \mu_l$ representing the market. All objects $\mu \in O_M$ are tuples of the form $\left(id, id_\sigma, id_\gamma, \delta_{id}, q_\sigma, p_\sigma, q_\gamma, p_\gamma\right)_\mu$, with id being the identifier of the transaction, id_σ being the identifier of the corresponding supply offer $\sigma \in O_\Sigma$, id_γ being the identifier of the corresponding demand $\gamma \in O_\Gamma$, δ_{id} being the id of the good, q_σ being the offered quantity, p_σ being the offered price, q_γ being the demanded quantity, and p_γ being the demanded price. Regardless of the particular functors that constructed C_M out of $C_\Sigma \times C_\Gamma$, O_M only contains those objects that have corresponding objects in C_Σ and C_Γ,

2. M_M as being the morphisms between the objects $\mu \in O_M$. A non-exclusive list of morphisms of M_M could include:

   ▪ $M_M^{average\_price}$ or $M^{average\_price}$, whereby $M^{average\_price}: O_M \to \mathbb{R}$ as "the average price of all transactions in the market",

   ▪ $M_M^{accumulated\_quantity}$ or $M^{accumulated\_quantity}$, whereby $M^{accumulated\_quantity}: O_M \to \mathbb{R}$ as "the accumulated quantity of all transactions in the market",

   ▪ $M_M^{lowest\_price}$ or M^{lowest_price}, whereby $M^{lowest\_price}: O_M \to \mathbb{R}$ as "the price of the cheapest transaction in the market",

   ▪ $M_M^{transparency}$ or $M^{transparency}$, whereby $M^{transparency}: O_M \to \mathbb{R}$ as "the transparency of the market",

   ▪ $M_M^{demander\_surplus}$ or $M^{demander\_surplus}$, whereby $M^{demander\_surplus}: O_M \to \mathbb{R}$ as "the consumer surplus of the market",

   ▪ $M_M^{supplier\_surplus}$ or $M^{supplier\_surplus}$, whereby $M^{supplier\_surplus}: O_M \to \mathbb{R}$ as "the supplier surplus of the market".

3. $\circ_M$ as composition of above morphisms. Examples of compositions are not limited to but may include:

■ $M_M^{welfare}$ or $M^{welfare}$, whereby $M^{welfare}: O_M \rightarrow \mathbb{R}$ as "sum of the consumer surplus and the supplier surplus (the welfare [EcoMac24]) of the market".

4. I_M as the identity morphisms of O_M.

3.1.5 Functors between Demand, Supply, and Markets

When demand is matched with supply, markets in general and electronic markets in particular underlie certain rules (or restrictions). In the following, these rules are expressed as functors $F: C_\Sigma \times C_\Gamma \rightarrow C_M$:

■ F_{PNZ} (price non-zero restriction): $price_\sigma, price_\gamma > 0$, which demands that the price of γ and the price of σ have to be larger than zero,

■ F_{QNZ} (quantity non-zero restriction): $quantity_\sigma, quantity_\gamma > 0$, which demands that the quantity of γ and the quantity of σ have to be larger than zero,

■ F_{PIR} (product identity restriction): $\delta_{id_\sigma} = \delta_{id_\gamma}$, which demands that both the good that is offered by the supply and the good that is requested by the demand are identical,

■ F_{PFR} (price fill restriction): $price_\sigma \leq price_\gamma$, which demands that the supply price of σ has to be smaller than or equal to the demand price of γ,

■ F_{QFR} (quantity fill restriction): $quantity_\sigma \geq quantity_\gamma$, which demands that the supply quantity of σ has to be larger than or equal to the demand quantity of γ,

■ F_{COR} (cheapest offer restriction): $quantity_\gamma \rightarrow min(\bigcup_{\sigma \in \Sigma} price_\sigma)$, which demands that the demand γ is fulfilled by the supply σ that has the cheapest price.

The combination of the above functors into $F_{Market}: F_{PNZ} \circ F_{QNZ} \circ F_{PIR} \circ F_{PFR} \circ F_{QFR} \circ F_{COR}$ describes what is necessary to form a market transaction. Thereby, F_{Market} incorporates the fundamental conditions with respect to matching supply with demand.

Other conditions might exist as well, but are more specific to certain characteristics of the consumer and the supplier, respectively. Trust, for example, is a concept that is of particular importance in electronic markets, and which might be modeled among other potentially important restrictions in future versions of the model.

3.1.6 Functor Category of Markets

Functors $F: C_\Sigma \times C_\Gamma \to C_M$ construct a new category C_M out of the product category $C_\Sigma \times C_\Gamma$. Objects of C_M are the transactions that occur within the market. Based on [Awodey 2010], there exists a category, which has as objects functors and which every locally small category can be embedded in. Such kind of category is named "Functor Category" and denoted as A^C –the functor category of all (covariant) functors from C to A.

Let $C_M{}^{C_\Sigma \times C_\Gamma}$ be the functor category of markets. Then, $C_M{}^{C_\Sigma \times C_\Gamma}$ naturally includes the basic functors $F_{PNZ}, F_{QNZ}, F_{PIR}, F_{PFR}, F_{QFR}, F_{COR}$. Additionally, O_M is augmented by functors that aim to describe different types of market coordination, such as monopolies, oligopolies, or competition. The functor category $C_M{}^{C_\Sigma \times C_\Gamma}$ consists of:

1. $O_M{}_{C_\Sigma \times C_\Gamma}$ as the functors from $C_\Sigma \times C_\Gamma$ to C_M. Examples of popular functors include:

   ▣ $F_{Monopoly}$, characterized by constructing a category C_M with all objects $\mu \in O_M$ having the same supplier,

   ▣ $F_{Oligopoly}$, characterized by constructing a category C_M with the objects $\mu \in O_M$ sharing a very limited number of suppliers in common,

   ▣ $F_{Competition}$, characterized by constructing a category C_M with the objects $\mu \in O_M$ showing a very high number of different suppliers,

2. $M_M{}_{C_\Sigma \times C_\Gamma}$ as the morphisms between the functors $F \in O_M{}_{C_\Sigma \times C_\Gamma}$. Morphisms of $M_M{}_{C_\Sigma \times C_\Gamma}$ are natural transformations between its objects, the functors. Natural transformations transform one functor into another. If, for example, F and G are functors between $C_\Sigma \times C_\Gamma$ and C_M, then there exists a natural transformation η from F to G that associates to every object X in $C_\Sigma \times C_\Gamma$

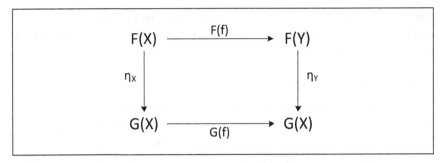

Figure 12: Commutative diagram of a natural transformation.

with that in C_M, using a morphism $\eta_x\colon F(X) \to G(X)$, such that for every morphism $f\colon X \to Y$ in $C_\Sigma \times C_\Gamma$ the following holds true [Walters 1991]:

$$\eta_y \circ F(f) = G(f) \circ \eta_x \tag{3.1.6.1}$$

Commutative diagrams are often used to visualize natural transformations. Figure 12 shows such a commutative diagram [Walters 1991] for (3.1.6.1).

With their characteristic of describing the transformations from one functor into another, the natural transformations $\eta \in M_M c_{\Sigma \times C_\Gamma}$ symbolize the transformations from one market type into another (e.g., $\eta\colon F_{Monopoly}(X) \to F_{Competition}(X)$). The natural transformations $\eta \in M_M c_{\Sigma \times C_\Gamma}$ are hence instruments to describe what is necessary to turn a market with a lower welfare, such as a monopoly, into a market with a (potentially) higher welfare, such as competition,

3. $\circ_M c_{\Sigma \times C_\Gamma}$ as composition of the above morphisms or composition of natural transformations. If $\eta\colon F_{Monopoly}(X) \to F_{Oligopoly}(X)$ and $\varepsilon\colon F_{Oligopoly}(X) \to F_{Competition}(X)$ are natural transformations between the functors $F_{Monopoly}, F_{Oligopoly}, F_{Competition}\colon C_\Sigma \times C_\Gamma \to C_M$, then their composition also yields a natural transformation $\eta \circ_M c_{\Sigma \times C_\Gamma} \varepsilon\colon F_{Monopoly}(X) \to F_{Competition}$. The composition $\eta \circ_M c_{\Sigma \times C_\Gamma} \varepsilon$ is associative and is called vertical. Horizontal compositions, contrarily, are also associative, but would instead describe a transformation of, for example, $F_{Monopoly}(X) \to F_{Monopoly}(Y) \to F_{Monopoly}(Z)$,

4. $I_M c_{\Sigma \times C_\Gamma}$ as the identity morphisms of $O_M c_{\Sigma \times C_\Gamma}$.

Together, the categories C_Σ, C_Γ, C_M, and $C_M{}^{C_\Sigma \times C_\Gamma}$ form a theoretical model that describes the mechanics of (electronics) markets. The model allows for comprehending how markets match supply with demand as well as for analyzing the transparency of markets. Thereby, the different degrees of transparency are modeled as functors. The following sections will comprehend the Internet of Products as an additional functor and show how it complements the model. Additionally, economic, ecological, as well as societal implications of an openly accessible Internet of Products, based on the above four categories are covered.

3.2 The Internet of Products

Section 2.1.6 stated the difference of electronic markets (as compared to traditional markets) as lying in higher coordination efficiency and in lower transaction cost. It was shown how electronic markets facilitate cheaper prices for goods and hence influence the overall welfare of an economy. Nevertheless, even in today's electronic markets transaction cost exists, not so much as transaction fees charged by the market provider, but rather in terms of search cost. Search cost evolves from the overall market in reality consisting of many small markets that are not integrated with each other. The concept of search cost expresses the time that is necessary to gain a sufficiently good overview of all (relevant) supplies available in a market. It furthermore maps the search time to a monetary unit, so that it can be included in pricing-related calculations.

As of today, various online markets exist. Once a consumer has entered one of these markets, finding the goods that are sought happens in a comparably efficient manner. Search tools, such as search engines or product indices, help the consumer to quickly navigate through the market. Individual online markets, however, do not associate with one another and are very limited in scope. If there existed a good in a market A as well as in a market B and the consumer, however, only knew about A, the suppliers in A could use their position to ask for potentially higher prices. Internet search engines[3] (e.g., Google, Bing, Yahoo, etc.) aim to compensate for this lack of efficiency by providing an aggregated view of both online markets A and B. Whenever consumers enter the name of a good

---

[3] Specialized price search engines (e.g., Google Products, Kayak) focus on finding the lowest price for goods in different markets.

into a search engine, the search engine should be able to discover the good being offered in both A and B.

In reality, however, search engines are biased and only provide a distorted view of the market. Search engine providers usually sell rankings in their result list in an auction to the supplier with the highest bid. The supplier, on the other hand, needs to compensate the price that was paid for the ranking in the search engine by raising the prices for his goods. This way, the expense for being ranked in the search engine becomes part of the suppliers' transaction cost again. The search engine has become a mediator, an information broker in an information economy. Instead of solely reducing prices, search engines also redistribute the margin that is made with the good.

Another problem lies in insufficient search technology making it often impossible for consumers to instantaneously find suppliers that could potentially fulfil their demand. The Internet of Products (IoP) describes an approach toward providing open and free access to unbiased product information. Its major goals are divided into macroeconomic and microeconomic as well as technical and search-related goals:

Macroeconomic & microeconomic goals:

[IOPMM01]   Marginal transaction cost,

[IOPMM02]   Maximum market transparency [Neumann 2011b], and

[IOPMM03]   Competition based on product quality and availability, rather than on information.

Technical & search-related goals:

[IOPTS01]   Cross-language product discovery,

[IOPTS02]   Cross-culture product discovery, and

[IOPTS03]   Dynamic products, which can adapt their content over time [Neumann 2010c].

The above six points require that at any given time consumers in the IoP gain an instantaneous overview of all supply in the market that matches their demand. More importantly, the concept of the IoP assumes that consumers are able to express their demand in a way, so that it can be efficiently understood by a machine and matched with the available supply, a capability that has never since the appearing of the internet been achieved.

3.2.1   Semantic Product Retrieval Benchmark

In order to illustrate the limitations of state-of-the-art technology with respect to [IOPMM01] – [IOPMM03] and [IOPTS01] – [IOPTS03], this section examines to which extent productive search engines, in this case Google (Shopping), eBay, and Amazon, are capable of processing semantic product search queries. All three examined search engines were benchmarked against a research prototype of a Semantic Product Server that was developed at the Department of Distributed Systems at the Otto-von-Guericke University.

The original tests were conducted in German language and for this thesis had to be translated into English language. Twenty reference queries that were originally designed for the ArbiterOne research prototype were run against the three before mentioned product search engines. As it will be detailed later in chapter seven, ArbiterOne represents an implementation of a Semantic Product Server that allows users for specifying product search criteria based on product attributes and their values. Furthermore, ArbiterOne allows for including operators in the search queries (e.g., ">", "<", ">=", "<=", etc.) that understand to automatically translate units into other unit systems (e.g., "kg"→"lbs"). ArbiterOne furthermore knows to automatically resolve differences in query language and product description language.

The following twenty reference queries use the ArbiterOne query syntax. It is observable that the syntax of the queries is very close to the syntax of a natural language.

1.   PS3 harddisk >= 60GB USB Ports=4

2.   MP3 Player harddisk >= 1GB batteries=AAA

3.   video card processor >= 600MHz memory >= 1000MHZ memory
     interface = 256bit

4.   jumper shoes size=44 material=leather

5.   property city=cologne central square meters >= 100

6.   wristwatch water-proof >= 200m format = 24h

7.   mobile manufacturer = Samsung price <= 200€ contract=no

8.   vacuum cleaner power>=2000Watt no bag

9.   digital camera memory card >= 16GB mega pixels >= 6

10. travel destination=Mallorca length >= 3days price <= 400€

11. hifi system price <= 100 type >= 5.1

12. book title = "Steve Jobs" price <= 30

13. massage chair price <= 200 color = black

14. refrigerator price <= 700 energy class >= A

15. comic name = Superman volume = 1 language=english

16. fish tank volume >= 112l price <= 35

17. fishing rod price <= 50 weight <= 80g

18. operating system name = "Windows 7" bit=64 Edition >= Pro-
     fessional price <= 60

19. drilling machine power >= 500Watts manufacturer = Bosch
     price <= 75

20. printer type=inkjet price <= 50

Since all of the three examined product search engines (Google, eBay, and Amazon) do not support operator semantics, the queries had to be modified, in order for the respective search engines to be correctly processed:

1. PS3 60GB 4 USB Ports

2. MP3 Player 1GB R6 batteries

3. video card 600MHz memory 1000MHZ 256bit

4. jumper shoes size 44 leather

5. property cologne central 100m2

6. wristwatch 200m water-proof 24h format

7. mobile Samsung 200€ no contract

8. vacuum cleaner 2000 watts no bag

9. digital camera 16GB memory card 6 megapixels

10. trvel Mallorca 3 days 400€

11. hifi system 100€ 5.1

12. book Steve Jobs 30€

13. massage chair 200€ black

14. refridgerator 700€ energy class A

15. comic superman volume 1 english

16. fish tank 1121 35€

17. fishing rod 50€ weight 80g

18. Windows 7 64bit professional 60€

19. drilling machine 500Watts Bosch 75€

20. printer inkjet 50€

Table 2: Search results for Google.

Test number	Results (max. 10)	Completely correct	Partially correct	Incorrect
1	3	1	0	2
2	2	0	0	2
3	0	0	0	0
4	10	10	0	0
5	0	0	0	0
6	10	8	2	0
7	10	9	1	0
8	10	7	3	0
9	10	0	0	10
10	10	0	1	9
11	10	2	5	3
12	10	10	0	0
13	10	0	10	0
14	10	0	8	2
15	10	1	3	6
16	10	0	7	3
17	10	2	8	0
18	10	0	0	10
19	1	0	1	0
20	10	3	6	1

The test counts for every examined product query system the number of returned results, the number of completely correct results, the number of partially correct results, as well as the number of incorrect results. Results can be any results returned, no matter whether they match the query or not. The number of inspected results, however, is limited to the top ten results, though in some cases there existed more than ten results.

Completely correct results are results that refer to a product that contains all of the characteristics/attributes defined in the query. Partially correct results are results that contain more than one of the characteristics/attributes defined in the query and that are not completely correct. Incorrect results do not contain any of the characteristics/attributes defined in the query. Table 2 summarizes the benchmark results for Google.

Table 3: Search results for eBay.

Test number	Results (max. 10)	Completely correct	Partially correct	Incorrect
1	0	0	0	0
2	0	0	0	0
3	0	0	0	0
4	10	10	0	0
5	0	0	0	0
6	0	0	0	0
7	0	0	0	0
8	10	10	0	0
9	0	0	0	0
10	0	0	0	0
11	0	0	0	0
12	0	0	0	0
13	0	0	0	0
14	0	0	0	0
15	0	0	0	0
16	0	0	0	0
17	0	0	0	0
18	0	0	0	0
19	0	0	0	0
20	0	0	0	0

In 20 tests with a potential 200 search results 156 results were returned by Google. Out of those 156, only 53 results were completely correct, 55 results were partially correct, and 48 results were incorrect. Analogously to Table 2, Table 3 summarizes the benchmark results for eBay.

In 20 tests with a potential 200 search results, 20 results were returned by eBay. All 20 results were completely correct. Occasionally, eBay suggested products that contained at least one of the search attributes. The eBay search engine, however, appears to be not capable of accepting and matching more than one search attribute with the products stored in its catalog.

Table 4: Search results for Amazon.

Test number	Results (max. 10)	Completely correct	Partially correct	Incorrect
1	10	0	0	10
2	0	0	0	0
3	0	0	0	0
4	10	8	2	0
5	0	0	0	0
6	0	0	0	0
7	0	0	0	0
8	10	9	1	0
9	10	0	1	9
10	0	0	0	0
11	5	1	3	1
12	0	0	0	0
13	0	0	0	0
14	0	0	0	0
15	1	1	0	0
16	0	0	0	0
17	0	0	0	0
18	0	0	0	0
19	0	0	0	0
20	0	0	0	0

The last test was performed on Amazon's product search engine. Table 4 summarizes the benchmark results for Amazon. In 20 tests with a potential 200 search results, 46 results were returned by Amazon. Out of the 46 returned results, 19 results were completely correct, 7 results were partially correct, and 20 results were incorrect. Similar to eBay, suggestions made by the Amazon search engine indicated that many products exist in the catalog with at least one attribute, but that do not fully comply with the attributes specified in the query.

Table 5 condenses the test results from Google, eBay, and Amazon.

Table 5: Summary of search results.

Product search engine	Completely correct	Partially correct	Incorrect
Google	53	55	48
eBay	20	0	0
Amazon	19	7	20

Another interesting result of the tests is the fact that none of the examined product search engines was capable of providing measures for the relevance (e.g., "how many of the specified characteristics are contained in a result?") of their search results. Contrarily, ArbiterOne (or Semantic Product Servers, respectively) provides relevance information on the returned search results (cp. section 5.2.1). The results in Table 5 bear important implications with respect to the formerly introduced transaction cost and market transparency. When consumers –with the given tools– are not able to effectively investigate markets for supply offers that could fulfil their demand, market transparency is significantly hindered, including all the undesirable effects that were elaborated upon in section 2.1.8. The following section provides a formal discussion around a concept that is referred to as "opaqueness margin", which represents the margin suppliers make with the lack of transparency in (electronic) markets.

3.2.2   Toward Total Commerce

The Internet of Products aims to provide consumers with a completely transparent view of the supply offers available in markets. It thereby aggregates individual markets to one big market. This infers that in the IoP product information is considered as commodity good, accessible at any time by anybody. In order to model the economic outcomes of non-transparent markets, contrarily, the earlier introduced concept of transparency (τ) is refined to (cp. $M_M^{transparency}$ in section 3.1.4):

$$\tau = \frac{1}{2^{m-n}} \tag{3.2.2.1}$$

with n being the number of investigated online markets and m being the total number of online markets (e.g., eBay, Amazon, Google (Shopping)). In a completely transparent market, where consumers have access to all available supply offers, the transparency equals 1:

$$\tau\left(U_{m \in M} \, \sigma_m\right) = \frac{1}{2^{m-n}} = \frac{1}{2^0} = 1 \tag{3.2.2.2}$$

When consumers only use one market (e.g., eBay) to procure goods from, the transparency equals the transparency of a single market:

$$\tau(\sigma_i) = \frac{1}{2^{m-n}} = \frac{1}{2^{m-1}} \tag{3.2.2.3}$$

When consumers investigate two markets before purchasing a good (e.g., eBay, Amazon), the transparency consequently increases (it doubles). Whenever consumers procure from non-transparent markets, they will likely not find the supply offer with the overall lowest price. Instead, in the average case, consumers will pay the average price for the good (cp. Figure 13).

In the case sampled in Figure 13, the supplier makes a margin on the good that is as high as the price of the supplier's offer reduced by the price of the lowest market bid. In [Neumann 2011b], this margin has been characterized as "opaqueness margin".

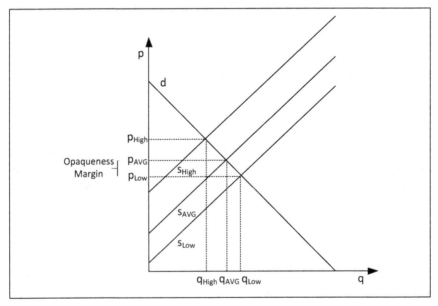

Figure 13: Average price vs. lowest price and opaqueness margin [Neumann 2011b].

In the Internet of Products, the opaqueness margin tends to be zero, since the market ensures complete transparency to the consumers. In contemporary electronic markets, however, the opaqueness margin (o) tends to be larger than zero:

$$o = \phi\left(\bigcup_{n \in N} \sigma_n\right) - \phi\left(\bigcup_{m \in M} \sigma_m\right) \geq 0$$

where

$$\phi: \Sigma \to min(p_\sigma), \forall \sigma \in \Sigma, p_\sigma \in \sigma \qquad (3.2.2.4)$$

Consequently, the following holds true:

$$o > 0 \leftrightarrow \phi\left(\bigcup_{n \in N} \sigma_n\right) \neq \phi\left(\bigcup_{m \in M} \sigma_m\right) \qquad (3.2.2.5)$$

By definition, in the IoP the consumer always finds the cheapest supply offer available ($\phi\left(\bigcup_{n \in N} \sigma_n\right) = \phi\left(\bigcup_{m \in M} \sigma_m\right)$). Further implications with respect to prices and quality can be derived from this. If, in the IoP consumers have the possibility to instantaneously discover the supply offer with the lowest price out of all supply offers in the market, those supply offers with a price different from the lowest price will likely not be matched any longer with demands, as long as they offer exactly the same good and/or exactly the same services as all the other suppliers. According to [EcoMic04] - [EcoMic15], those suppliers will either have to lower their prices to match with the lowest price available or will have to exit the market as no revenue is generated any longer. Higher prices than the lowest price will only be acceptable by consumers, if the supply offer differentiates itself from others in terms of quality of service. If, for example, additional services are included in the supply offer (e.g., fast shipping, insurance, etc.), then consumers might still want to pay the higher price for the good. In summary, there exist three strategies for suppliers to conduct business ([Porter 1998], p. 35) in the IoP:

- ▪ Adapt their prices to the lowest market price (cost leadership strategy),

- ▪ Differentiate by offering a higher quality of service (differentiation strategy), or

- ▪ "Focus on particular buyer group, segment of the product line, or geographic market" (segmentation strategy) ([Porter 1998], p. 38).

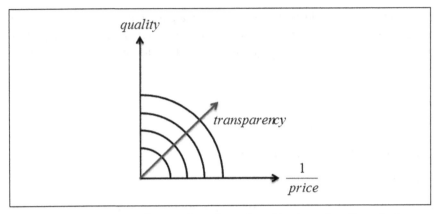

Figure 14: Iso-transparency lines are formed out of combinations of quality and price.

Figure 14 demonstrates how quality of service and price relate to each other. Iso-transparency lines thereby indicate that for a given transparency level there might exist multiple combinations of quality and price (cp. [Varian 1999], p. 562). Though Figure 14 samples a concave type of an iso-transparency line, hypothetically iso-transparency lines can have any shape, but with different weights for quality and price.

Based on the previously introduced market categories, the IoP can be comprehended as an additional functor $F_{IoP}: C_\Sigma \times C_\Gamma \to_{IoP} C_M$. This a fundamental difference to the state of the art (SotA), where there exist m functors $F_{SotA_1}: C_{\Sigma_1} \times C_\Gamma \to_{SotA_1} C_{M_1}, \ldots, F_{SotA_m}: C_{\Sigma_m} \times C_\Gamma \to_{SotA_m} C_{M_m}$. According to (3.2.2.1) and (3.2.2.2), the cheapest offer in SotA could only be found, if all markets were investigated. The IoP, contrarily, implicitly contains the cheapest offer $(M_{\Sigma_{IoP}}^{price\_leader} = M_{\Sigma_{M_1 \cup \ldots \cup M_m}}^{price\_leader})$.

While F_{IoP} adds to $F_{Monopoly}$, $F_{Oligopoly}$, and $F_{Competition}$ (the objects $O_M c_\Sigma \times c_\Gamma$ of the functor category of markets) as another functor, in reality it approaches an idealized economic concept, which is called "perfect competition" ([Samuelson 2005], p. 35), from an information systems point of view. The transformation from F_{SotA_i}, $i = 1, \ldots, m$ or $F_{Monopoly}$, $F_{Oligopoly}$, and $F_{Competition}$, respectively to F_{IoP} is characterized as the natural transformations $\chi_{Monopoly}: F_{Monopoly}(X) \circ F_{IoP}(X)$, $\chi_{Oligopoly}: F_{Oligopoly}(X) \circ F_{IoP}(X)$, and $\chi_{Competition}: F_{Competition}(X) \circ F_{IoP}(X)$.

3.2.3 Reverse Commerce in the IoP

Search cost and hence opaqueness margin originate from:

▪ Consumers not being able to precisely express their demand due to insufficient tools,

▪ Search engines being biased with respect to the ranking of results,

▪ Search engines not being able to discover the entire online market,

▪ Search engines not being able to include the consumers' search preferences, and

▪ Traditional markets paralleling electronic markets.

The Internet of Products aims to provide solutions for the above four points. As it will be shown in chapters 5, 6, and 7, the IoP is based on a network of Semantic Product Servers (SPS) that use a Semantic Product Description Language (S-PDL), in order to communicate with clients and users. The S-PDL allows consumers for describing goods based on their actual attributes/characteristics. A query (q) for a BMW car, for instance, with more than 250HP and a price that is less than $40.000 would be expressed in the S-PDL as the following example shows:

$$q = (BMW)(power > HP250)(price < \$40000)$$

Listing 1: Sample PDL query.

Upon reception of q, the SPS performs an on-attribute-level matching of every attribute/characteristic of the sought good in q with every product description that exists in its catalog. The SPS only returns those products in its catalog that implement the above three attributes/characteristics.

The capability of the SPS to precisely express the attributes/characteristics of the goods consumers seek led the author to envision a way of conducting e-commerce, where the matching is done by suppliers and not by consumers anymore. "Reverse Commerce" describes a concept where consumers, instead of investigating the market by themselves, solely announce their demand in a way as it was sampled in Listing 1, whereby their demand is automatically matched with the available supply. Based upon the attributes of a search query, suppliers have the option to provide a bid for a good that implements the attributes of q. If all received bids refer to the same good, the consumer will likely decide for the bid with the lowest price. In the IoP, this process is highly automated, whereby ideally, the provisioning and matching of bids is performed automatically by the SPS. Consumers can furthermore provide matching preferences together with the query, if, for example, they value the reputation of suppliers higher than their prices for goods.

The idea of Reverse Commerce is to be understood as consequence of the IoP. As Reverse Commerce aims to entirely remove all market insufficiencies that exist in electronic markets, it might also be referred to as "Total Commerce". Though closely related, Total Commerce (TC) –analogously to $F_{IoP}(X)$– adds as another Functor $F_{TC}(X)$ to the objects of the functor category of markets $O_M c_{\Sigma \times C_\Gamma}$ (cp. section 3.1.6).

3.3 The Triple Bottom Line

With the ratification of the United Nations and ICLEI TBL in 2007, the Triple Bottom Line (short: 3BL) became a standard for public sector full cost accounting. 3BL attempts to evaluate business performance based on its impacts on the environment, interested stakeholders, as well as profitability concerns [Dao 2011]. The acronym 3BL stands for people, planet, and profit [Bader 2008], and demands that in order to sustainably measure and evaluate any economic activity, the profit that is generated, the people that are affected by the economic activity as well as ecological consequences have to be evenly assessed. An activity A, for example, that generates a lot of profit but in turn significantly pollutes the environment cannot be sustainable and thus will be gauged lower than an activity B that generates less profit than A but is eco-friendly. Other factors, which are not covered by 3BL but which might be of particular interest for an even more holistic approach than 3BL, are discussed in [Drake 2011].

3.3.1   The Category 3BL

In order to highlight certain characteristics of the 3BL, a new category is introduced. Let C_{3BL} be the category of 3BL. Then, C_{3BL} consists of:

1. O_{3BL} as the entirety of economic activities,

2. M_{3BL} as the following morphisms between the economic activities $act \in O_{3BL}$ that symbolize the three elements of the Triple Bottom Line:

▣ M_{3BL}^{people}, or M^{people}, whereby $M^{people}: O_{3BL} \rightarrow \mathbb{R}$, as "a measure for the impact an economic activity has on the people",

▣ M_{3BL}^{profit}, or M^{profit}, whereby $M^{profit}: O_{3BL} \rightarrow \mathbb{R}$, as "a measure for the impact an economic activity has on the profit being generated",

▣ M_{3BL}^{planet}, or M^{planet}, with $M^{planet}: O_{3BL} \rightarrow \mathbb{R}$, as "a measure for the impact an economic activity has on the environment".

3. $\circ_{3BL}$ as composition of the above morphisms. Particularly, the composition of all three of the above morphisms $\xi(X): M_{people}(X) \circ_{3BL} M_{profit}(X) \circ_{3BL} M_{planet}(X) \rightarrow \mathbb{R}$ incorporates the actual concept of the Triple Bottom Line. Contemporary literature has been discussing and suggesting ways of blending M^{people}, M^{profit}, and M^{planet} into one objective function ξ [Langella 2011], [Drake 2011], but there has been no sufficiently good solution to this problem yet. In order to comprehend the difficulties with finding an objective blending function, the following example can be considered: Let $act_1, act_2 \in O_{3BL}$ be two economic activities. Let furthermore the following values be given for their morphisms:

$M^{people}(act_1) = 0, M^{profit}(act_1) = 100, M^{planet}(act_1) = 0,$

$M^{people}(act_2) = 33, M^{profit}(act_2) = 33, M^{planet}(act_2) = 33$ (3.3.1.1)

If, in the trivial case, ξ was defined as $\xi(X) = M_{people}(X) + M_{profit}(X) + M_{planet}(X)$ and furthermore $\xi_1 \geqslant \xi_2 \leftrightarrow \xi_1 \geq \xi_2$, then act_1would be considered as "better than" act_2, though the distribution of gains in act_2 appears to be much fairer. A unilateral maximization of one of the three factors as shown in the above example is indeed completely counter-intentional to the 3BL. This is why ξ requires balancing of the three factors and/or punishment of badly balanced activities. Other sources of literature ([Krikke 2003], [Langella 2011]) propose assigning weights, so that, for example, $\xi(X) = w_{people} * M^{people}(X) + w_{profit} * M^{profit}(X) + w_{planet} * M^{planet}(X)$. Finding objective weights, however, might be as difficult as finding an objective blending function.

4. I_{3BL} as the identity morphisms of O_{3BL}.

Especially, the discussion about finding an objective blending function appears to be one of the major hurdles on the way toward the implementation of the 3BL in practice. Due to the complexity and interdependence of the three factors of the 3BL, comparing two activities $act_1, act_2 \in O_{3BL}$ with another might be very difficult. If, however, one of the three factors $M^{people}(X), M^{profit}(X), M^{planet}(X)$ can individually be optimized, so that, for instance,

$$M^{people}(X') + M^{profit}(X') + M^{planet}(X')$$

$$= M^{people}(X) + M^{profit}(X + \Delta_{profit}) + M^{planet}(X)$$

with

$$\Delta_{profit} > 0 \qquad\qquad\qquad\qquad\qquad\qquad\qquad (3.3.1.2)$$

then this would mean a Pareto optimization ([Varian 1999], p. 15) and $\xi(X') > \xi(X)$ would really infer that $\xi(X') \succcurlyeq \xi(X)$ (or $\xi(X')$ dominates $\xi(X)$). The remainder of this thesis builds upon Pareto improvements, which are caused through independent factor optimizations by the IoP. The next sections will briefly highlight the impact of the IoP on each of the three 3BL factors.

3.3.2   The IoP Impact on the 3BL

The Triple Bottom Line represents a unified and ratified concept that –for the first time ever– measures the impact of economic activities on the three dimensions people, profit, and planet. Possible consequences of the IoP with respect to the three 3BL dimensions are the focus of the remainder of this chapter. Thereby, the following three sections are to be understood as a general framework that approaches the potential gains of the Internet of Products from three different perspectives.

3.3.2.1   The IoP Impact on People

The 3BL criterion "People" aims to measure the impact of economic activities on the people who are affected by that activity. Thereby, the impact can be very diverse and reaches from income-related and health-related to time- and stress-related factors. [Becker 2010] names the concept of corporate social responsibility (CSR) and states that "organizations must recognize their responsibilities to all stakeholders, including communities, […], business relationships, and consumers". By nature, finding a measure that sufficiently respects all of the aspects that decide over the wellbeing of a society is very difficult and requires a lot of balancing. Throughout this thesis, the earlier introduced economic measure of welfare is used to represent the IoP's impact on the "People" criterion of the 3BL.

3.3.2.2 The IoP Impact on Profit

Enterprises need to generate profit, in order to be able to invest into their future operations. Without profit, companies cannot grow; they cannot even replace old factor inputs with new ones (e.g., machines, computers, etc.).

The discussion about opaqueness margins in section 3.2.2 focused upon enterprises that generate profit, based on their market visibility and not on the competitiveness of the goods they offer or produce. By chasing the idea of creating completely transparent markets, the IoP aims for removing those enterprises that in a completely transparent market would not be able to keep up their business activity.

Nevertheless, those enterprises that are able to maintain their operations in the IoP will generate sufficient profit, in order to finance future investments. A concept that is very close to the IoP is perfect competition, where enterprises generate just enough profit to sell their goods at (marginal) production cost ($p = MC$) ([Varian 1999], p. 302).

The IoP focuses upon the discovery of inferior supply; that is a supply offer A that is dominated by another supply offer B in terms of prices, whereby A and B are referring to exactly the same good. The IoP differs from perfect competition in a way that it does not assume an infinite number of supplies for the same good. In the IoP's perfectly transparent market, suppliers of identical goods can yet differentiate themselves by:

- Offering the lowest price in the market (price leadership),

- Offering additional services (service leadership), or

- Having the cheapest shipping option, which is directly influenced by the distance to the consumer.

Especially the distribution of ordered goods through an efficient logistics facility and with that the last point out of the above list represents an important aspect in electronic commerce in general and in the IoP in particular. It is next shown that a cheap shipping option not only serves as a way for suppliers to differentiate, but even more importantly has a significant impact on the "Planet" criterion of the 3BL.

3.3.2.3   The IoP Impact on Planet

A research of the ECMT [ECMT2007] presented to the International Transport Forum shows that about 27% of the total CO_2 emissions originate from transport, and this number is persistently growing year by year. Transport sector emissions grew up to 1,412 million tons worldwide (31%) between 1990 and 2003, and have increased by 820 million tons (26%) in OECD countries [ECMT 2007]. In Germany, transport caused about 21% of the total CO2 emissions in 2008 (see Figure 15).

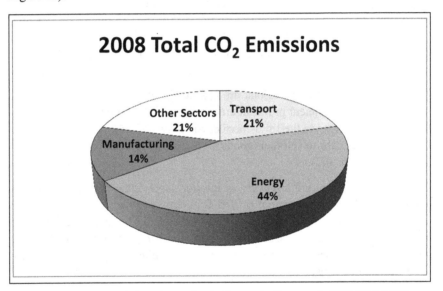

Figure 15: Transport and Greenhouse Gas Indicators in Germany in 2008 [ITF 2008].

A report by The Climate Group on behalf of the GeSI (Global e-Sustainability Initiative) [Climate Group 2008] predicts that, in total, Information and communication technologies (ICT) could account for approximately 7.8 Giga tons of CO_2 emissions savings in 2020. As compared to the 2003-based CO_2 emissions, this would mean an 11% reduction down to 15% of emissions in 2020 [Climate Group 2008]. Moreover, in 2020 CO_2 emissions could even drop below the 1990 levels. In economic terms, the ICT-enabled energy efficiency translates into approximately €600 billion ($946.5 billion) of cost savings [Climate Group 2008]. Clearly, electronic commerce in general and the Internet of Products in particular will play a major role in the above mentioned reductions in CO_2 emissions.

In 2010, the author together with a student conducted an analysis of how the planet criterion of the 3BL could be affected by the IoP, assuming that the vast majority of suppliers turned online and accepted online orders. The analysis aimed to find a measure for how much CO_2, time, and money (cp. 3BL's profit, planet, people) could be saved, if consumers procured their entire goods online and if the goods were dispatched by local logistics service providers (LSPs). Contrarily, the state of the art was assumed as consumers relying upon in-store shopping and having to individually travel to stores, in order to pick up their goods. Furthermore, the analysis solely focused upon:

- The routes an individual consumer would have to travel in order to pick up the goods from the store vs.

- The routes an LSP would have to travel in order to dispatch the orders.

Three mathematical models were developed in order to quantify the routes that need to be traveled by both parties:

- The triangle inequality-based model,

- The ellipse-based model, and

- The segment-based model.

All three models tend toward the same result, but with a different accuracy and granularity. While the triangle-based model works very well for simple setups with only a few suppliers and a few consumers, its complexity increases very fast. The ellipse-based model is also only suitable for simple setups with very few suppliers and consumers, but yields the highest accuracy out of all three. It precisely calculates the area around which an LSP is more effective than individual consumers travelling themselves to the stores. Further evolutions of this model showed that –comparable to the triangle inequality-based model– it quickly achieved a complexity that is difficult to handle. The segments-based model remains simple, even in setups where there are many suppliers and many consumers. This is because it trades accuracy for simplicity. It operates upon the average route lengths; that is the average length of all possible routes, which LSPs and consumers could travel. The segments-based model counts the segments that are required for either the LSP or the individual consumer, in order to dispatch the purchases. The outcomes of the segments-based model are as follows:

■   If at least three consumers procure from the same supplier, an LSP travels less distance,

■   If all consumers procure from different suppliers, an LSP travels a longer distance, and

■   If there are N consumers and M suppliers involved, then the LSP's travel distance is longer, until at least one of the suppliers received orders by more than two consumers, or at least one consumer procures from more than two suppliers. The savings of the LSP in travel distance will be even more significant, the more often the same supplier received orders from different consumers.

The results of the segments-based model are comparable to the results of the other two models, but scale up to an indefinite number of suppliers and consumers. All three models, the triangle inequality-based model, the ellipse-based model, as well as the segments-based model, can be reviewed in detail in Appendix A. Though none of the three models produces an entirely correct answer toward the question of how the IoP affects the 3BL (and in particular its Planet component), they at least provide strong indicators for an enhanced eco-balance, in combination with the fact that consumers spend less time on travelling in order to pick up their purchases.

3.3.3   3BL Impact Analysis Criticism

Points, which the above 3BL Impact Analysis did not cover, originate from simplifications that were made in order to keep the complexity of the models at a comprehendible level. All three models, for example, omit the fact that there arises significant cost from maintaining a local LSP fleet. Furthermore, the models are not capable of determining the number of LSPs that are necessary for operations in an entire city or municipality. Clustering a geographic area into multiple zones, whereby every zone is served by one LSP bears potential for further optimization, but at the same time causes the question of how deliveries are dealt with that involve multiple zones. Other points of criticism aim at involving 3BL-related considerations of the information systems that are necessary to run the IoP. Other sources of literature, for example, warn that "[…] online shopping can increase carbon emissions" [url$_3$]. The research results in [url$_3$] reveal that environmental savings can be achieved if online shopping replaces 3.5 traditional shopping trips. This number is very close to what the models and in particular the segment-based model in the 3BL Impact Analysis predict. Other points that the 3BL Impact Analysis disagrees with, but which are stated in [url$_3$], are that online shopping might be more sustainable, if

■   25 orders are delivered at the same time or

■   The distance travelled to where the purchase is made is more than 50km.

Though [url$_3$] states that "otherwise the impact on the environment is likely to be worse than traditional shopping", all three models of the 3BL Impact Analysis suggest that all three factors of the 3BL could contrarily even benefit from mid to short range delivery of electronically procured goods. The reason for this is that in particular recent enhancements in the reduction of the TCO of information systems (e.g., Cloud Computing) appear to have an even greater impact on the 3BL of the IoP.

3.4 Chapter Summary

This chapter introduced the Internet of Products (IoP) as a form of market coordination that is backed by information technology and aims to provide for maximum market transparency. A category-based market model was developed that declaratively describes the properties and functions of demand and supply in markets. The IoP was fit into the category-based market model as a new functor in addition to other forms of coordination, such as oligopoly or competition, whereby its special characteristic is a maximum market transparency.

Reverse Commerce or Total Commerce were discussed as consequences that might result from the IoP's maximum transparency property. It was outlined that when –in the IoP– suppliers are not able to differentiate themselves from other suppliers through prices any longer, they would need to implement new means of differentiation, such as, for example, an increased quality of service.

Throughout the second half of this chapter, the Triple Bottom Line (3BL), which is a composition of the impact economic activities might have on people, planet, and profit, was introduced as a novel concept for public sector full cost account-

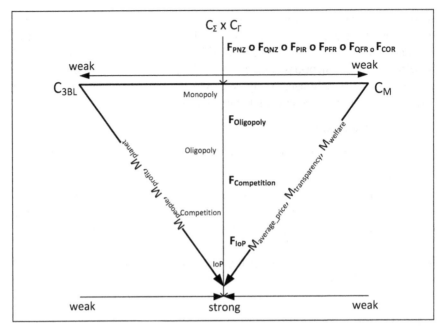

Figure 16: The category-based ecosystem of the Internet of Products.

ing. Based on the 3BL, several possibilities of how the IoP could positively influence the information society were elaborated upon. It was argued that the IoP's increased market transparency would lower supply prices with an eventually positive impact on the welfare. Additionally, more competition would lead to new business models and new services, in order for suppliers to differentiate themselves from others. One business model that might evolve from the transportation and logistics sector, for example, was referred to as "shared logistics service providers", which are LSPs that focus on the fast delivery of remotely ordered goods to the customers. Finally, ecological improvements through enhancements in transportation efficiency were covered under the Planet component of the 3BL.

Figure 16 summarizes the relations between the categories and functors that were developed throughout this chapter and depicts them in a unified diagram.

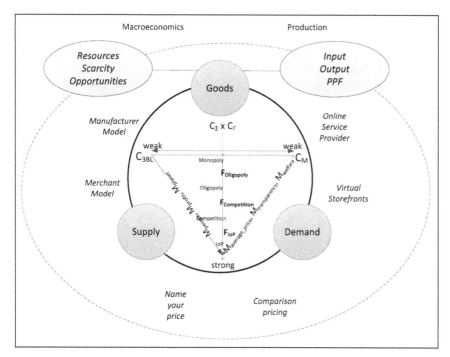

Figure 17: Categories in electronic markets.

The essence of the above diagram lies in the Internet of Products facilitating reduced transaction cost, lower prices, higher transparency, and higher welfare on the market side (C_M). On the side of the 3BL (C_{3BL}), the IoP bears significant potential to positively affect people, profit, and planet. With respect to market transactions ($C_\Sigma \times C_\Gamma$), the IoP can be considered as an information system-based form of competition, with maximum efficiency in terms of market coordination.

Figure 17 integrates Figure 11 with Figure 16 and shows how the concepts elaborated upon throughout this chapter complement the transparency of contemporary electronic markets, through openly accessible product information in the Internet of Products.

The following chapters cover the design and development of an information system that serves as the technological backbone of the IoP.

Part II:
Technologies and Paradigms
of the Internet of Products

Part I of this thesis provided an extensive discussion around the economic, ecological, and societal gains of an openly accessible Internet of Products, as well as
their sustainability. Due to the complexity of aspects that are involved (e.g.,
suitable information technology, shared logistics, consumer and supplier acceptance, etc.), realizing the Internet of Products is a complex enterprise. There
are three major research objectives that deal with very different aspects of the
Internet of Products:

■ How can electronic markets be made more transparent (cp. sections 2.1.8 &
  3.3.2.1)?

■ How can suppliers/consumers be convinced to contribute to and use the
  Internet of Products (cp. section 3.3.2.2)?

■ How can goods ordered online be efficiently dispatched to customers (cp.
  section 3.3.2.3)?

Each of the three above questions involves different research disciplines. Question 1, for example, mainly covers an information systems related problem.
Question 2 investigates how an incentive system can be created to stimulate
suppliers and consumers to make effective use of the Internet of Products and
contribute to it. Question 3 finally involves logistics-related aspects, such as
route planning, repository planning, vehicle planning, etc.

Though this thesis contains research insights from all of the three above mentioned problem domains, questions 2 and 3 are only briefly covered and are
backed by some initial research findings (cp. sections 3.3.2.2, 3.3.2.3, and Appendix A). Since questions 2 and 3 are completely orthogonal to question 1 and
due to limitations in space, they would need to be covered in detail as part of
future work or through other researchers (e.g., [Langella 2011], [Dao 2011],
[Becker 2010]).

The following chapters focus solely upon providing a suitable solution to question 1. It is shown how a Semantic Product Description Language (S-PDL) in combination with a Semantic Product Server (SPS) assists users with product discovery in a novel semantic product search engine. Hence, throughout the remainder of this thesis, the Internet of Products is approached from an information systems point of view. The elaborations and conceptual models developed throughout chapters 5, 6, and 7 are based upon the following four pillars:

■   Semantic and Web 2.0 principles (section 4.1),

■   Semantic Product models and classification (section 4.2),

■   Semantic product query systems technologies and paradigms (section 4.3), and

■   Semantic product query systems quality assurance (section 4.4).

Chapter 4 covers the fundamentals of the above four mentioned disciplines in the respective sections 4.1, 4.2, 4.3, and 4.4. Chapters 5, 6, and 7, which belong to Part III, cover the design of the S-PDL, the implementation of the SPS, as well as the validation of these two concepts in form of prototypical applications, including a selection of particularly interesting quality-related aspects of the developed technology.

4 Foundations of Semantic Product Query Systems

"Everything should be made as simple as possible, but not simpler." (Albert Einstein)

This chapter examines the technological foundations of Semantic Product Query Systems (SPQS). It is divided into four sections. The first section covers the principles of the Semantic Web and the Internet of Things, with a focus upon means of information representation. The second section aims to provide a literature overview of the origins and the state of the art of semantic product data modeling. The third section reviews technology paradigms that might be of particular importance with respect to the design and development of semantic product query systems. The fourth section details a selection of quality-related aspects of semantic product query systems, before section five wraps-up the content of this chapter.

4.1 Semantic and Web 2.0 Principles

The Semantic Web and the technologies and concepts that evolved from it play a major role with respect to finding a suitable information architecture for a semantic product query system. This section reviews the Internet of Things and projects its ideas onto the Internet of Products. Furthermore, a selection of means of storing and representing information is introduced and detailed.

4.1.1   The Internet of Things

The idea of an Internet of Products is inspired by the vision of the technology pioneer Kevin Ashton to build something that he referred to as the "Internet of Things" (IoT) [Ashton 2009]. The IoT consists of uniquely identifiable objects ("things") and their virtual representations on the Internet. CERP, the Center for European Research Projects (On the Internet of Things), defines the IoT as an "integrated part of Future Internet" and could be seen as "a dynamic global network infrastructure with self-configuring capabilities based on standard and interoperable communication protocols where physical and virtual 'things' have identities, physical attributes, and virtual personalities and use intelligent interfaces, and are seamlessly integrated into the information network" [url4]. [Uckelmann 2011] adds that things are any identifiable physical objects, independent of the technology that is used for identification or providing status information of the objects and their surroundings. According to [Reed 2012], "the number of things connected to the Internet greatly exceeds the number of people using them".

4.1.1.1 The "Internet of Things" Category (IoT)

The Internet of Things can be considered as a category IoT, where

$$IoT = (Ob(IoT), Mor_{IoT}(X,Y), \circ, id_{IoT}) \tag{4.1.1.1.1}$$

with $Ob(IoT)$ being the objects of the Internet of Things (e.g., the actual "things") and $Mor_{IoT}(X,Y)$ being the arrows between two objects $X, Y \in Ob(IoT)$. $\circ$ defines a composition operator between two morphisms $f1, f2 \in Mor_{IoT}(X,Y)$. id_{IoT} are the identity morphisms for each element $X \in Ob(IoT)$.

In the IoT, there exists an arrow $f_{URL}(X,Y): X \to Y$, if X is a URL and Y is an object that is accessible via X. In the Internet of Things, objects are accessed via their uniform resource locators (URL), a subclass of uniform resource identifiers (URI), and served by web servers. The object's URL typically consists of two parts: the web server's internet address (an IP address or a DNS) and the object's virtual address on the web server. The object's virtual address (together with other mapping information) contains the identifier of the object.

The morphism f_{URL} is injective. URLs are assigned at maximum one object. If f_{URL} is furthermore surjective, every URL in the Internet of Things is assigned exactly one object. In this case, f_{URL} is bijective. f_{URL}, however, is never only surjective as this would mean that several URLs pointed to multiple objects. Objects would not be uniquely identifiable any longer.

Web servers store objects and make them accessible to requests by other objects, thereby managing the object's lifecycle. Typical tasks of web servers include:

- Creation, destruction, and persistence of objects,

- Authentication and authorization of access requests for objects,

- Traffic and performance management of object requests (e.g. caching, replication),

- Integrity and consistency management between multiple object storages (database, cache).

All publicly accessible web servers together form what is known as the World Wide Web (WWW). The WWW organizes its web servers into a hierarchy of Domain Name Servers (DNS's). By being routed through all intermediate DNS's, one web server in the WWW can discover and access every other web server in the WWW - they form a web of web servers, the World Wide Web.

In terms of category theory, the WWW and as such the Internet can be described by the category PoSet (cp. section 3.1.1) with objects of PoSet being partially ordered sets (posets) and morphisms being arrows from $f: X \to Y$, if $X \geq Y$, meaning that X precedes Y in the hierarchy. Elements of these posets are (RESTful) [Fielding 2000] web servers.

4.1.1.2   The "Cloud of Things" Category (CoT)

If many web servers are grouped together within an intranet, this constellation can be seen as a grid of web servers (or "Grid of Things"). If additionally this grid can elastically scale out and scale in, it is called a Cloud of Things. The Cloud is the glue that binds the Internet of Things together [Reed 2012]. Clouds of Things implement the Platform-as-a-Service paradigm (PaaS). They are platforms because they serve the purpose of hosting web objects in general and web applications in particular (cp. 4.3.4). Clouds of Things facilitate semantic application development, as they abstract various parts of the object's lifecycle away from developers. Cloud developers, for example, surrender their responsibility for data safety and security, fail-over, fault-tolerance and the elastic adaptation to varying traffic loads entirely to the Cloud (cp. 4.3.4).

Similarly to the Internet of Things, Clouds of Things can be described as:

$$CoT = (Ob(CoT), Mor_{CoT}(X,Y), \circ, id_{CoT}) \qquad (4.1.1.2.1)$$

The elements of CoT are defined analogously to IoT. $Ob(CoT)$ are the objects of the Cloud of Things. $Mor_{CoT}(X,Y)$ are arrows between two objects $X, Y \in Ob(CoT)$, if X is a URL and Y is an object. $\circ$ defines a composition operator between two morphisms $f1, f2 \in Mor_{CoT}(X,Y)$. id_{CoT} are the identity morphisms for each element $X \in Ob(CoT)$. Furthermore, there exists a functor F from IoT to CoT that maps the objects, morphisms, the composition, and the identities of IoT to CoT.

4.1.1.3   The "Internet of Products" Category (IoP)

This thesis considers a sub domain of the IoT, where things are comparable products that are language and culture-independent, and that are hosted on an extensible and customizable platform. This IoT sub domain is referred to as "Internet of Products" (IoP). Let IoP be a subcategory of IoT, such that $Ob(IoP)$ is a subclass of $Ob(IoT)$. Furthermore, for two objects $X, Y \in Ob(IoP)$ the following holds true: $Mor_{IoP}(X, Y) \subseteq Mor_{IoT}(X, Y)$.

$$IoP = (Ob(IoP), Mor_{IoP}(X, Y), \circ, id_{IoP}) \qquad (4.1.1.3.1)$$

$Ob(IoP)$ represents the class of objects of the Internet of Products. Objects are semantic product descriptions that are accessible through their identifiers. Semantic product descriptions are introduced and detailed later in chapter 5. $Mor_{IoP}(X, Y)$ are arrows between two semantic product descriptions $X, Y \in Ob(IoP)$. These arrows can be any arrows $f1, f2, ..., f_n \in Mor_{IoT}(X, Y)$. $\circ$ defines a composition operator between two morphisms $f1, f2 \in Mor_{IoP}(X, Y)$. id_{IoP} are the identity morphisms for each element $X \in Ob(IoP)$.

In the IoP, products are accessed via their Uniform Product Identifier (UPI), which is essentially a URI. Analogously to the Internet of Things, objects in the Internet of Products are hosted and served by product servers. Product servers are web servers that define certain operations on the objects they serve: products. These operations are detailed later in section 5.2.

Product servers inherit the property of web servers of sharing their DNS with all other participants of the IoP. Every product server can discover and interact with every other product server in the IoP. While this allows for exchanging products between product servers, all processing of products remains within the product server that hosts the product.

4.1.1.4   The "Cloud of Products" Category (CoP)

If Semantic Product Servers are run in a Cloud, they can be thought of as "product Clouds". Product Clouds can be considered Software-as-a-Service (SaaS), if servers are rented out to customers for the purpose of hosting the customer's products (cp. section 4.3.4). Product Clouds can furthermore be considered Platform-as-a-Service (PaaS), if application developers are able to enhance the product server's functionality by developing and deploying custom extensions. It is detailed later in section 6.5 how custom extensions can be developed for product servers.

As compared to individually hosting product servers, product Clouds exhibit the following benefits [Armbrust 2009]:

- Reduced TCO,

- Reduced maintenance complexity,

- Data safety and security,

- Elasticity, and

- Consumption-based pricing.

Analogously to Clouds of Things (CoT), Clouds of Products are described by a category CoP:

$$CoP = (Ob(CoP), Mor_{CoP}(X, Y), \circ, id_{CoP}) \tag{4.1.1.4.1}$$

CoP is a subcategory of CoT. Again, there exists a functor F from IoP to CoP that maps the objects, morphisms, the composition, and the identities of IoP to CoP. Since IoP is a subcategory of IoT, there also exists a functor from IoT to CoP.

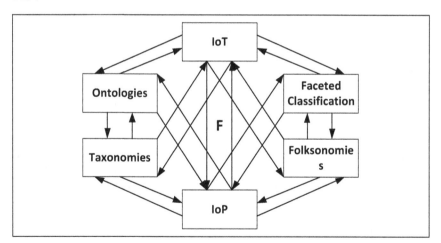

Figure 18: Functors mapping objects and morphisms between categories of the IoT/IoP.

Technologies of the Semantic Web in general and IoT, CoT, IoP, and CoP in particular are ontologies, taxonomies, faceted classifications, or folksonomies. All of them provide means of knowledge/information representation. Thereby, they represent own categories, with functors mapping things and morphisms to other categories. Figure 18 shows that there exist functors from *IoT* to *IoP* as well as from Ontologies, Taxonomies, Faceted Classification, and Folksonomies to *IoT* and *IoP*. Though not depicted in Figure 18, similar functors also exist for *CoT* and *CoP*.

The following sections 4.1.2 – 4.1.5 provide an overview of the concepts behind ontologies, taxonomies, faceted classification, and folksonomies, since they are considered as the fundamental structures behind the IoT/IoP.

4.1.2   Ontologies

The Semantic Web aims to integrate content through semi-structured data models that explicitly specify data semantics through ontologies [Volz 2003]. The word Ontology refers to the branch of philosophy that studies the nature of existence and the structure of reality [Jacob 2003]. According to [url$_8$], an ontology investigates "the categories of things that exist or may exist" in a particular domain and produces a catalog that details the types of things and the relations between those types, which are relevant for that particular domain [Jacob 2003]. Ontologies have been variously construed as classification schemes, taxonomies, hierarchies, thesauri, controlled vocabularies, terminologies and even dictionaries [Jacob 2003].

According to ([Neches 1991], p. 40), "an ontology defines the basic terms and relations comprising the vocabulary of a topic area as well as the rules for combining terms and relations to define extensions to the vocabulary". Ontologies furthermore refer to a formal representation of knowledge in a specified domain. The word ontology thereby refers to a formal, explicit specification of a shared conceptualization [Gruber 1995]. Ontologies model any knowledge domain, the objects, concepts and their properties that exist in that domain, and the relations between them [Milde 2011]. Ontologies are classified into two categories [Uschold 1996]:

- ▪ Domain ontologies and
- ▪ Foundation ontologies.

Domain ontologies model things and their properties with regard to a specific domain [Uschold 1996]. Since things can be shared across domains with different meanings, domain ontologies are not universally applicable, but only within the same domain [Milde 2011]. An example is the concept of a bank that can be distinguished into a financial institution and into a seating. The above example shows that ontologies and with this ontology-based applications suffer from heterogeneity [Volz 2003]. Foundation ontologies, contrarily, are designed to be used throughout different domains [Sanchez-Alonso 2006], [Niles 2001]. Foundation ontologies are required to be general enough to be applicable in various scenarios, but at the same time should have enough features to be still of practical use [Milde 2011].

A popular example of a foundation ontology is Dublin Core3 [url$_9$], a structural representation of metadata elements that use classifiers (e.g., title, creator, subject, description, type, format, etc.) to describe products and articles of various kinds [Milde 2011]. The friend-of-a-friend ontology (FOAF) [url$_{10}$] is another example of a foundation ontology. The FOAF ontology is used to describe the relations of people to other people on a global scale [Milde 2011].

Figure 19 shows that the main components of an ontology consist of instances, classes, attributes, relations, restrictions, rules, axioms, and events [Gruber 1995]. Instances are concrete objects (e.g., persons, animals, cars, etc.) [Milde 2011]. Classes are more general abstractions of instances and can be used across multiple instances [Milde 2011].

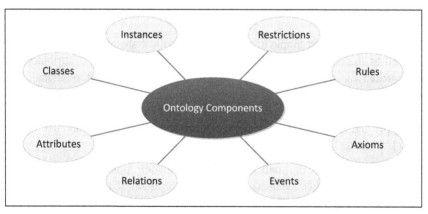

Figure 19: Ontology components [Milde 2011].

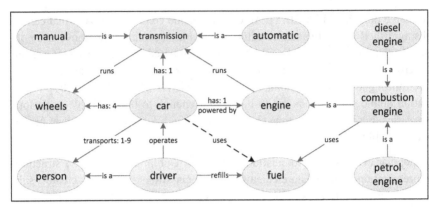

Figure 20: An example ontology within the knowledge domain about cars [Milde 2011].

Similarly to object-oriented programming, classes support inheritance, which means that classes can have super and sub classes [Milde 2011]. Attributes describe objects within an ontology in more detail and provide information about the associations of these objects with other objects [Milde 2011]. Lastly, relations specify how objects in an ontology are related to other objects [Milde 2011]. The fundamental advantage of ontologies is based on its capability to define arbitrary relations for the description of how objects are interrelated [Neches 1991].

Figure 20 depicts an example of an ontology that illustrates various parts of a car as well as the relations between them [Milde 2011]. Classes and attributes are represented through green ellipses. Arrows represent directed relations. The relation "is a", for example, stands for a hierarchical relationship [Milde 2011]. The "has" relation, on the other hand, is often bound to a restriction that provides the upper and lower boundaries of the respective parts that are contained [Milde 2011]. As it can be seen from the example in

Figure 20, ontologies that only contain "is a" relationships and no restrictions, rules, axioms, or other elements, are structurally identical to taxonomies (covered in section 4.1.3). In this respect, ontologies can be regarded as a generalizations of the taxonomies ([Priebe 2005], p. 149).

In his vision of the Semantic Web, Tim Berners-Lee referred to ontologies as the core element that is used to store human knowledge in a machine-readable and machine-understandable format [Berners-Lee 2001]. In this Semantic Web, computers and human users would operate in a similar knowledge domain [Milde 2011]. Ontologies can furthermore be used automatic reasoning as well as knowledge discovery. In Figure 20 (dashed arrow), for example, a machine could automatically conclude that cars consume petrol, since cars are equipped with a combustion engine, which again is an engine that uses petrol.

Several formats exist that can be used to model, encode, and persist ontologies. The probably most popular approach to modeling ontologies is the Web Ontology Language (OWL) [Horrocks 2003], which is maintained by the World Wide Web Consortium (W3C). OWL is the successor of the Resource Description Framework (RDF) [Wang 2004]. Since for later chapters of this thesis, neither OWL nor RDF will be of particular relevance, it is refrained from detailing the syntax of both. Nevertheless, it is important to understand the purpose and feasibility of ontologies and their description languages.

Though they represent the foundation of the Semantic Web, ontologies suffer from a multitude of problems when being applied in practice. [Svátek 2004] states that with respect to the Semantic Web the following three ontology-related qualities are of particular importance:

- Accuracy: ontologies should reflect the true state of affairs that represent the reality, with few or no tacit assumptions. Tacit assumptions would lead to incorrect use beyond the original context,

- Transparency: if ontologies are to be shared, their meaning must be comprehensible for other people than just their designers, and

- Reasonability: in terms of usability for inference by existing semantic web reasoners.

[Svátek 2004], however, adds that many ontologies fail in at least one of the before mentioned quality criteria, due to reasons of:

- Inaccuracy: inaccurate ontologies produce wrong results, as soon as their implicit assumptions are violated,

- Opaqueness: opaque ontologies will either not be used outside their native application or will be mapped on an inadequate state of affairs,

- Inferences: ontologies unusable for inference will not be usable with OWL (as inference–oriented language that is based on description logics).

[Silva 2002] lists problems of ontologies when applied in practice, especially when knowledge is shared among multiple different ontologies:

■ Sharing and reusing knowledge of multiple overlapping ontologies,

■ Sharing inferential knowledge; that is, knowledge that is implicit to the ontology and that is made explicit through inference engines,

■ Sharing semantic knowledge through semantic links between the inferences within individual ontologies,

■ Sharing group knowledge out of a cluster of multiple ontologies.

Though they represent a very powerful basis for the Semantic Web, when being applied in practice ontologies suffer from a variety of problems. Despite the internal but avoidable problems with ontologies (as summarized in [Svátek 2004]), even more severe, sometimes non-avoidable problems occur when different ontologies are used in practice and among different organizations [Silva 2002]. Taxonomies represent a kind of ontology, but with only certain semantic relations, which makes them easier to comprehend and transform.

4.1.3   Taxonomies

Taxonomies are another type of classification which is used to group related things together [Taylor 2006]. Based on [Garshol 2004], the term taxonomy refers to a subject-based classification that arranges the terms in the controlled vocabulary into a hierarchy, without doing anything further. Based on certain characteristics, concepts are grouped into categories or classes that best describe the properties of the concept [Taylor 2006]. Taxonomies usually refer to mono-hierarchical structures [Jaksch 2005]. Mono-hierarchical structures assign each class exactly one super class (except for the root node) [Taylor 2006]. Thereby, each class has exactly the same properties as its super class, possibly extended by some more specific information [Taylor 2006]. Furthermore, the more deeply nested a class within a taxonomy is, the more specific the properties of the class are (e.g., the number of constraints that adhere to it) [Taylor 2006].

Figure 21 provides an example of a taxonomy for countries. The root node represents the domain "world", which all subordinate concepts are contained within

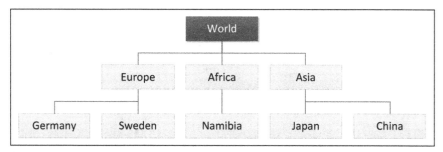

Figure 21: An example taxonomy that categorizes countries by the continent [Milde 2011].

[Milde 2011]. Furthermore, the world consists of continents, which again consist of countries. It is also to be noted that the relations between classes are not bidirectional [Milde 2011]. While, for example, Germany is a part of Europe, Europe is not a part of Germany; that is, Germany is more specific than Europe.

Many modern product catalogues use taxonomies to categorize products. Thereby, products that are related to each other or that share common properties might be grouped in the same class [Milde 2011]. The number of different classes as well as the hierarchy's depth depend on the number and the type of products that are being categorized [Milde 2011]. A high diversity of products within the catalog often leads to a broad [Skadron 2000] and flat taxonomy, whereas very specialized products result into a narrow [Xing 2008] and deep taxonomy.

The advantage of using a taxonomy for product categorization is that taxonomies expose an explicit underlying structure to the user [Milde 2011]. This characteristic might be helpful when users are looking for products but do not know exactly where to start searching or how to specify search queries [Milde 2011]. On the contrary, however, taxonomies also feature a number of problems. One major disadvantage of taxonomies is that they have to be maintained manually [Milde 2011]. Manual editing of the taxonomy can be tedious, especially when many products are to be added to the taxonomy [Ziegler 2004]. A second major disadvantage is that taxonomies are usually fixed, which means that the number or type of categories cannot easily be altered [Milde 2011]. If the categories of a taxonomy are still being altered, it might be required to manually recategorize every single element of the taxnonomy. Furthermore, concepts should generally be assigned to only one category, but often products could very well fit in two or

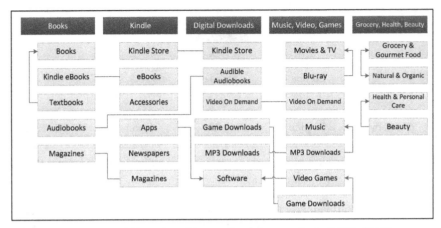

Figure 22: The top-level hierarchy of Amazon's product catalogue [Milde 2011].

more categories [Milde 2011]. If, for example, Russia was to be added to the taxonomy in Figure 21, it could be listed under Europe but also under Asia. Figure 22 provides an extract of a real-world taxonomy that was extracted from the top-level taxonomy used by Amazon [url$_{11}$].

Since Amazon started as online store for books, it has its own category for books. Over time, additional product types were added and the taxonomy grew bigger [Milde 2011]. It can furthermore be seen that the categories are not mutually exclusive or that some categories –for the sake of browsability– were grouped together, even though they do not share much in common [Milde 2011].

Despite their shortcomings, taxonomies also provide for certain benefits, when applied in electronic product data modeling. Similar to indices for relational data, taxonomies make search and access more efficient [Ziegler 2004], with a positive impact on system performance. Especially in large-scale systems, the performance advantage of taxonomies over ontologies might play a major role. The before mentioned problem of taxonomies having to potentially restructure all their elements, when an element is added or deleted, is mitigated in [Ziegler 2004] through an automatic system that performs this task.

4.1.4   Faceted Classification

Faceted classification is related to taxonomies, but is yet different. In faceted classification, concepts are described by a set of terms (facets) and facet values

[Poulin 1993]. According to [Taylor 2006], a facet consists of clearly defined, mutually exclusive, and collectively exhaustive aspects, properties, or characteristics of an item. Thereby, every item exposes all facets of the scheme [Taylor 2006]. Figure 23 depicts an example of a faceted classification, which provides quick and diverse access to the names and information of Nobel laureates. Facets in Figure 23 are "Gender", "Country", "Prize", and "Year". There are, for example, 698 male and 44 German laureates. 138 laureates received the Nobel Prize for chemistry (and so on).

Faceted classification can be considered as constructing several parallel taxonomies, which all describe the same set of data [Denton 2009]. Thereby, every taxonomy represents a single facet. Every facet, on the other hand, categorizes the underlying data from a different point of view, which allows for search queries being authored in different ways with different aspects of the sought item. [Denton 2009] describes another way to look at faceted classification by highlighting the similarity to the relational database model. The classification itself may represent a database table, while the individual facets may represent the columns in the table [Denton 2009]. Then, browsing a faceted classification may equal a database search on the selected columns using a WHERE clause [Denton 2009]. Selecting more than one value per facet, however, compromises the strict original definition of faceted classification [Denton 2009].

Gender		Country		Prize		Year	
Male	698	Germany	44	Chemistry	138	1900s	57
Female	33	Japan	11	Economics	55	1940s	43
		Sweden	30	Physics	166	1950s	72
		France	48	Literature	101	1970s	103
		USA	279	Medicine	182	1990s	98
		UK	104	Peace	108	2000s	56

Figure 23: An example of a faceted classification [Milde 2011].

There are multiple examples that make use of faceted classification. The Colon Classification, for instance, is used in libraries to organize books, articles, and magazines [Ranganathan 2006]. It consists of five facets: "personality", "matter", "energy", "space", and "time". These five facets are so general that all publications fit at least one of them. Despite the fact that the Colon Classification could not replace traditional taxonomies, both are widely used side by side in Indian libraries [Ranganathan 2006].

The success of faceted classification is much more eminent in online product catalogues. Online retailers who offer searchable catalogues adopted faceted classification to provide more diverse ways of data exploration. Very often online product catalogs use faceted classification in combination with taxonomies, in order to leverage the individual strengths of both. While taxonomies are used to provide a general hierarchy that divides products into smaller sets of features, additional search capabilities are provided through facets of these feature sets. One way of persisting facets is to store them in a relational database. Contrarily, the Exchangeable Faceted Metadata Language (XFML) represents an open XML format, which stores and exchanges faceted classification data.

The information explosion of the digital age led to the development of greatly improved index languages, which are widely based on facet analysis [Mills 2004]. In a way, facets are similar to the attribute-value method [Poulin 1993], but with a limited choice of values. In this respect, the problem of ambiguity in deciding on the best value for a term or attribute is eliminated [Poulin 1993]. If the facet, for example, is "Car", valid values might be "BMW", "Mercedes", "Audi", "Volkswagen", or "Opel". Since facets limit the choice of terms, they promise a very good search performance [Poulin 1993] and might be of particular relevance to large-scale systems.

4.1.5   Folksonomies

The term folksonomy is an artificial word that consists of "folks" and "taxonomy". Other sources of literature also refer to folksonomies as "collaborative tagging" [Halpin 2007], "social tagging", or "social indexing" [Marlow 2006]. Folksonomies are used by normal users to tag resources, and thus provide them with a searchable description. The process of tagging is defined as the common practice of adding keywords to resources for later retrieval [Marlow 2006]. Tags are thereby organized in a flat hierarchy without any hierarchical relationship between the tags [Mathes 2004]. According to [Milde 2011], tags can be considered as categories, whereas the act of assigning a tag to a resource is similar to assigning a resource to a category. While in folksonomies resources can be assigned as many tags (categories) as users deem, in taxonomies, contrarily, resources are restricted to being assigned to exactly one category. Every folksonomy consists of the following three main components [Halpin 2007]:

- Users,

- Tags, and

- Resources.

Users are individuals who perform the tagging. Tags can be single words, compound words, or phrases that describe the content, the context or any other relation to the resource being tagged [Halpin 2007].

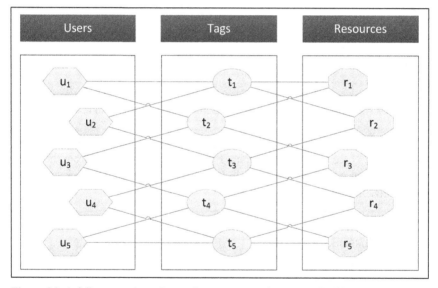

Figure 24: A folksonomy is made up of users, tags, and resources [Milde 2011].

Resources are the content which the tags are attached to and which will be retrieved when searching for the tags [Halpin 2007]. Every component of a folksonomy can be regarded as a separate space that contains a set of nodes, whereas edges exist between nodes in different spaces [Halpin 2007]. These spaces are the user space, the tag space, and the resource space (see Figure 24).

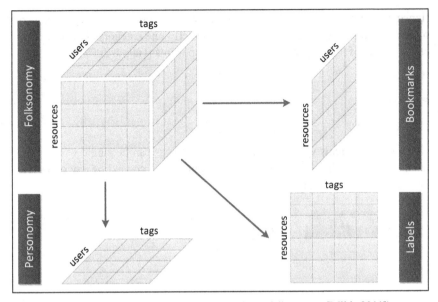

Figure 25: The tripartite data structure that describes a folksonomy [Milde 2011]).

A tagging instance consists of one user, one resource, and one or more tags between them. Three bipartite subgraphs (Figure 25) can be derived from the original tripartite graph [Wetzker 2010] in Figure 24. The subgraphs thereby represent [Wetzker 2010]:

■   The personomy,

■   The bookmarks, and

■   The item labels.

The personomy contains information regarding the resources that were labeled by a specific user. Personomies reveal the tagging preferences of users, which is why they are called "personal" [Wetzker 2010]. Bookmarks, on the other hand, describe the tags that were employed by a certain user to annotate a certain resource [Wetzker 2010]. Lastly, item labels contain information regarding the tags that a user has assigned to resources [Wetzker 2010]. The novelty in folksonomies is that users themselves annotate content, instead of experts [url7].

Folksonomies come with both benefits and drawbacks over traditional taxonomies and ontologies. One advantage of folksonomies is that they offer much higher adaptability [Milde 2011]. While taxonomies assign an object exactly to one category, folksonomies provide users with the flexibility to assign as many tags as they like. Furthermore, tags can be both precise and general and therefore suit all users [Milde 2011]. Taxonomies, contrarily, are predefined and might not serve all users. Since taxonomies (and ontologies as well) operate on a controlled set of vocabulary, search operations performed on them always return all relevant resources. Folksonomies, on the other hand, categorize content after its creation. Since tags originate from uncontrolled vocabulary, problems with synonymy and polysemy are implicit.

Figure 26: An example of a tag cloud [Milde 2011] (data taken from Flickr [url12]).

If resources, which contain synonyms in their tags, are searched by users, the search will not unrestrictedly be successful. If a user searches for a polysemous word, the result will also contain resources that are not related to the meaning of a search term [Milde 2011]. [Golder 2006], however, provides evidence for tags in broad folksonomies (with many users tagging the same resources) eventually stabilizing. This is due to the fact that users who tag resources often make reuse of already existing tags [Golder 2006]. Tag recommendation can facilitate the stabilization of folksonomies, since users are provided a selection of popular tags and encouraged to reinforce the usage of those tags [Golder 2006]. The problem of different vocabulary between users is addressed through tag translation techniques [Noh 2009], where –upon viewing and based on their tagging history– users are presented a translation candidate for a tag that was assigned to a resource. [Schrammel 2009] describes a common way of graphically presenting tags to users as "tag cloud". In a tag cloud, a tag's font size reflects its importance, whereas the tag ordering can be based upon the alphabet, popularity, etc. Figure 26 contains an example tag cloud with data taken from Flickr. The most popular tags are highlighted through their large size.

4.1.6   Section Summary

This section discussed the fundamentals of The Semantic Web and provided an overview of some of the most important technologies for information retrieval. Ontologies, taxonomies, faceted classification, as well as folksonomies were mentioned as means of organizing information through specific relations. Though ontologies represent a very powerful concept, severe problems exist when applying them in practice and across different organizations. Among those problems are knowledge sharing of overlapping ontologies, sharing of inferential knowledge [Silva 2002], or inaccuracy and opaqueness [Svátek 2004].

Taxonomies were introduced as a subject-based classification that arranges terms in a controlled vocabulary into a hierarchy [Garshol 2004]. Taxonomies are easier to read for human beings and provide for a potentially high performance [Ziegler 2004], when being applied in large-scale systems. Taxonomies are also easy to map to existing data exchange formats, such as XML, JSON, YAML, etc., which makes them especially interesting for industrial applications. Though taxonomies are potentially difficult to maintain –especially if new/existing items are added/deleted– software tools, as proposed in [Ziegler 2004], help with automating maintenance-related efforts.

Being closely related to taxonomies, faceted classifications were introduced as structures where concepts are described by a set of terms (facets) and facet values [Poulin 1993]. Conceptually, faceted classification can be seen as multiple parallel taxonomies, whereby each of the taxonomies stands for a single facet [Denton 2009]. Though facets limit the choice of terms, at the same time they provide the possibility for multiple alternative classifications of a concept. Regarding their feasibility for large-scale web applications, they promise a very good search performance [Poulin 1993] that is comparable to the search performance of taxonomies.

The fourth classification scheme that was discussed throughout this section is called a folksonomy. Folksonomies pursue the idea of allowing users to participate in classification efforts. Folksonomies are based on tagging, whereby tags are structured in a flat, non-hierarchical structure. Though folksonomies might potentially show a very high search performance, their biggest drawback is the uncontrolled and potentially redundant usage of tag vocabulary for multiple concepts [Noh 2009]. This might result in the generation of erroneous or confusing search results.

Based on the advantages and disadvantages of the four previously mentioned classification schemas, chapter 5 chooses one classification schema as fundamental basis for a Semantic Product Description Language. Moreover, it will be shown how by employing the notion of category theory a formal model of the Semantic Product Description Language can be mapped to algorithms in software.

4.2 Semantic Product Models and Classification

After topological basics of the Semantic Web were laid in the previous section, this section examines the fundamentals of semantic product models and classification.

On their very basis, SPQS' feature a product model. Product models are distinguished into industrial product models and end-consumer product models. Industrial product models serve the purpose of modeling complex products in very high detail and exchanging product information with up and downstream partners of the same supply chain. Industrial product models are found in manufacturing industries, such as automotive, and are developed through so called CAD/CAM tools. The focus of this thesis, however, lies upon product models for electronic commerce. Both product models differ in the type and granularity of product information that is being exposed. While industrial product models might contain assembly lists of parts the product is composed of, electronic commerce product models might contain data on pricing, discounts, and quantities. Also, the technical details of a product being exposed through an electronic commerce product model focus primarily on information that is relevant to customers.

4.2.1 Origins of Product Modeling

The major requirement of a product model is to support "communication, interpretation, or processing of product information" [ISO 1994] between different systems. In order to be machine-interpretable, product models rely upon so called product modeling structures. Several product modeling structures were analyzed by [Eastman 1998]. The earliest attempts date back to the 1970s and were sponsored by the British government. [Bijl 1975] proposed a CAD-based housing site layout system for the British real estate market. Other efforts were named OXSYS and BDS [Hoskins 1976], the Harness System for hospital design [Meager 1973], Eastman's group GLIDE [Eastman 1977], as well as the Archway Model by [Borkin 1982]. All of the before mentioned systems aimed to provide support for modeling of one specific type of products: buildings.

Efforts that aimed to implement product data exchange capabilities evolved through early efforts of CAD data exchange (IGES, DXF, SAT, etc.) [Eastman 1998]. These efforts turned into PDES in the US and into ISO-STEP in Europe. The General AEC Reference Model (GARM) [Gielingh 1988] and RATAS [Bjork 1995] were projects that attempted to apply data exchange technology in the construction industry. In the mid-1990s, the two EU-funded projects PISA (Platform for Information Sharing by CIME Applications) [Gielingh 1996] and ATLAS (Architecture, Methodology and Tools for Computer-Integrated Large-Scale Engineering) [Böhms 1993] were dedicated to contribute to the harmonization of ongoing product development technologies. While PISA represented an approach toward integrating STEP with CORBA, ATLAS introduced means for modeling data exchange between different disciplines and on different levels of abstraction [Eastman 1998]. Many concepts that were engineered in ATLAS went into early versions of the building construction core model (PCCM), which eventually produced the STEP application protocol 106 (AP106) [Eastman 1998].

4.2.2   Semantic Product Models

The ISO standard 10303 [ISO 1994] for product data representation and exchange, whose official title is Standard for the Exchange of Product Model data (STEP), represents a standard initiative for describing product data. STEP allows for the representation and exchange of product data throughout the entire product lifecycle [Mannistö 1998] and was ratified by the ISO in 1994. STEP provides so called application protocols for Computer-aided Design (CAD), Computer-aided Manufacturing (CAM), etc. Some of the application protocols are:

■   AP203: Configuration Controlled Design,

■   AP212: Electronical Design and Installation,

■ AP214: Core data for automative mechanical design processes,

■ AP218: Ship structures,

■ ...

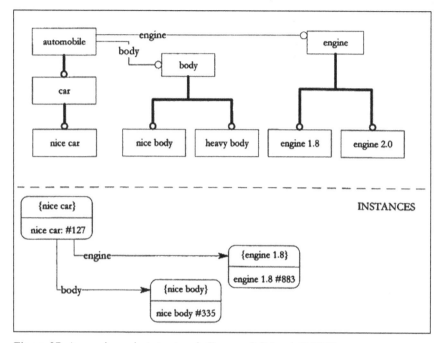

Figure 27: A generic product structure in Express-G [Mannistö 1998].

Application protocols are refinements of so called Integrated Generic Resources to meet the needs of different industrial areas. Data models in STEP are defined with the language EXPRESS [Mannistö 1998]. Figure 27 shows an example of a product model designed in EXPRESS-G, a graphical form of EXPRESS. As it can be seen, classes (e.g., "engine") can be used to derive subclasses (e.g., "engine 1.8" and "engine 2.0"). Furthermore, relations between classes can exist. Step also allows for the definition of product variants (Figure 28).

Though the EXPRESS language is formal, [Böhms 2008] outlines the major drawback of STEP as the objects represented by EXPRESS being not formal and thus not semantically interpretable. [Böhms 2008] adds that the resulting schema

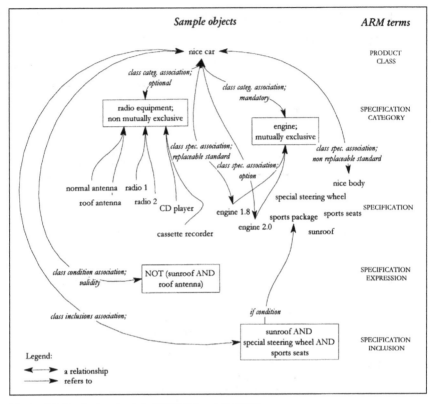

Figure 28: Product variants in STEP [Mannistö 1998].

is complicated and surrounded by "implementers' agreements, which are necessary for reliable exchange" [Böhms 2008]. Those implementers' agreements, however, are case-specific and hence incompatible across multiple different corporations.

Another, European initiative for product data exchange is pursued with the BMECat standard. BMECat represents an XML-based approach to describing product data that organizes product characteristics in a hierarchy (cp. section 4.1.3). BMECat furthermore defines a set of standardized characteristics that are quantifiable for every product. Most of the attributes of products in BMECat, however, contain order-relevant information, such as order details, shipping addresses, prices, etc. For the actual description of the features of a product, the BMECat standard only defines the tags <ARTICLE_DETAILS> and <REFER-

ENCE_FEATURE>. Though BMECat tags are organized in XML and thus hierarchical, the actual description of the product itself is not. Listing 2 features a sample product description authored in BMECat.

```
<?xml version="1.0" encoding="UTF-8"?>
<!DOCTYPE BMECAT SYSTEM "bmecat_new_catalog.dtd">
<BMECAT version="1.2">
<HEADER>
<CATALOG>
<LANGUAGE>EN</LANGUAGE>
<CATALOG_ID>124sd34f</CATALOG_ID>
<CATALOG_VERSION>120</CATALOG_VERSION>
<CATALOG_NAME>
A simple catalog
</CATALOG_NAME>
<CURRENCY>DEM</CURRENCY>
</CATALOG>
...
</HEADER>
...
</BMECAT>
```

Listing 2: BMECat sample [Fraunhofer 2001].

In 2008, the W3C started a Product Data Modeling Incubator Group that discussed product modeling in the context of the Semantic Web [Böhms 2009]. The expert group's intent was to create a product ontology, so that semantic statements about products can be made [Böhms 2008]. If product data was semantically interpretable, users could also be better assisted through product search engines, etc. Though results are not yet available, the Incubator Group's approach aims to integrate existing standards, such as STEP, within a description logic framework, such as OWL [Böhms 2008]. According to [Böhms 2008], the Incubator group will furthermore add an ontology that represents quantities, units, and scales, which would even further benefit the quality of semantic product retrieval.

[Graves 2010] is following an approach toward semantic product modeling that is based on OWL. Types and so called binary properties are used to formalize a structural block diagram model; that is "a model that does not have behavior in the sense that values of properties do not change" [Graves 2010]. However, a model may include properties, variables, and operations, which can be included throughout semantic search operations.

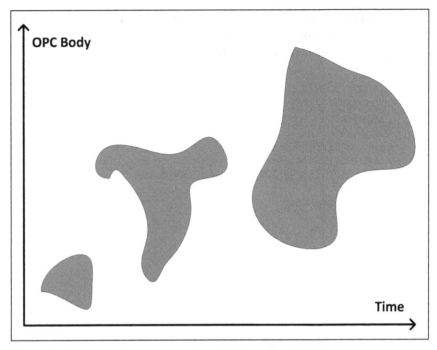

Figure 29: The (organic) momentum of an OPC [Neumann 2011b].

Lee 2007] introduces a method for generating product models from user data and derives twelve design patterns for resolving conflicts throughout the integration and normalization of product data. In [Lee 2007], it is furthermore assumed that product entities consist of attributes. Among the design patterns are "conflicts between attribute definitions", "attributes shared by two entities", "optional vs. mandatory relations", "conflicts between subtype definitions", etc. The extraction of product models from user data and the associated problems that might occur are fundamental to a technology-mediated participation of end-users in the process of generating product data for search and retrieval.

[Neumann 2010b] and [Neumann 2010c] proposed a TMSP-based approach for product data modeling and retrieval that is referred to as "Organic Product Catalogs" (OPCs). The idea behind OPCs is to derive classification schemas from user input. If the OPC detects a certain similarity or relatedness between two product descriptions, it will try to merge both descriptions into a common schema and this way create a product class (see Appendix B). Instances of classes are configurable, so that product authors may choose only a subset of the class attributes. Depending on the extent at which the automatically extracted product class is used by product authors, it will either be withdrawn or used for further merge and extraction with other similar product descriptions. The OPC is hence called organic, because it organically develops its repository of product classes together with the product descriptions that were provided by its users (Figure 29).

4.2.3   Product Model Persistence

Another important aspect concerns the persistence of product models. In many cases, product models implement a predefined schema. The schema serves the purpose of mapping the product model to a relational schema, which is implemented by a database management system. However, as long as product models are based upon fixed schemas, there will always exist certain flexibility-related limitations. Especially if new product types need to be registered frequently and on a daily basis, changing a data base schema or program code is no satisfactory option. [Frank 2002] propose a way of how changing product definition can be registered at runtime. [Frank 2002] furthermore formulates requirements of a versatile product model. These requirements are summarized as:

[PM01]   the product model should be able to support any type of product,

[PM02]   the registration of new product types should not require changes in program code or in the database schema,

[PM03]   the stored product models should support users with searching for suitable products, and

[PM04]   The information contained within the product model should provide sufficient content to be discovered through a variety of different search queries.

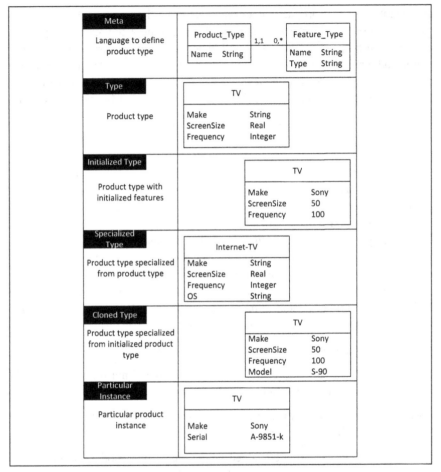

Figure 30: Levels of abstraction in product representation [Frank 2002].

Other requirements are added through the Product Data Modeling Incubator Group of the W3C [Böhms 2009] and through Lockheed Martin [Graves 2010]:

[PM05]   The quality of semantic product search operations to a big extent depends on how the underlying system deals with quantities, units, and scales,

[PM06]   Product models can exhibit a certain behavior that results from values and properties of the model changing over time.

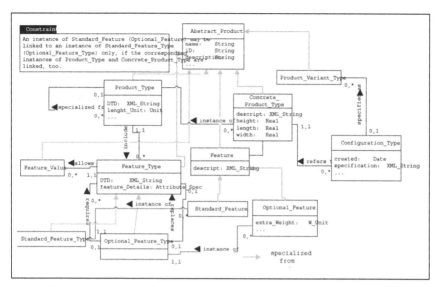

Figure 31: General and reusable product model [Frank 2002].

In order to implement [PM01] – [PM06], [Frank 2002] proposes a general architecture for a product model that consists of six layers, with each layer representing an additional layer of abstraction (Figure 30). In particular, the layers provide meta information, such as the product name, information about the product type, information about standard configurations, specialized types, etc.

Based on Figure 30, [Frank 2002] defines three versions of product models that differ in certain aspects, such as flexibility, generality, or reuse. The version that provides for the highest generality and the highest reuse is depicted in Figure 31.

[Frank 2002] suggests persisting the above product model into an XML representation and storing the XML representation in a database. It is, however, not detailed the feasibility of this approach from a system performance point of view. Furthermore, [Frank 2002] does not provide recommendations for whether to store the XML representation as XML type and making it accessible through, for instance, XPath or whether to transform the XML representation into a relational schema that is based on reference tracking of parent nodes. [Neumann 2011d] analyzed both of the before mentioned alternatives from a performance point of view and concluded that access to products through XPath in many cases outperforms the relational alternative.

4.2.4   Product Configurators

Configurators add an additional layer on top of the product model that allows for maintaining configurations of a product. [Erens 1995] state that configurators serve as key decision support system for users, when they search for products. [Huang 2007] adds that configurators play an important role in generating and managing product variants. Configurators maintain constraints for a product model. These constraints, thereby, indicate which individual parts, or features, of a product can exist together. In many cases, configurators maintain a list of product features that are mutually exclusive on the one extreme or might require other features on the other extreme.

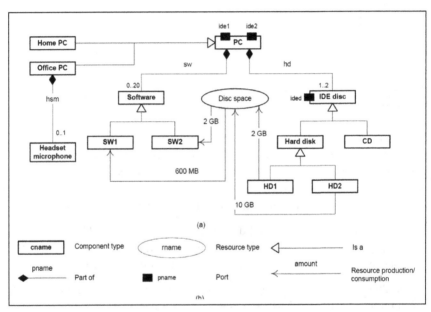

Figure 32: UML-based configuration ontology [Asikainen 2003].

[Asikainen 2003] proposes a configurator approach that is based on an ontology. Ontologies can be used in order to resolve constraints for valid configurations. Figure 32 samples a configuration ontology for a Personal Computer (PC). Other means of providing support for configuration are proposed in [Asikainen 2004]. Here, constraints are solved as parts of alternative feature constraints. Figure 33 samples a text editor that is based on a feature tree.

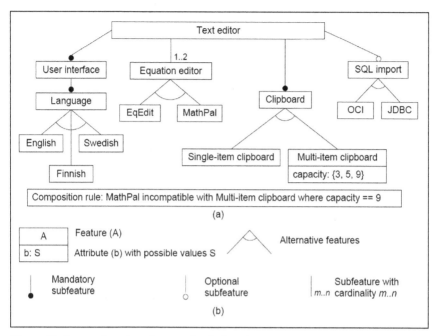

Figure 33: Feature-based configurator [Asikainen 2004].

Resolving constraints, especially for larger configuration ontologies or feature trees, can consume quite a reasonable amount of processing power. [Hadzic 2004] proposed to precompile all possible configurations (the solution space) into a symbolic representation in an offline-phase. In the online phase, that is the phase when the system is to resolve user input for valid configurations, the precompiled symbolic representation is then used for fast, complete, and backtrack-free interactive product configuration [Hadzic 2004]. The system was benchmarked against a car example provided through Renault with $2.8x^{12}$ possible solutions. The average response time of the system was measured as 0.127 seconds [Hadzic 2004].

4.2.5 Product Classification

Related or similar products are often considered as being part of the same product family. According to [Hansen 2003], configurators are enablers for mass customization, as "they allow customers to transform their perceptions regarding

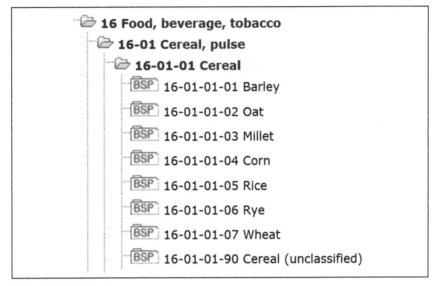

Figure 34: Sample of an eCl@ss classification [Milde 2011].

a desired product into a precise product specification". Customers thereby choose options within so called set limits that best match the customers' configuration goal. [Pels 2006] states that product families can be viewed as classes of product types, whereas product types are seen as classes of product instances. In order to define relations between product families and classes, which provide certain semantic information about, for instance, the semantic distance or closeness of two products special means of topological ordering were developed. Those means are summarized under the terminology "product classification systems".

There exist several formats for classification systems for different types of products, languages and translations. The following are examples for product classification, which are being used in Europe and North America.

eCl@ss: is a format primarily used in German-speaking countries, but it is also expanding towards North America and Asia. The fundamental basis of eCl@ss is implemented by a taxonomy that consists of four levels: "segments", "main groups", "groups", and "commodity classes" (Figure 34). The fourth level contains property bars with standardized properties and value tables, which allow for

List of all classes

List of all classes	Change requests	Search class	Selection filter classes	Last found result(s)	Requested RFCs

1 2 3 4 5 6 7 8 9 10 11 12 13 14 15 16 17 18 19 20 21 22 23 24 25 26 27 28 29 30 31 32 33 34 35 36 37 38 39 40 ... >>

ID	Version	Description	Description (EN)
EC000001	4	Busbar terminal	Busbar terminal
EC000003	5	Residual current circuit breaker (RCCB)	Residual current circuit breaker (RCCB)
EC000005	4	Cable end sleeve	Cable end sleeve
EC000006	5	Cover plate for installation units	Cover plate for installation units
EC000007	5	Cover frame for domestic switching devices	Cover frame for domestic switching devices
EC000008	4	Tap off unit for busbar trunk	Tap off unit for busbar trunk
EC000009	4	Hammer set anchor	Hammer set anchor
EC000010	5	Starter combination	Starter combination
EC000011	5	Cover plate for switches/push buttons/dimmers/venetian blind	Cover plate for switches/push buttons/venetian blind
EC000012	5	Slotted cable trunking system	Slotted cable trunking system
EC000013	5	Base plate for flush mounted installation	Base plate for flush mounted installation
EC000014	5	Tube-shaped incandescent lamp	Tube-shaped incandescent lamp
EC000016	5	Explosion proof CEE socket outlet	Explosion proof CEE socket outlet
EC000017	5	Explosion proof CEE-plug/-coupler	Explosion proof CEE-plug/-coupler
EC000018	5	Insert/cover for communication technology	Insert/cover for communication technology
EC000019	4	Coaxial cable	Coaxial cable
EC000020	5	Combination switch/wall socket outlet	Combination switch/wall socket outlet
EC000022	4	Bracket for cable support system	Bracket for cable support system
EC000023	4	Cover for wall duct	Cover for wall duct
EC000024	4	Installation box for underfloor-installation	Installation box for underfloor-installation
EC000025	5	Dimmer	Dimmer
EC000026	4	Low Voltage HRC solid link	Low Voltage HRC solid link
EC000028	5	Threaded rod	Threaded rod

Figure 35: ETIM sample [url13].

description and identification of products and services [Milde 2011]. In order to facilitate the retrieval of a class for a given product or service without having to know the entire taxonomy, commodity classes are often given keywords. Though having originated from mechanical engineering, eCl@ss today covers a wide area of products and services with different levels of detail [Milde 2011]. Classes are maintained in more than six languages, which allows for automated translingual exchange of product information [Milde 2011].

ETIM: is a format similar to eCl@ss, which focuses on electrical engineering [Milde 2011]. Similarly to eCl@ss, ETIM was also developed and is mostly used in Germany. ETIM consists of a two level taxonomy (with "categories" and "classes"), whereby each class consists of certain properties and keywords (Figure 35).

UNSPSC: stands for United Nations Standard Products and Services Code and represents a classification system, which is most widely being used in the United States, but also in other countries and on other continents [Milde 2011]. UNSPSC consists of a five level taxonomy ("Segment", "Family", "Class", "Commodity", and "Business Function"). Since its original focus was not upon the identification of individual materials but on statistical evaluation, UNSPSC does not have any properties or keywords [Milde 2011]. Its current version consists of more than 18,000 terms and is available in 14 languages. Due to UNSPSC being a government initiative, its taxonomy does not focus on any particular industry branch and is supposed to be suitable for a wide range of products and services [Milde 2011].

The typical usage scenario of classification systems aims at suppliers creating product classifications using eCl@ss, ETIM, UNSPSC, or any other format, and storing it in a format, such as BMECat. The products, on the other hand, are defined in a product model and are persisted into a product catalog. This catalogue is then provided to upstream members of the supply chain, which might require the supplier's products or services for their own production. If both suppliers and consumers rely on the same format, they can easily import the catalog into their own catalog management or e-procurement system. In case of both organizations, however, using different product models or different terminology within a common product model, product classification systems are required to resolve the differences for a common format and naming.

The comparison between different products is hindered by the lack of standards (or, "the proliferation of standards") that describe and classify products. This causes enterprises to reclassify goods and services according to different standardization models [Bergamaschi 2002]. [Mohanty 2005] proposes a system that is based upon fuzzy logic, in order to handle conflicting, imprecise, and non-commensurable product attributes. [Leukel 2002] proposes an XML-based common structure model for product classification systems that can be used for the "transmission of classification systems". In this sense, the work in [Leukel 2002] represents a meta classification system. [Ding 2002] proposes a system, called GoldenBullet, that aims at removing the heterogeneity of information descriptions used by multiple vendors and customers. GoldenBullet does so by mechanizing the process of structuring, classifying, aligning, and personalizing product data through techniques known from information retrieval. At its basis, GoldenBullet uses the vector-space model for automatic product classification in UNSPSC. [Ding 2002] claims accuracy rates between 70% and 98%, which indicate that the process of product classification can be automated, at least to a certain degree, by employing information retrieval techniques.

4.2.6   Section Summary

This section provided an introduction to semantic product modeling. It was shown how contemporary product modeling approaches, such as STEP or BMECat, are limited in their capabilities to allow for semantic product data retrieval. In order to fix these shortcomings, since 2008 the Product Data Modeling Incubator Group of the W3C has been working on adding an ontology to STEP that represents quantities, units, and scales, which would even further benefit the quality of semantic product retrieval.

Other points that were covered include the problem of product data model persistence as well as the requirements [PM01-PM06], which a persistence technology would need to fulfill. Product configurators were mentioned as an end-user tool that would operate upon the before mentioned persistence technology. Finally, three different product classification systems (eCl@ss, ETIM, and UNSPSSC) were briefly examined, whereby especially their capability to provide certain semantic information about the semantic distance or closeness of two products was outlined.

4.3 Distributed SPQS Technologies and Paradigms

This section provides an overview of technological aspects of semantic product query systems. In particular, the component-based (CBSE), the service-oriented (SOSE), the agent-oriented (AOSE), and the Cloud paradigm are investigated, regarding their suitability to serve as base technology for semantic product query systems. Earlier paradigms (e.g., object-orientated software engineering (OOSE), procedure-based software engineering (PBSE)) are –due to their low relevance with respect to this thesis– not further detailed.

4.3.1   Component-based Software Engineering

The roots of Component-based Software Engineering (CBSE) go back to Douglas McIlroy who in 1968 suggested that software could be built from prefabricated components [McIlroy 1968]. CBSE emphasizes the reuse of loosely coupled components, which –at the time of the so called software crisis [Randell 1996]– promised to be an effective means to build high-quality software.

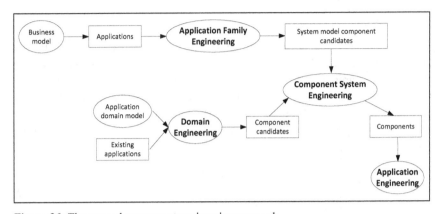

Figure 36: The general component engineering approach.

Software components can be classified into "commercials off-the shelf (COTS)", qualified components, adapted components, assembled components, and updated components, which depends on their flexibility and adaptability with respect to system building [Brown 1998]. The main goal of CBSE is to achieve software reuse, which is characterized as "the systematic practice of developing software from a stock of building blocks, so that similarities in requirements and/or architecture between applications can be exploited to achieve substantial benefits in productivity, quality and business performance" [Ezran 1998]. Typical methods of software reuse are black box reuse, defensive reuse, explicit reuse, glass box reuse, external reuse, implicit reuse, etc.

The general approach to CBSE modeling is based upon component engineering (as characterized in Figure 36). For a detailed description of Domain Engineering (DE), Application Family Engineering (AFE), Component System Engineering (CSE), and Application Engineering (AE) it is referred to [Albani 2003], [Schmietendorf 2002a], and [Sodhi 1999].

When components are used for software development, this usually happens based concrete technologies (Figure 37), such as COM/DCOM (Component Object Model/ Distributed COM), CORBA (Common Object Request Broker Architecture), or EJB (Enterprise Java Beans) ([Sarang 2001], [Schmietendorf 2002b]). Component-based implementation is characterized as "assembling of components", whereby those components that might serve parts of the software's tasks are assembled and combined into a new program/component.

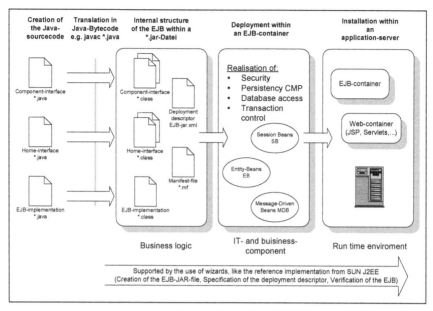

Figure 37: The EJB modeling and implementation approach.

The San Francisco Component Framework represents a famous CBSE approach for modeling business components [Monday 2000]. Originally initiated by IBM (together with over 130 independent software vendors), the San Francisco project encapsulated business process components that provide distributed solutions for mission-critical business applications [Bohrer 1998]. Another interesting CBSE-related idea is based on [Aßmann 2003] and is referred to as invasive software composition (ISC). In ISC, generic classes of domain-related components are combined. [Turowski 2001] coined the term "business component" and outlined the importance of CBSE for large-scale enterprise applications (e.g., SAP ERP, etc.). Many other types of components and component composition exist, but –due to limitations in space– are not further detailed.

Component-based software testing and evaluation is based upon analyzing the relationships between different components, thereby determining certain quality aspects. The complete software measurement process, including a variety of quality-related aspects, is later covered in detail in section 4.4. Figure 38 shows quality-related aspects of a software component [Dumke 1997].

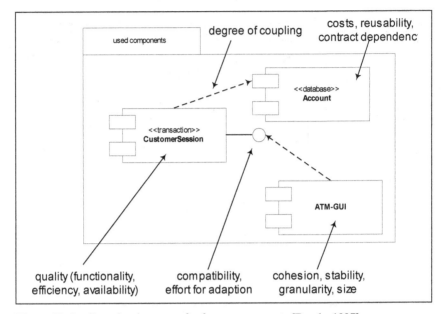

Figure 38: Quality-related aspects of software components [Dumke 1997].

Feature-oriented development (FOD) [Kang 1998] can be considered as a special extension to CBSE. FOD is based on Higher Order Software (HOS) [Dumke 1990] and involves further techniques of CBSE-based rapid prototyping, domain languages, and model-driven development.

4.3.2   Service-oriented Software Engineering

Service-oriented Software Engineering (SOSE) is based upon the general concept of SOA (Service-Oriented Architectures) and combines software (web) services with (worldwide) business processes [Schmietendorf 2007a]. The main intuition behind SOSE –similar to CBSE– is upon reuse of loosely coupled services. Some of the essential differences between CBSE and SOSE are described in Table 6 [Xiong-Yi 2009].

With the beginning of the first decade in 2000, web services started replacing component-based applications, due to their lighter application interface, eased programmability, and platform independence. The first implementations of web

Table 6: CBSE vs. SOSE [Xiong-Yi 2009].

	CBSE	SOSE
[CS01] Design goal	Designed to implement requirements	Designed to adapt to changes
[CS02] Development cycle	Long development cycle	Development of interaction and reusability
[CS03] Focus	Cost-centered	Service-centered
[CS04] Composition	Blocked applications	Harmonious services
[CS05] Coupling	Tight coupling	Flexible and loose coupling
[CS06] Technologies	Isomorphic technologies	Isomeric technologies
[CS07] Orientation	Object-oriented	Information-oriented
[CS08] Implementation details	Deep understanding of the implementation details required	Independent of the implementation details

services were based on an initiative driven by OASIS in the year 2000. OASIS suggested the (web) service technologies SOAP, WSDL, and UDDI for message exchange, interface description, and service discovery, respectively [url5] (see Figure 39).

Web services rely upon so called SOAP messages for communication with clients. SOAP represents an XML dialect that defines a standardized pattern for message exchange. Due to SOAP being platform-independent, clients that run on various platforms, such as Java, .Net, Windows32, etc., access the service in a unified way. The service-specific definition of the SOAP message format is contained as part of the WSDL of a service. Clients can publicly access a service's WSDL and implement the SOAP format for later message exchange.

Base technologies for web services are JAX-WS, WSFL, WSOL, XLANG, etc. ([Alonso 2004], [Chappell 2002], [Papazoglou 2008], [Schmietendorf 2007b], [Zimmermann 2003]). Web services are distinguished into web services in the narrower sense (a.k.a "big web services") and RESTful services. Thereby, the terminology "SOAP services" is synonymously used for "big web services" ([Friesen 2011], p. 754).

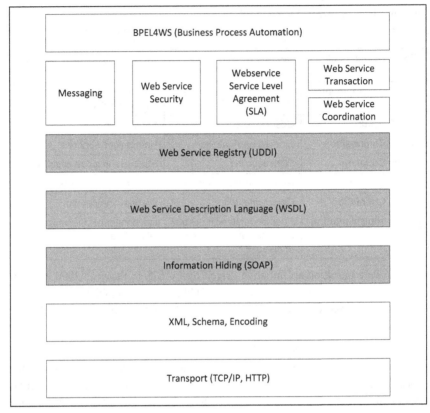

Figure 39: Basic Web service technologies [url5].

One essential characteristic of (web) services is that they hide business logic from their clients behind a standardized service interface. For (web) service clients, this means that they do not have any insights into the way of how services transform inputs into outputs. That is why (web) services can also be considered as black boxes.

Another characteristic of SOSE, which results from the previous paragraph, is that –compared to OOSE and CBSE– (web) services are coarser grained. Figure 40 details how together with the paradigm shifts from OOSE over CBSE to SOSE the granularity of software artifacts also changed towards coarse.

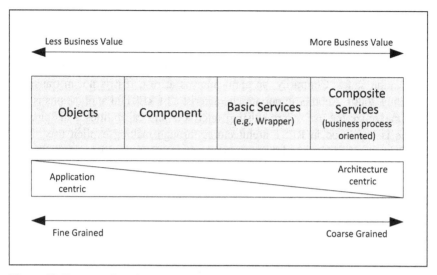

Figure 40: Degrees of service granularities by [Hanson 2003].

Other (web) service granularity analysis approaches employ software metrics. [Griffel 1998], for example, proposes the following set of metrics to indirectly measure the service granularity:

▪ Size of the service interface (operations, parameter, etc.),

▪ Share of the service of the complete application (e.g., supported business processes), and

▪ Size of the effective source code (lines of code, number of classes, etc.).

In the year 2000, Roy Thomas Fielding declared the WWW and the Internet as a RESTful (service) system [Fielding 2000]. In his dissertation, Fielding formulated a set of constraints for systems in order to be RESTful. These constraints are [Fielding 2000]:

[REST01] Client-server: clients and servers are separated via uniform interfaces,

[REST02] Statelessness: servers do not maintain client context,

[REST03] Cachability: resources define themselves as cacheable or not,

[REST04] Layered systems: system layers are invisible to the client,

[REST05]   Code on demand: clients can request executable code, and

[REST06]   Uniform interface: simplified and decoupled architecture.

According to [Fielding 2000], an application is in transition, if it moves between application states. Contrarily, an application is at rest, if it is not in transition [Fielding 2000]. Another important characteristic of RESTful applications is that they maximize the use of pre-existing interfaces and capabilities. This circumstance is harnessed in REST architectures through making explicit use of the HTTP protocol and its capabilities. In particular, RESTful applications define the operations PUT, POST, GET, and DELETE on hosted objects:

[ROP01] $f_{PUT}(X,Y): X \rightarrow Y$, puts an object X to a URL Y,

[ROP02] $f_{POST}(X,Y): X \rightarrow Y$, posts an object X to a URL Y,

[ROP03] $f_{GET}(X,Y): X \rightarrow Y$, gets an object Y from a URL X, and

[ROP04] $f_{DELETE}(X,Y): X \rightarrow Y$, deletes an object Y from a URL X.

Contrary to REST, SOAP services define their own vocabulary of operations, usually by overlaying POST. The big disadvantage of SOAP services is that clients –in order to communicate with a service– will first have to learn the service's protocol. SOAP services expose the service protocol via their WSDL file to clients. The WSDL file contains a definition of operations that are defined on the service:

[SOP01] $f_{POST}(X,Y): X \rightarrow Y$, posts a SOAP message X to a URL Y, and

[SOP02] $f_{WSDL}(X,Y): X \rightarrow Y$, obtains a WSDL file Y from a URL X.

[ROP01] – [ROP04] and [SOP01] - [SOP02] underline the fundamental difference between SOAP and RESTful (web) services. RESTful (web) services always define the same operations PUT, POST, GET, and DELETE on an object. SOAP services, on the other hand, overlay POST for their vocabulary definition. RESTful web services can but do not necessarily have to expose a WSDL file to clients –in fact it is not necessary at all.

4.3.3   Agent-oriented Software Engineering

Agent-oriented software engineering (AOSE) is based upon software agents and involves essential characteristics, such as intelligence, self-management, autonomy, knowledge-based activities, etc. ([Ciancarini 2001], [Ferber 1999], [Knapik

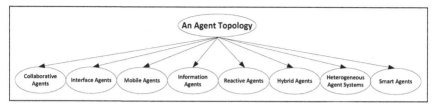

Figure 41: Kinds of software agents [Nwana 1998].

1998], [Liu 2001]). According to Figure 41, agents can be distinguished into collaborative, mobile, reactive, etc. [Nwana 1998]:

Implementations of agent systems are based on concrete languages and infra-structures, such as JADE, KQML, ShopBots, Agent-0, JADL, Aglets, COOL, sACL, AML, Telescript, TRUCE, etc. [Dumke 2009]. Agents are hosted and maintained by a special execution environment that is referred to as the Multi Agent System (MAS) [Wille 2005]. According to [Ferber 1999], the term MAS is applied to a system that comprises the following elements:

▪ An environment E,

▪ A set of objects O. These objects are situated, which means that it is possible at a given moment to associate any object with a position in E. These objects are furthermore passive, which means that they can be perceived, created, destroyed and modified by agents,

▪ An assembly of agents A, which are specific objects (A ⊆ O), that represent the active entries of the system,

▪ An assembly of relations R, which link objects (and thus agents) together, and

▪ An assembly of operations Op, which makes it possible for the agents of A to perceive, produce, consume, transform, and manipulate objects from O.

Software agents can be applied to electronic commerce and e-business scenarios. The following listing names some of the applications of software agents in the before mentioned domain:

▪ Distributed trust management, as described in [Negri 2006], for e-travelling applications,

▪ Mass-customized e-commerce through agents [Turowski 2002],

▪   Special pricing-related operations, such as dynamic pricing in electronic market systems, as mentioned in [Maes 1994],

▪   An agent-based micropayment system for e-commerce [Liu 2001],

▪   Digital signatures through mobile agents [Liu 2001],

▪   Privilege negotiation for e-commerce as described in [Au 2003]. This approach defines an ISP-side authorization agent (AA), a client-side credential management agent (CMA), and a server-side recommendation agent (RA),

▪   An agent-based implementation of the Haggle protocol for e-commerce transactions (Figure 42).

▪   The Market Internet Format (MIF), which was defined in order to support e-commerce transactions [Papadopoulos 2001]. In MIF, agents share a common language, which is a formalized subset of commerce communication. A sample MIF expression of interest is sampled in Listing 3:

```
(def car "trade-object"
color (instance "red"))
.  .  . )
(instance "contract"
data(interval 1/1/2000 1/1/2001)
buyer(instance "person"
(name "John Brown")
(address ...) ...)
goods(instance "car"
color(instance "red") ...)
```

Listing 3: MIF expression of interest [Papadopoulos 2001].

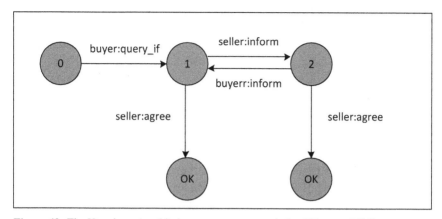

Figure 42: The Haggle protocol in in e-commerce negotiation [Dignum 2000].

Finally, Table 7 compares SOSE [Xiong-Yi 2009] and AOSE with another.

Table 7: SOSE vs. AOSE.

	SOSE	AOSE
[CS01] Design goal	Designed to adapt to changes	Designed to use knowledge and roles to cooperatively solve problems
[CS02] Development cycle	Development of interaction and reusability	Development of agent roles and tasks
[CS03] Focus	Service-centered	Collaboration-centered
[CS04] Composition	Harmonious services	Agent communication
[CS05] Coupling	Flexible and loose coupling	Autonomous agents
[CS06] Technologies	Isomeric technologies	Isomorphic technologies
[CS07] Orientation	Information-oriented	Knowledge-oriented
[CS08] Implementation details	Independent of the implementation details	Agents depend on MAS

4.3.4   Cloud-based Software Engineering

The commoditization of web services led to a new computing paradigm, namely Cloud Computing, whose goal is to provide computing power as well as software services on demand. "Cloud computing is the Internet-based development and use of computer technology (computing), whereby dynamically scalable and often virtualized resources are provided as a service over the Internet. Users need not have knowledge of, expertise in, or control over the technology infrastructure 'in the cloud' that supports them" [Birman 2009].

An essential idea of Cloud Computing was the adaptation of the service paradigm [Banerjee 2011], [Cusumano 2010], [Papazoglou 2011]). Despite other X-as-a-Service paradigms, the three most popular ones are Software-as-a-Service (SaaS), Platform-as-a-Service (PaaS), and Infrastructure-as-a-Service (IaaS).

In the Cloud, resources are provisioned "on demand" [Armbrust 2009] and "as a service" [Assunção 2009]. In pre-Cloud times, resource provisioning and capacity management (cp. [Grossman 2009]) were hindered because of (cp. Figure 43):

- Differences in load forecast and real load,

- Investment hurdles with a high up-front investment, and

- Overbuy and underbuy, due to discrete provisioned capacity units [PWC 2011], [Vertica 2008].

Overbuy means that over a certain time period the available IT capacity was underutilized (cp. [PWC 2011]). Overbuy results from firms buying IT capacity ahead of times and in comparably large timely intervals, even when the capacity is not fully needed yet. In Figure 43, overbuy is represented by the area between the two curves "provisioned IT capacity" and "real "load".

Underbuy, on the other extreme, is even more critical than overbuy as it might affect the quality of service of the Cloud application. Underbuy results from the application –at a certain point in time– not having sufficient resources available, in order to efficiently deal with the real load. Even though capacity is well planned ahead (e.g., there exists a large overbuy), in certain peak times, when the application is especially heavily utilized, underbuy might still occur. Increasing IT capacity, just to meet the capacity requirements for certain peak times, might significantly increase overbuy and thus IT expenses. However, if the current IT

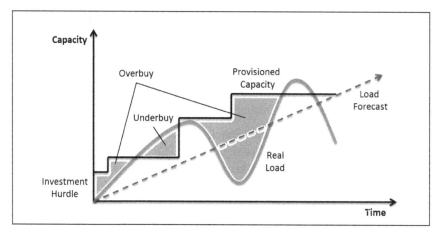

Figure 43: Pre-Cloud overbuy and underbuy.

capacity management cannot avoid underbuy, the performance of the Cloud application might be affected, which ultimately might result in users stopping to use the Cloud application.

Figure 44 shows how IT provisioning in the Cloud avoids underbuy and significantly reduces overbuy through a dynamic capacity management. Cloud applications can automatically scale their utilized resources together with the load, acquire additional computing resources when they are needed, and release overcapacity when the resources are not needed [Krishnan 2010].

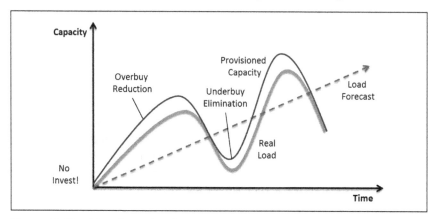

Figure 44: Cloud-based capacity alignment.

[CloudEco01] - [CloudEco03] summarize the economic benefits of Cloud Computing as depicted in Figure 44:

[CloudEco01]   No up-front investment,

[CloudEco02]   No underbuy, and

[CloudEco03]   Significantly reduced overbuy.

In addition to the capacity-related characteristics of Cloud Computing, other technical and non-technical characteristics exist. [Cloud01] - [Cloud14] give an overview and summarize the individual characteristics of Cloud Computing:

[Cloud01]   Software-as-a-Service (SaaS): Cloud computing is mainly based on the SaaS service paradigm [Armbrust 2009]. Market-leading SaaS/Cloud applications are Google Gmail/Calendar, Microsoft Dynamics, NetSuite, Oracle CRM On Demand, RightNow, Salesforce.com, SuccessFactors, Workday, and Microsoft Windows Azure [Narasimhan 2011]. According to [Vasan 2011], "as a result of the impact of the Web, Cloud Computing, and mobility, technology companies had to radically rethink how they build, package, deploy, market, and sell their solutions",

[Cloud02]   Federated Cloud Model (FCM): challenges in the field of federated Cloud Computing technologies relate to the discovery of particular workload requirements and quality of service aspects. Technologies in FCM are dynamic service elasticity, admission control, policy-driven placement optimization, cross-Cloud virtual networks, and cross-Cloud live migration [Rochwerger 2011]. Another kind of Cloud integration is based on application identities, as described in [Olden 2011] as "cloud-scale identity fabric" (e.g., identity as a service),

[Cloud03]   Cloud Computing standardization: according to [Ortiz 2011], Cloud Computing standards have not yet gained traction, with a potential impact on the future adoption of the technology. Cloud standardization, however, is an important task for future Cloud technology-based system deployments and evolutions [Ortiz 2011]. Table 8 summarizes the essential communities and their standardization activities:

Table 8: An overview of cloud computing standards.

Organization	Standard
Distributed Manage-ment Task Force	Open Virtualization Format (OVF)
IEEE	P2301: Guide for Cloud Portability and Interoperability Profiles (CPIP)
	P2302: Standard for Intercloud Interoperability and Federation (SIIF)
Open Grid Forum	Open Cloud Computing Interface (OCCI)
OASIS	Cloud process supports such as ID Clouds and communities
Storage Networking Industry Association	Cloud Data Management Interface (CDMI)

[Cloud04]   Global Cloud Computing testbed: also referred to as "Open Cirrus", it supports the test of heterogeneous distributed data centers for systems, applications, services and open source development research world-wide, thereby involving institutions from the USA, Germany, Russia, South Korea, and Malaysia [Avetisyan 2010]. This approach includes an Open Cirrus economic model that analyzes storage size, networks rates, and server utilization,

[Cloud05]   Maturity model of Cloud Computing: defines five different maturity levels, thereby considering business perspectives, Cloud governance, procurement methods, Cloud applications, information perspective, and infosec [Jaatun 2009],

[Cloud06]   Cloud provider selection: different models of harnessing the benefits of Cloud Computing (e.g., Cloud leasing) are discussed in [Walker 2010] and [Ojala 2011]. Fundamentally, decisions for or against one specific Cloud provider are based on capital costs, disk price trends, disk replacement rates and disk salvage value [Dustdar 2011]. Special energy-related effects of Cloud Computing in mobile/offloading computation are discussed in [Kumar 2010]. A business-driven optimization of Cloud architectures is described in [Litoiu 2010]. With respect to the marketization of Cloud services, [Kim 2009] estimates that Cloud Computing will have an annual growth rate of 17% through 2011 for CRM (customer relationship management), ERP (enterprise resource planning) and SCM (supply chain management) markets in the SMB (small and medium business) sector (see also [Cooper 2010], [Hofmann 2010] and [Leavitt 2009]),

[Cloud07]   Cloud-based trust architecture: Cloud architectures for building and establishing trust were described and discussed in [Jaatun 2009],

[Cloud08]   Cloud Computing and e-Governance: The general benefits of Clouds in e-Government involving SOA are discussed in [Cellary 2009] as dynamic load of resources, professional maintenance and administration, timely software updates, higher security, higher performance, shift from investment cost to operational cost, and dissemination of good practices. Future e-governance-related aspects that are based on cost, expertise, maintenance, and green ICT are discussed in [Pokharel 2009],

[Cloud09]   Green Cloud: different principles and technologies for achieving a "Green Cloud" with a possibly high eco efficiency are discussed in [Jaatun 2009]. Figure 45 classifies different types of Clouds and underlines the "Green Cloud" as an essential criterion that applies to all types of Cloud,

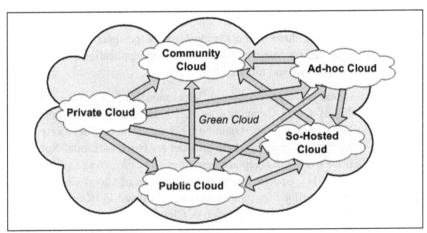

Figure 45: Example of a Cloud infrastructure [Jaatun 2009].

[Cloud10]   Cloud-based service recommendation: the efficiency of service recommendation in a Cloud Computing market is described in

[Han 2009]. This efficiency is based on resource rank analysis, including QoS analysis, performance testing of virtual machines, and rank analysis itself. The general relationships between Cloud Computing and service computing are discussed in [Wei 2010],

[Cloud11]   High performance Cloud Computing: a service composition framework for a market-oriented high performance computing Cloud is discussed in [Pham 2010]. This approach/technology is based on an ontology using OWL, which defines the required architectural knowledge (see also [Yeo 2011]),

[Cloud12]   Scaling, management, and controlling in Clouds: scaling technology for the dynamic scaling of Cloud applications is described in [Vaquero 2011]. This approach is based on NaaS (network as a service) and considers the container-level and database scalability. The controlling approach of Lim is based on decoupled control, control granularity, and control parameters, such as CPU time and workload estimation ([Lim 2009], [Agapi 2011]). The virtual infrastructure management in private and hybrid Clouds, using the OpenNebula tool, is described in [Sotomayor 2009],

[Cloud13]   Cloud data management: replaces relational databases with non-relational (noSQL) databases. Especially, in scenarios with many concurrent transactions and a high scale-out ratio, the lock mechanisms and the foreign key restrictions of relational databases are not appropriate any longer,

  [Cloud13a]   Fault tolerance: large data centers/Cloud providers have the possibility to provide high levels of fault tolerance to their customers [Abadi 2009]. In Microsoft's Windows Azure, for example, data is mirrored at least three times [Krishnan 2010]. Data-based fault tolerance is also referred to as "partition tolerance". Fault-tolerant data storages, however, trade fault tolerance for consistency. The CAP theorem states that it is not possible to exhibit availability and partition tolerance along with (strong) consistency [Lynch 2002]. This is where eventual consistency comes into play. Service-based fault tolerance is achieved through maintaining at least one replica/instance of the service,

[Cloud13b]   Cloud data management: loosens consistency in favor of performance. General characteristics of consistency are strong consistency, sequential consistency, causal consistency, weak consistency, and eventual consistency. Client-side, consistency surfaces as "read your writes", "write follows read", "monotone read", and "monotone write". Server-side consistency aims at avoiding dirty read, dirty write, and lost updates. Non-relational databases often implement eventual consistency [Vogels 2008],

[Cloud13c]   Transactions: represent a means of allowing for techniques that implement data consistency. In traditional data consistency theory, transactions were an important component of ACID (atomicity, consistency, isolation and durability). In times of large-scale web applications, however, ACID hinders scale-out, with a negative impact on performance. BASE (Basically available, soft state, eventual consistency) represents the counterpart to ACID [Fox 1997] and trades performance for strong consistency,

[Cloud14]   Cloud Computing benefits: as improved server utilization, improved reliability, greener IT, clear business models, user-oriented benefits as commodification of compute resources, managing surge requirements with on-demand resources, ease of deployment, and virtual ownership of resources [Lee 2010]. Standard technologies for these challenges are OCCI (Open Cloud Computing Interface), OVF (Open Virtualization Format), and CDMI (Cloud Data Management Interface). Related concepts and tooling are identity management, virtual organizations, the GLUE schema for describing computing resources, and data access and transfer standards (e.g., OGSA-DAI, GridFTP, and SRM, etc.). [Lee 2010] states that –as concepts concerning distributed infrastructure management and dynamic provisioning– "grid and Cloud are not in competition, but are rather quite complementary" [Lee 2010]. Standard organizations for Cloud Computing are OGF, DMTF, SNIA, OCC, CSA, TMF, OMG, and OASIS (see also [Borenstein 2011]),

[Cloud15]   Windows Azure: Microsoft's Cloud Computing platform adheres
             to the name "Windows Azure" [Khalidi 2011]. Figure 46 depic-
             tures a simplified view of Azure's Cloud infrastructure [Chappell
             2010]. The components of Windows Azure are "Compute" (runs
             applications in the Cloud), "Storage" (stores binary and structured
             data in the Cloud), "Fabric Controller" (deploys, manages, and
             monitors applications), "Content Delivery Network (CDN)"
             (speeds up access to Azure Storage), and "Connect" (for creating
             IP-level connections between on-premises computers and Win-
             dows Azure applications) [Chappell 2010].

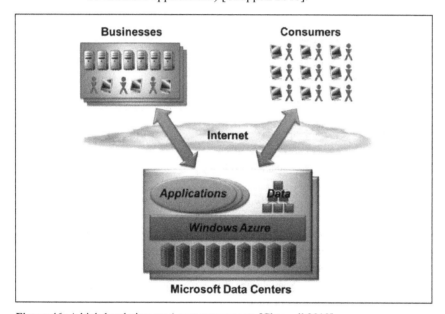

Figure 46: A high-level view on Azure components [Chappell 2010].

4.3.5   Section Summary

This section covered the development of (recent) software engineering paradigms and outlined the typical characteristics of every paradigm. Classical paradigms, such as procedure-based software engineering and object-oriented software engineering –due to their subordinate relevance with respect to SPQS
development– were not further detailed.

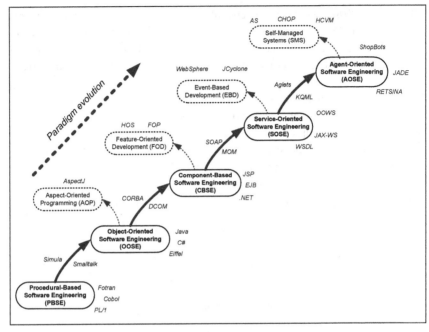

Figure 47: Technology-based paradigm evolution.

While component-based software engineering incorporated a first attempt to facilitate software reuse among system boundaries, its major drawbacks were to be found in its complexity and the lack of support for interop scenarios. In 2000, web services took over the lead in distributed software development. Compared to components, web services are easier to implement and easier to consume for clients. Their (standard) XML-based interfaces thereby ensure platform independence. The latest iteration of (distributed) software engineering paradigms was referred to as agent-oriented software engineering. Though software agents might expose web service interfaces, they differ from services in a way that they are capable of acting autonomously (either alone or in a network) and might maintain a knowledge base for (intelligent) decision making. Figure 47 summarizes the evolution of software engineering paradigms from (procedures, objects, and) components over services to agents. Since Cloud Computing is characterized as a (new) combination of existing paradigms and technologies (an instantiation of the service-oriented paradigm), it is not contained in Figure 47.

4.4 Quality Assurance in SPQS

Semantic Product Query Systems underlie certain quality-related constraints, such as high availability, short response times, high throughput, etc., in order to be truly useful. Chapter seven details a selection of runtime performance-related issues of a reference implementation of an SPS, called "ArbiterOne", which had to be dealt with. Measurements were conducted and empirical data was collected in order to profile the "ArbiterOne" system and locate the performance bottlenecks. This section examines the fundamentals of software measurement, details the components of the measurement process, and briefly discusses the many aspects of the measurement process. Eventually, the theory provided throughout this section is applied in chapter seven.

4.4.1   Software Measurement Definition

Based on (general) systems theory [Skyttner 2005], a software measurement system can be declaratively defined as [Ebert 2007]:

$$MS = (M_{MS}, R_{MS}) = (\{G, A, M, Q, E, V, T, P, E', A'\}, R_{MS}) \qquad (4.4.1.1)$$

where G represents the set of measurement goals, A represents the set of measured artifacts, M represents the set of measurement methods, Q represents the set of measurement quantities, E represents the set of measurement-based experiences, V represent the set of measurement values, T represents the set of measurement (CASE/CAME) tools, P represents the set of measurement personnel, E' represents the extended measurement experiences, and A' represents the extended measurement artifacts. R_{MS} defines the relations between the elements of M_{MS}.

The business software measurement process BMP (as an instantiation of the general software measurement system) can be defined as ([Ebert 2007], [Fenton 1997]):

$$BMP: (G \times A \times M)_{T,P} \to (Q \times E)_{T,P} \to (V)_{T,P} \to (E' \times A')_{T,P} \qquad (4.4.1.2)$$

4.4.2   Measurement Objects in Business Software

The tuple $(G \times A \times M)$ (measurement goals, artifacts, and methods) describes the input and basis for any software measurement. The detailed characteristics of G, A, M are:

4.4.2.1 Measurement Goal G of Business Software Quality Assurance

■ Evidence of business software quality: is based on the general viewpoint of evidence levels (see the measurement graduation in the ISO/IEC product quality standard [ISO 2003]) and can have the following characteristics:

$$evidence \in \{internalGoal, externalGoal, goalsInUs\} \qquad (4.4.2.1.1)$$

■ Viewpoint of the business software: goals depend on their special viewpoint, such as the development phase, the kind of software product [Bundschuh 2008]), and the use of the product in the market:

$$viewpoint \in \{development, product, market\} \qquad (4.4.2.1.2)$$

■ Intention of business software usage: as understanding, evaluation, improvement, and management. This enumeration corresponds with an increasing level of measurement goals (see the classification in [Basili 1986]):

$$intention \in$$
$$\{understanding, evaluation, improvement, management\} \quad (4.4.2.1.3)$$

■ Purpose of the business application: goals depend on their purpose of application (e.g., characterization, evaluation, and motivation), which is based upon the distinctions of motivation by [Basili 1986]):

$$purpose \in \{characterization, evaluation, motivation\} \qquad (4.4.2.1.4)$$

The above four components of G lead to a general characterization of the measurement goal as:

$$BMPGoals = {}^{evidence}_{viewpoint}G^{intention}_{purpose} \qquad (4.4.2.1.5)$$

4.4.2.2 Measurement Artifacts A of Business Software Infrastructures

■ Domain of business software: includes parts of the general classification after [Fenton 1997]), such as software as products (systems), processes (e.g., projects), and resources, including their different parts or aspects (e.g., product model, process phases, or personal resources):

$$purpose \in \{product, process, resource\} \qquad (4.4.2.2.1)$$

■ Dependence of business software infrastructure: is distinguished into integrated, associated, and monolithic (based on the measurement difficulties by [Laird 2006]):

$$dependence \in \{integrated, associated, monolithic\} \qquad (4.4.2.2.2)$$

- Origin of business software: could be pendant, analogy, or original. Analogy could further be distinguished into tuning, where a pendant in the same class of software systems is used, or as adaptation, where another pendant of artefact is used (see the Pandian graduation in [Pandian 2003]):

$$origin \in \{pendant, analogy, original\} \qquad (4.4.2.2.3)$$

- State of business system: depending on the measurement process goals and methods, the artifact could be understood, evaluated, improved, managed, or controlled (after the graduation in [Bundschuh 2008], [Ebert 2007]):

$$state \in \{referred, understood, improved, managed, controlled\}$$
$$(4.4.2.2.4)$$

The above four components of the measurement artifact lead to the following general characterization:

$$BMPArtefacts = {}_{dependence}^{domain}A_{origin}^{state} \qquad (4.4.2.2.5)$$

4.4.2.3 Measurement Methods M of Business Software Evaluation

- Usage of business software: depends on the IT process environment and considers aspects, such as outsourced, global production, or inhouse [Dumke 2009]):

$$usage \in \{outsourced, globalProduction, inhouse\} \qquad (4.4.2.3.1)$$

- Method of business application measurement: classified as experiment/case study, assessment, improvement, or controlling. It must be noted that an extensive use of experiences might lead to estimation or simulation (considering the Munson classification in [Munson 2003]):

$$method \in \{experiment, assessment, improvement, controlling\}$$
$$(4.4.2.3.2)$$

- Application of business application components: is enclosed in IT processes and can, for example, be differentiated into closed component, remote application and web service, etc. (see the measurement infrastructure in [Dumke 2009]):

$$application \in \{closedComponent, remoteApplication, webService\}$$
$$(4.4.2.3.3)$$

■ Kind of business software evaluation: depending on the measured artifact, it is distinguished between analogical conclusion, estimation, simulation, and measurement (using the measurement overview by [McConnel 2006]):

$$kind$$
$$\in \{analogicalConclusion, estimation, simulation, measurement\}$$

(4.4.2.3.4)

These characteristics lead to the following description of the measurement methods as:

$$BMPMethods = {}_{mathod}^{usage}M_{kind}^{application}$$

(4.4.2.3.5)

4.4.3   Measurement Subjects of Business Software Evaluation

Measurement subjects consist of quantities (Q), which are interpreted by measurement personnel through their experience (E), together described as (Q × E). Typical properties of these sets are:

4.4.3.1   Measurement Quantities Q as Business Software Indicators

■ Evaluation of the business software: includes aspects, such as threshold, (min, max) criteria, gradient, and formula (see the criteria classification in [Pandian 2003]):

$$evaluation \in \{threshold, minMaxCriteria, gradient, formula\}$$

(4.4.3.1.1)

■ Exploration of the business application: analysis of the measurement output (based on the experience E) through principles, such as intuition, rules of thumb, trend analysis, or calculus (as detailed in the measurement exploration in [Abran 2006] and [Endres 2003]):

$$exploration \in \{intuition, ruleOfThumb, trendAnalysis, Calculus\}$$

(4.4.3.1.2)

■ Value of the business application: characterizes a qualitative measurement and is based on a nominal scale or ordinal scale (see the metrics scale classification in [Whitmire 1997]):

$$value \in \{nominalScale, ordinalScale\}$$

(4.4.3.1.3)

■ Structure of the e-business system: measured values can be structured into different kinds of presentation and transformation, such as single value, normalization, or aggregation (adapting the measurement evaluation in [Juristo 2001] and [Pfleeger 1998]):

$structure \in$
$\{singleValue, normalization, transformation, aggregation\}$ (4.4.3.1.4)

The above aspects of quantities are summarized as:

$$BMPQuantities = \,^{evaluation}_{exploration}Q^{value}_{structure} \qquad (4.4.3.1.5)$$

4.4.3.2 Measurement Experience E of Business Software Applications

■ Kind of e-business experiences: can be axioms, correlations, intuitions, trends, lemmas, formulas, conjectures, etc. (cp. the different kinds of experience in [Basili 2007], [Davis 1995], [Shull 2008] and [Wohlin 2000]):

$$kind \in \left\{ \begin{array}{c} axoims, correlations, intuitions, \\ trends, lemmas, formulas, conjectures \end{array} \right\} \qquad (4.4.3.2.1)$$

■ Content of business software evaluation: contents/subjects of experience could be thresholds, lower and upper limits, gradients, proofs, etc. (after the causal-based levels of experience in [Dumke 2006]):

$$contents \in \{limit, threshold, gradient, proof\} \qquad (4.4.3.2.2)$$

■ Source of e-business experience: experience can be derived from different sources, such as case studies, project-based practice, etc. (adapting the Kitchenham classification in [Kitchenham 2007]):

$$source \in \{caseStudy, practice\} \qquad (4.4.3.2.3)$$

■ Extension of e-business experience: explains the extended knowledge based on the measurement, evaluation and exploration, and can produce formula correction, principle refinement, criteria approximation and axiom extension (see the Pandian graduation in [Pandian 2003]):

$$extension \in \left\{ \begin{array}{c} correction, refinement, approximation, \\ adaptation, extension \end{array} \right\} \qquad (4.4.3.2.4)$$

The above four aspects are summarized as the following description of the measurement experience:

$$BMPExperience = {}_{content}^{kind}E_{extension}^{source} \qquad (4.4.3.2.5)$$

4.4.4 Measurement Results of Software Quality Assurance

As a result of a measurement process, it is desirable to obtain real values, including their units. Characteristics of the elements of the sets in V are:

4.4.4.1 Measurement Values V of Business Application Measurement

- Measure of business software quality: characterizes a quantitative measurement and is given as interval scale or ratio scale (after the metrics scale analysis in [Zuse 1998]):

$$measure \in \{intervalScale, ratioScale\} \qquad (4.4.4.1.1)$$

- Aggregation of business software evaluation: values can be obtained as different structures and aggregations, such as measurement repositories, simple visualizations (e.g., diagrams, plots, etc.), dashboards, or cockpits (see the measurement process description in [ISO 2001]):

$$aggregation \in \left\{ \begin{matrix} repository, visualization, \\ dashboard, cockpit \end{matrix} \right\} \qquad (4.4.4.1.2)$$

- Unit of business software quality measurement: depends on the measurement method (e.g., CFP for (COSMIC FP functional size), kilo delivered source instructions (KDSI), etc. (cp. measurement units in [Ebert 2007]):

$$unit \in \left\{ \begin{matrix} economicalUnit, physicalUnit, \\ hardwareUnit, softwareUnit \end{matrix} \right\} \qquad (4.4.4.1.3)$$

- Interpretation of quality measurement values: measurement values are interpreted, based on experiences (e.g., analogous projects, IT projects, database projects, or the (international) ISBSG project database (adapting the benchmark concept of the International Software Benchmark Standard Group (ISBSG) in [ISBSG 2003]):

$$interpretation \in \left\{ \begin{matrix} analogousProject, ITProject, \\ databaseProject, ISBSG \end{matrix} \right\} \qquad (4.4.4.1.4)$$

The above characteristics lead to the following description of the measurement values as

$$BMPValues = {}_{aggregation}^{measure}V_{interpretation}^{unit} \qquad (4.4.4.1.5)$$

4.4.5   Measurement Resources of Software Measurement

Every phase of the business software measurement process is supported by tools, which are used by personnel. The detailed characteristics of these sets are:

4.4.5.1   Measurement Tools T of Business Applications

■ Level of business software measurement: is classified as manual (without any tools), semi-automatic, and automatic (using the support classification in [Pfleeger 1998]):

$$level \in \{manual, semi - automatic, automatic\} \qquad (4.4.5.1.1)$$

■ Support of business application evaluation: tools might be applied internally (as internal measurement) or through external vendors (as external measurement) [Bundschuh 2008]):

$$support \in \{external, internal\} \qquad (4.4.5.1.2)$$

■ Context of business software measurement: measurement tools can be applied as simple task application, embedded in a measurement task sequence, or as an integrated part of the measurement process (cp. Munson's graduation in [Munson 2003]):

$$context \in \{simpleTask, taskSequence, integratedTask\} \qquad (4.4.5.1.3)$$

■ Degree of business application evaluation: classifies the tool as decision-support tool or experience-based measurement and evaluation tool (see the measurement levels described in [Dumke 2008]):

$$degree \in \{simple, experience, evaluation\} \qquad (4.4.5.1.4)$$

These descriptions lead to the general characterization of the measurement tool as:

$$BMPTools = {}_{support}^{level}T_{degree}^{context} \qquad (4.4.5.1.5)$$

4.4.5.2   Measurement Personnel P for Business Application Evaluation

■ Kind of business software measurement personnel: personnel involves different kinds of intentions and can be distinguished into measurement researchers, practitioners, or managers (cp. the different IT roles in [Pfleeger 1998]):

$$kind \in \{researcher, practitioner, manager\} \qquad (4.4.5.2.1)$$

■   Area of business software measurement personnel: personnel can be divided
    into measurement staff per se (e.g., measurement analyst, certifier, librarian,
    metrics creator, user, validator, etc.) and into other IT staff that indirectly
    performs software measurement (e.g., administrator, analyst, auditor, de-
    signer, developer, programmer, reviewer, tester, maintainer, customer, user,
    etc.) [Pandian 2003]:

$$area \in \{expert, IT\}$$ (4.4.5.2.2)

■   Qualification of business software measurement personnel: the qualification
    of the measurement personnel can be distinguished into beginners, certified
    users, or experienced users (according to the experience classification in
    [Ebert 2007]):

$$qualification \in \{beginner, certified, experienced\}$$ (4.4.5.2.3)

■   Intention of business software measurement personnel: considers the moti-
    vation and intention of the measurement personnel and can be distinguished
    into engaged users, external motivated users, self-motivated users, etc.
    (adapting the different roles as introduced in [Dumke 2008]):

$$intention \in \{engaged, external, self-motivated\}$$ (4.4.5.2.4)

Therefore, the measurement personnel is characterized by:

$$BMPPersonnel = {}^{kind}_{area}P^{qualification}_{intention}$$ (4.4.5.2.5)

4.4.6   Measurement Repercussions of E-Business Software Improvement

Finally, software measurement might lead to extensions of the experience and to
improvements of the measured artifacts, explained as the tuple $E' \times A'$.

4.4.6.1   Extended Measurement Experiences E' of Measurement Personnel

After the measurement concluded, it will likely have gained additional experience that might positively influence future measurements. The properties of E'
are analogous to E (see section 4.4.3.2).

4.4.6.2   Extended Measurement Artifacts A' of Business Software Measurement

After the measurement concluded, the measurement artifact will likely have
changed in a way, so that it now includes the properties that were defined as part

of the measurement goal. The properties of A' are analogous to A (see section 4.4.2.2).

4.4.7 Detailed Measurement Process BMP for Business Software Quality Assurance

The business software measurement process BMP itself is characterized by the level of covered/measured artifacts (as approach), the kinds of IT relationships (as IT process), the solution, and the realization. The detailed measurement process is characterized through (adapted from [Ebert 2007] and [Georgieva 2009]):

$$
\begin{aligned}
&{}^{ITProcess}_{\ solution}BMP^{approach}_{realization}: \\
&\left({}^{evidence}_{viewpoint}G^{intention}_{purpose} \times {}^{domain}_{dependence}A^{state}_{origin} \right. \\
&\left. \times {}^{usage}_{method}M^{application}_{kind} \right)\ {}^{level}_{support}T^{context}_{degree}\ kind_{P}{}^{qualification}_{,area}{}^{intention} \\
&\rightarrow \left\{ \begin{array}{l}
\left({}^{evaluation}_{exploration}Q^{value}_{structure} \times {}^{kind}_{content}E^{source}_{extension} \right)\ {}^{level}_{support}T^{context}_{degree}\ kind_{P}{}^{qualification}_{,area}{}^{intention} \\
\left({}^{measure}_{aggregation}V^{unit}_{interpretation} \right)\ {}^{level}_{support}T^{context}_{degree}\ kind_{P}{}^{qualification}_{,area}{}^{intention}
\end{array} \right\} \\
&\rightarrow \left({}^{kind}_{content}E'^{source}_{extension} \times {}^{domain}_{dependence}A'^{state}_{origin} \right)\ {}^{level}_{support}T^{context}_{degree}\ kind_{P}{}^{qualification}_{,area}{}^{intention}
\end{aligned}
$$

$$(4.4.7.1)$$

The classification of the business software measurement process BMP itself is based upon the measured characteristics. In a first approximation, the IT process is characterized through quality evaluation, quality improvement, and quality assurance:

$$ITProcess \in \left\{ \begin{array}{c} quality, evaluation, qualityImprovement, \\ qualityAssurance \end{array} \right\}$$

$$(4.4.7.2)$$

The solution aspect refers to the measurement process in a way, so that it details certain characteristics of the measurement methodology, such as ad hoc, scheduled, or ubiquitous (as in [Dumke 2008]):

$$solution \in \{adHoc, scheduled, ubiquitous\}$$

$$(4.4.7.3)$$

The measurement of aspects (aspect of a product, process, or resource) leads to aspect-oriented measurement. The measurement of all aspects of a product, a process or a resource is referred to as capability-oriented measurement. If all software artifacts (products, processes, and resources) were involved, this would be referred to as a whole measurement. These characteristics represent the "approach" attribute of a measurement process [Ebert 2007]:

$$approach \in \{aspect - oriented, capability - oriented, whole\} \quad (4.4.7.4)$$

The "realization" attribute of BMP defines the measurement process, based on research approaches, wide-used methodologies, or established standards (cp. [Dumke 2008]):

$$realization \in \{research, methodology, standard\} \quad (4.4.7.5)$$

4.4.8   Section Summary

This section provided an overview of the many aspects that are involved in the business software measurement process. In chapter 7, business software measurement (and in particular performance measurement) will be conducted on a prototype of a semantic product query system, in order to validate the practicability of the chosen approach. The measurement fundamentals that were laid throughout this section will thereby help to interpret the measurement results.

4.5 Chapter Summary

Throughout this chapter, the basic technologies and concepts of semantic product query systems (SPQS) were examined. It was shown that state-of-the-art technology for semantic product data modeling lacks substantial capabilities for smooth and truly useful semantic product data retrieval.

Based on the elaborations in this chapter, the following chapters contain the design (chapter 5), development (chapter 6), and validation (chapter 7) of a Semantic Product Description Language (S-PDL) and an environment that hosts semantic product descriptions, the Semantic Product Server (SPS). The proposed solutions thereby particularly address the vital need of the IoP for highly transparent product data discoverability, which was emphasized in chapters 2 and 3.

Table 9 summarizes how the theory contained within this chapter maps to the core concepts and software artifacts of the following chapters. It can be seen that semantic techniques (e.g., ontologies, taxonomies, etc.) substantially influence the design of the S-PDL in chapter 5. Furthermore, topics (e.g., product model persistence) and paradigms (e.g., components, services, etc.) determine the conceptual modeling of the SPS in chapter 6. Both the S-PDL and the SPS are finally implemented in chapter 7 as software prototypes (e.g., ArbiterOne, eVoces, etc.) and assessed with respect to quality-related aspects (e.g., real-time query performance) in chapter 7.

Table 9: How theory maps to concepts and artifacts.

Paradigms & Technologies	Concept	Implementation	Validation
Ontologies	S-PDL (chapter 5)	ArbiterOne, eVoces, EscapeMisery, & SpotCrowd (chapter 7)	Measurement Process, Performance Measurement, & HCSF (chapter 7)
Taxonomies			
Faceted Classification			
Folksonomies			
Semantic Product Model			
Product Model Persistence	SPS (chapter 6)		
Components			
Services			
Agents			
Cloud			

Part III:
S-PDL and SPS as Technological Backbone of the Internet of Products

Part II provided an overview of the technological state of the art in semantic product modeling and laid the conceptual foundations for the development of a novel semantic product description language (S-PDL) that allows for highly accurate product search queries in online markets.

Part III consists of three chapters that cover the development of the S-PDL, the implementation of an execution environment for the S-PDL (the SPS), as well as quality-related aspects of the developed technology, which influence its real-time capability.

Chapter 5 contains a theoretical model of a semantic product description language that addresses the following questions:

- How to ensure that a product description language is general enough to describe any kind of product or service (section 5.1)?

- Which specific requirements exist for a semantic product description language and how can they be modeled (section 5.2)?

- What is the general schema of a semantic product description language (section 5.3)?

- How does this schema translate into technology (section 5.4)?

Chapter 6 covers the design and development of an execution environment for semantic product descriptions and attempts to answer the following questions:

- What are the particular requirements of an execution environment that is capable of hosting and interpreting semantic product descriptions (section 6.1)?

- How can clients access semantic product descriptions within the catalog and perform search queries on them (section 6.2 and 6.3)?

- Which specific components exist within a reference architecture of the execution environment and which technologies can be used to implement these components (section 6.4)?

- How can the dynamic behavior of semantic product descriptions be reflected in code and which mechanisms exist to ensure real-time performance (section 6.5)?

- How are semantic product descriptions matched with search queries (section 6.6)?

- Which different options of deployment of the execution environment exist and what are the advantages/disadvantages of the individual options (section 6.7)?

Chapter 7 deals with quality-related aspects of the S-PDL and the SPS and investigates the following points:

- Which prototypes were developed and how did they validate the concept of the S-PDL and the SPS (section 7.1)?

Which particularly interesting quality-related aspects exist, how did they influence the real-time capability of the SPS, and which measures were taken to mitigate the issues?

5 Semantic Product Description Language

"People do product research by searching an open web of products, rather than having to go to Amazon.com, cnet, epinions, and a thousand other web sites." (Jay Myers, Best Buy)

The semantic product data retrieval benchmark in chapter 3 and the elaborations in chapter 4 revealed the limitations of contemporary product search engines with respect to semantic search capabilities. This chapter covers the conceptual details of a semantic product description language (S-PDL) in a category-based model and translates this model into real technology. The goal of the S-PDL is to provide a structural foundation for semantic product search queries with a high detail of product search results.

5.1 Hierarchy-based Product Descriptions

Chapter 4 discussed the suitability of ontologies, taxonomies, faceted classification, and folksonomies with respect to their application in electronic product data modeling. Ontologies were assessed as being a very powerful instrument, at least from a conceptual point of view. In practice, however, ontologies suffer from various problems. One problem occurs when different parties use different ontologies. In this case, a meta ontology might be necessary in order to resolve ambiguity between the other two ontologies. Ontologies might furthermore suffer from high processing requirements, which makes them somewhat difficult to use in practice.

Folksonomies appear to be an interesting approach for letting the community describe the characteristics of a concept. As the basis for a Semantic Product Description Language, which requires that product descriptions are standardizable, folksonomies seem rather impractical.

Since faceted classification is very related to taxonomies (in fact, every facet is its own taxonomy), and taxonomies (or more generally "hierarchies") provide for real-time processing capabilities, the S-PDL that is developed throughout this chapter is based upon hierarchies.

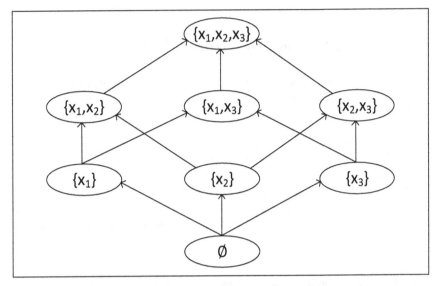

Figure 48: Hasse diagram of the power set of $\{x_1, x_2, x_3\}$.

Hierarchies have always been a tool for human beings to add structure to something with an apparently high level of complexity. There is evidence from research that when people can perceive a thing as a hierarchy of multiple smaller things, they tend to make much more rational decisions than without hierarchical order (cp. the Analytic Hierarchy Process (AHP) in [Saaty 2001]).

A hierarchy describes an order in which items are characterized with respect to the position of other items within the same hierarchy. Mathematically seen, hierarchies are partially ordered sets, so called posets. A hierarchy, or poset, can be graphically depicted by its Hasse diagram [Marte 2008]. For a poset $(S, \leq)$, each element of S is represented as a vertex in a plane. Furthermore, lines are drawn upward from x_1 to x_2, whenever x_2 is above x_1 in the hierarchy. This is exactly the case, whenever $x_1 < x_2$ and there exists no x_3, such that $x_1 < x_2 < x_3$. The following Hasse diagram represents the power set of $\{x_1, x_2, x_3\}$:

Just as every "thing", products can also be better understood by arranging their individual components in a hierarchy. The individual features of the products (e.g., the power of an engine, the size of the wheels, etc.) are thereby referred to as attributes. Figure 49 gives an example of a hierarchical product description, which describes the features of a car as a hierarchy of attributes.

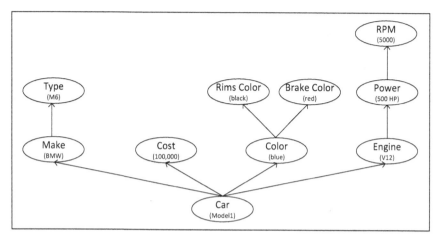

Figure 49: Sample of a hierarchical product description (a) and its Hasse diagram (b).

The node Car (Model1) serves as the root node for the product description. The four child nodes Make (BMW), Cost (100,000), Color (blue), and Engine (V12) describe top-level characteristics of the car. Furthermore, the node Make (BMW) is detailed by Type (M6). The node Color (blue) is again detailed by the two nodes Rims Color (black) and Brake Color (bed). The node Engine (V12) is detailed by a child node Power (500 HP), which is again detailed by a child node At Rounds Per Minute (5000). It must be noted that –other than the Hasse diagram in Figure 48– the nodes in Figure 49 do not have multiple predecessors. This might, however, be the case for product components that are used multiple times by other components, which are lower in the hierarchy.

The power of hierarchically ordered product descriptions lies in the semantics that can be derived from their structure. These semantics are extensively exploited during the transformation of input queries into result sets. From here on, semantic product descriptions are considered as hierarchies of key-value pairs. A key-value pair is thereby named an "attribute". Hence, a semantic product description consists of a hierarchy of attributes.

5.2 Semantic Product Description

Semantic product descriptions differ from traditional product descriptions (cp. section 4.2) in the way they provide product information. The S-PDL does not depend on web search engines or crawlers to extrapolate semantic information from product descriptions. Instead, the S-PDL provides a native interface to the information that is contained within a product description. The eight fundamental characteristics of a semantic product description language, as it is proposed in this chapter, are:

Generality	the property to describe every arbitrary product or service (characteristics),
Attribute-based schema	the property to describe products based on their attributes (characteristics),
Internationalization	the ability to allow for searching across multiple languages and cultures,
Interpretation through semantic operators	the capability to interpret semantic operators contained in search queries,
Language localization	the ability to localize the language of a product description into the language of the query, before the matching is performed,
Culture localization	the ability to localize the culture (e.g., units) of a product description into the culture of the query, before the matching is performed,
Dynamic binding of functionality (attribute handlers)	the ability to equip product descriptions with a behavior that depends on the sender of the query and the time when the query was sent. Behavior thereby is to be understood as capability of the product description to adapt (recompute) the values of its attributes based on the context of the query,
Relevance	the capability to provide a quality measure for how relevant a search result is, with respect to the corresponding search query.

All of the above eight points in one way or another aim to provide a basis for making product descriptions discoverable by their characteristics. The Internet of Products leverages the discoverability of product descriptions by providing consumers with an undistorted, cross-language, and cross-cultural view of electronic markets. This principle originates from and is mainly based upon the welfare and the 3BL analysis in sections 2.1.8 and 3.3.

Figure 50 summarizes the above eight points in a conceptual overview and shows how the single components of a semantic product description are interrelated with another.

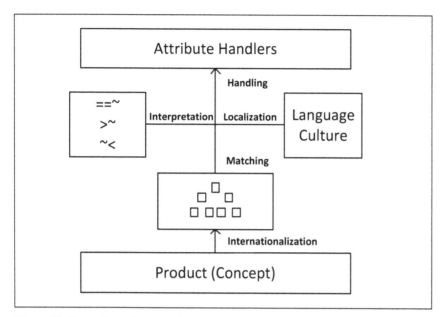

Figure 50: Semantic Product Description Process.

At the very bottom, a product concept, which is any unstructured representation of product data, is transformed into a semi-structured, general schema (the S-PDL). The schema is based upon a hierarchy of product attributes. This process is referred to as "internationalization", since it prepares the product data in a way, so that it can later be queried by any language or culture. After the product description was internationalized, it is ready to be included in the process of matching it with semantic queries. One of the core characteristics of semantic queries is that they can contain operators, which are used to specify quantitative restrictions on product characteristics. This process is called "interpretation". Furthermore, products need to be adapted to the language and the culture that is contained within the query. This process is referred to as "localization". Localization allows for cross-culture and cross-language queries. In the last step, dynamically bound functionality in form of the so called attribute handlers is executed on the product description. Attribute handlers modify the value of an attribute (e.g., price) in correspondence with the context of the query. The context of the query thereby consists of the language and the culture of the query (defined by the caller), as well as the time when the query was received. This is where the processing of a semantic query concludes and the result is returned back to the caller.

The following sections detail the individual process steps and are based upon a number of categories.

5.2.1   Explicit vs. Implicit Semantics

As compared to traditional product descriptions, semantic product descriptions differ in the mechanics they offer for product information retrieval. While traditional product descriptions –due to their very nature– are limited to text-based semantics (e.g., string comparison and string transformation), semantic product descriptions explicitly provide product information through a well-defined interface, the Semantic Product Description Language (S-PDL).

In section 3.2.1 (Semantic Product Retrieval Benchmark), it was shown how contemporary product search engines aim to discover implicit product information from text-based product descriptions –with fairly limited success. Contrarily, semantic product descriptions provide explicit product information that is highly reliable and does not require interpretation or extrapolation in order to be discovered. Reliability, thereby, is measured in terms of relevance of the search results. Relevance is a semantic search concept that is detailed later on in this chapter. Essentially, semantic product descriptions are capable of calculating their own relevance and expressing it on a numerical scale.

Semantic product descriptions rely upon semi-structured information, whereas traditional product descriptions most often have no structure at all. In case of the latter one, information discovery solely relies upon text mining or other, more sophisticated extrapolation methods. Semantic product descriptions, contrarily, do not require extrapolation as they provide a generic interface to their information content. Table 10 opposes the characteristics of explicit and implicit product information to each other.

The benefits of explicit product information in semantic product descriptions are manifold. One of the benefits is based upon the accuracy of search results. Search queries can contain an explicit listing of product characteristics, whereby product descriptions stored within a product catalog are matched with the product characteristics in the query, on a characteristic level. Moreover, semantic

Table 10: Implicit and explicit semantic product information.

Characteristic	Explicit	Implicit
Structure	Semi-structured	Plain, no structure
Information discovery	–	Text mining, extrapolation
Interface	Generic	–

product descriptions –if they contain units– are capable of transforming values into other but related unit systems, for example [kg] to [lb] (see section 5.2.7.2 for details). Performance-wise, traditional product descriptions require significant preprocessing due to search engine indexing. On the other hand, once the indexing is completed, queries can very fast be served as there is almost no need for runtime processing. Semantic product descriptions, contrarily, especially if advanced semantic operations are requested, might require substantial runtime processing. In turn, no indexing is needed. Table 11 summarizes the advantages of semantic product descriptions over traditional product descriptions.

Table 11: Advantages of explicit and implicit product information.

Feature	Semantic Product Descriptions	Traditional Product Descriptions
Attribute-based search	Yes	No
Search accuracy	High	Low
Unit system transformation	Yes	No
Preprocessing and indexing	No	Yes
Runtime processing	Possibly substantial	Low

5.2.2 Category-based Fundamentals of Semantic Product Descriptions

Section 3.1.1 gave an overview of commonly known categories. Some of them might be used as basis for a semantic product description language. Regarding the theoretical foundation of the S-PDL, only the categories Set and PoSet are further examined. The final model of the S-PDL will be based upon the category PoSet.

5.2.2.1 Product Descriptions as Objects of Set

Assuming that product descriptions are assemblies of product attributes, the category "Set" could be used as categorical representation of product descriptions. In the context of product descriptions, the term "ProductSet" is chosen to refer to Set as being a category that has as objects "product sets". Given all "product sets" A, B, C, ... to be objects and all functions $f: A \rightarrow B, g: B \rightarrow C, ...$ to be morphisms, this represents the category ProductSet (in analogy to ([Walters 1991], p. 5)).

Let A_{Se} be the set-based category of product descriptions:

$$A_{Se} = \left(Ob(A_{Se}), Mor_{A_{Se}}(X, Y), \circ_{A_{Se}}, id_{A_{Se}}\right) \qquad (5.2.2.1.1)$$

Then, A_{Se} consists of:

- ■ $Ob(A_{Se})$ as the set-based product descriptions,

- ■ $Mor_{A_{Se}}$ as the morphisms between the objects $PD_{Se} \in Ob(A_{Se})$. Morphisms of $Mor_{A_{Se}}$ are functions on product descriptions,

- ■ $\circ_{A_{Se}}$ as composition of the morphisms in $Mor_{A_{Se}}$. Composition means composition of functions with $g \circ f(\alpha_{Se}) = g(f(\alpha_{Se}))$, and

- ■ $I_{A_{Se}}$ as the identity morphisms of $Ob(A_{Se})$.

Set-based product descriptions do not innately support hierarchies. In fact, set-based product descriptions represent a list of attributes in a flat hierarchy. In this sense, set-based product descriptions correspond with features (cp. section 4.2). For semantic product descriptions, however, hierarchies are a fundamental requirement (cp. section 4.2.3). The category PoSet provides native support for hierarchies.

5.2.2.2 Product Descriptions as Objects of PoSet

Semantic product descriptions are resembled by a hierarchy of attributes. Mathematically seen, a hierarchy is an ordered set. The term hierarchy is used as synonym for poset, whose elements are classes of objects of increasing complexity. The category PoSet is defined as $(P, \leq)$. Objects of PoSet are members of the set P. The morphisms of PoSet are binary relations $a \leq b$ [Awodey 2010]. Analogously to "ProductSet", the term "ProductPoSet" was chosen to refer to PoSet as being a category that has as objects posets of product attributes.

Let A_{Po} be the category of poset-based attributes:

$$A_{Po} = \left(Ob(A_{Po}), Mor_{A_{Po}}(X, Y), \circ_{A_{Po}}, id_{A_{Po}}\right) \qquad (5.2.2.2.1)$$

Then, A_{Po} consists of:

▪ $Ob(A_{Po})$ as the poset-based product descriptions,

▪ $Mor_{A_{Po}}$ as being the morphisms of the objects $PD_{Po} \in Ob(A_{Po})$. Morphisms of $Mor_{A_{Po}}$ are arrows $f: \alpha \in PD_{Po} \rightarrow \alpha' \in PD'_{Po}$, if $\alpha \le \alpha'$,

▪ $\circ_{A_{Po}}$ as *composition* of the morphisms in $Mor_{A_{Po}}$, and

▪ $I_{A_{Po}}$ as the identity morphisms of $Ob(A_{Po})$.

PoSet-based product descriptions natively provide support for hierarchical product descriptions. Hierarchically structured product attributes are an important prerequisite for performing semantic search queries.

5.2.3 Product attributes

Semantic Product Descriptions consist of product attributes. Product attributes $\alpha \in PD_{Po}$ represent a quadruple that consists of the elements *name, value, base_unit*, and *handler*. These four elements are the basic building blocks of a semantic product description:

$$\alpha = (name, value, base\_unit, handler) \tag{5.2.3.1}$$

with

▪ *name* being the unique identifier of the attribute. This can, for example, be an integer-based auto-increment, a global unique identifier, or any kind of string,

▪ *value* representing the attribute's non-handled (or static) value. When an attribute handler is called on an attribute, its attribute value is transformed into a handled (or dynamic) value,

▪ *base_unit* being the unit in which the non-handled value is defined. base_unit is furthermore relevant, when values are transformed into other units, and

▪ *handler* containing an ordered list of attribute handlers that are bound to the attribute. The detailed mechanics of attribute handlers are later detailed in section 5.2.8.

The following sections detail how *name, value, base_unit*, and *handler* are used to provide for the capabilities outlined in section 5.2.

5.2.4   Internationalization of Product Descriptions

Internationalization represents an engineering effort to build software in a way, so that it natively supports multiple languages and cultures, without changes in code being necessary. Without internationalization, product descriptions would neither be culturally neutral nor language-independent. Despite the fact that a trans-lingual search of product descriptions would be impossible, this also implied that clients from cultural backgrounds other than the culture of the product description would not be able to run quantitative queries against the catalog, as units and scales would not match. When product authors define a new product description, they do this in a language of their choice $L \in Lang$, whereby L defines the "locale" of this language (cp. section 5.2.7).

Internationalizing the language of product descriptions means transforming a language-biased product description PD_L into a language-independent representation PD, and linking a set of translations, the so called "translation sets", to PD. The functor $Transl$ sends every $Ob(A_{Po}) \in A_{Po}$ to a new category $A_{PoTransl}$. Objects of $A_{PoTransl}$ are "translation sets" $TranslSet \in Ob(A_{PoTransl})$ of translated product posets:

$$A_{PoTransl} = \left(Ob\big(A_{PoTransl}\big), Mor_{A_{PoTransl}}(X,Y), \circ_{A_{PoTransl}}, id_{A_{PoTransl}}\right)$$
$$(5.2.4.1)$$

For every product description $PD \in Ob(A_{Po})$, there exists a "translation set" $TranslSet \in Ob(A_{PoTransl})$ that has as elements the translated product posets PD_L. Moreover, there exists a translated product poset $PD_L \in TranslSet, \forall L \in Lang$. Queries against the catalog will later resolve product descriptions for their translation sets and perform the matching of query attribute names with product attribute names based on their respective $TranslSet$.

The PDL supports culture internationalization by design and does not require runtime processing. Culture localization, contrarily, is not implicit and requires runtime processing, which is covered in section 5.2.7.2.

5.2.5   Matching Product Descriptions with Queries

Upon reception of a query, a matcher will match the query with all product descriptions available in the catalog. The category M of queries and product descriptions has as objects query posets and product description posets, and as morphisms arrows from Q to PD, if the product description PD matches the query Q, denoted as $Q \asymp PD$:

$$M = (Ob(M), Mor_M(Q, PD), \circ_M, id_M)$$

$$Q \asymp PD \Rightarrow \exists m \in Mor_M : m(Q, PD) \geq 1 \tag{5.2.5.1}$$

The matcher morphism m is a function of a query Q and a product description PD, both consisting of a poset of a $(name, value, base\_unit, handler)$ quadruples. Thereby, Q and PD match, if there is at least one $\alpha^{PD} \in PD$ that matches at least one $\alpha^Q \in Q$.

$$m(Q, PD) \geq 1 \Leftrightarrow \exists \alpha^{PD} \in PD : f(\alpha^{PD}, \alpha^Q) = 1, \forall \alpha^Q \in Q$$

$$m(Q, PD) = \sum_{\alpha^Q \in Q} \sum_{\alpha^{PD} \in PD} f(\alpha^{PD}, \alpha^Q) \tag{5.2.5.2}$$

Furthermore, one $\alpha^{PD} \in PD$ can be considered as a match for one $\alpha^Q \in Q$, if both their names $\alpha^{PD}_{name} \in \alpha^{PD}$ and $\alpha^Q_{name} \in \alpha^Q$ and their values $\alpha^{PD}_{value} \in \alpha^{PD}$ and $\alpha^Q_{value} \in \alpha^Q$ match:

$$f(\alpha^{PD}, \alpha^Q) = \begin{cases} 1, \alpha^{PD}_{name} \asymp \alpha^Q_{name} \wedge \alpha^{PD}_{value} \asymp \alpha^Q_{value} \\ 0, else \end{cases} \tag{5.2.5.3}$$

According to (5.2.5.1), the purpose of m and f is to find all those product descriptions PD in the catalog, for which there exists an attribute $\alpha^{PD} \in PD$ and an attribute $\alpha^Q \in Q$, so that the name of α^{PD} matches the name of α^Q (denoted as $\alpha^{PD}_{name} \asymp \alpha^Q_{name}$) and the value of α^{PD} matches the value of α^Q (denoted as $\alpha^{PD}_{value} \asymp \alpha^Q_{value}$), respectively. Thereby, matches are distinguished into exact match and partial match. An exact match of PD and Q is given, if:

$$\left(\sum_{\alpha^Q \in Q} f(\alpha^{PD}, \alpha^Q) \right) \geq 1, \forall \alpha^{PD} \in PD \tag{5.2.5.4}$$

It must be noted that the match of a query attribute $\alpha^Q \in Q$ with PD is an "overdetermined exact match", if there exists more than one attribute α^{PD} that matches α^Q ($\sum_{\alpha^Q \in Q} f(\alpha^{PD}, \alpha^Q) \geq 1$). If there is exactly one attribute α^{PD} that matches the query attribute α^Q, then the match is a "straight exact match" ($\sum_{\alpha^Q \in Q} f(\alpha^{PD}, \alpha^Q) = 1$). In all other cases, the match is a partial match (at least one $\alpha^{PD} \in PD$ matches at least one $\alpha^Q \in Q$) or a non-match (no $\alpha^{PD} \in PD$ matches any $\alpha^Q \in Q$). In case of a partial match, it is important to determine the relevance of the partial match. Relevance thereby measures to which extent PD

matches Q. If only a fraction of query attributes match the product description, then this fraction is what measures the relevance (R):

$$R(Q, PD) = \frac{\Sigma_\alpha Q_{\in Q}(\chi(\Sigma_\alpha PD_{\in PD}(f(\alpha^{PD}, \alpha^Q))))}{|Q|} \qquad (5.2.5.5)$$

with

$$\chi(x) = f\colon x \to \{0,1\} = \begin{cases} 1, if \ x \geq 1 \\ 0, else \end{cases} \qquad (5.2.5.6)$$

Relevance is particularly important, when search results are to be put into a ranking. A ranking thereby represents a partially ordered set. The rank r of a product description PD is higher than or equal to the rank r' of a product description PD', if there exists an arrow from r to r', so that $r(PD) \geq r'(PD')$. Essentially, there exists a mapping $g\colon R(Q, PD) \to r(PD)$ that assigns the relevance R of a product description with respect to a search query Q a rank r in a ranking.

Based on the above matching semantics, semantic search query results contain accurate information about the degree at which a product description in a catalog matches a query. Moreover, the above matching semantics provide for an objective measure of how to rank multiple search results, based on their relevance. If only exact matches are of particular interest, search results can be filtered for a maximum relevance of "1".

5.2.6   Query Refinement through Semantic Operators

Operators are used in semantic product queries in order to provide more fine-granular matching semantics that allow for the specification of quantitative aspects of attributes (e.g., prices, weights, length, etc.). Operators are interpreted during the matching process at runtime. Thereby, operators are identified by their particular symbol. The S-PDL can define any arbitrary symbol as operator ω. Basic operators are binary or unary operators. Tertiary, or generally spoken n-ary operators, are specializations of binary and unary operators.

The following listing contains the definitions of operator functions for the five basic binary operators $=, >, \geq, <, \leq$. Both sides of the five basic binary operators have to strongly match (math. *strong equivalence*) a product attribute for an exact match. Furthermore, $\doteq_L, \doteq_R, \doteq, \gtrdot, \gtrsim, \lessdot, \lesssim$ represent specializations of the five basic binary operators, which indicate that either the left argument, the right argument, or both arguments of the operator might weakly match (math. *weak equivalence*) a product attribute. Thereby, the notion of weak equivalence and the dotted operators originate from [Zuse 1998], and are mapped to semantic product attributes. It must be noted that –other than $\doteq$ with its two specializations $\doteq_L$ and $\doteq_R- >, \geqslant, <, \leqslant$ implicitly apply to the right operator argument. The reason for this lies in the right argument (in case of the latter four mentioned operators) being numeric, whereby the operator by itself already weakens the equivalence. The exact meaning of a weak match (or weak equivalence) is specific to the individual implementation and is not further detailed throughout this chapter.

The following formal expressions detail the meaning of the five basic binary operators and their weak-matching versions. Thereby, the notation

$$\alpha^{PD} \asymp {}^{\omega}\alpha^{Q} \rightarrow f_{\omega}(\alpha^{PD}, \alpha^{Q}) = 1 \tag{5.2.6.1}$$

means "for the operator ω: if α^{PD} matches α^{Q}, then there exists a morphism f_{ω} from α^{PD} to α^{Q} for that holds: $f_{\omega}(\alpha^{PD}, \alpha^{Q}) = 1$. For the purpose of readability, the following listing of operators omits the "= 1" from the notation.

The operator " = " (left: strong, right: strong) is defined as:

$$\alpha^{PD} \asymp_{=} \alpha^{Q} \rightarrow f_{=}(\alpha^{PD}, \alpha^{Q})$$

with

$$f_{=}(\alpha^{PD}, \alpha^{Q}) = \begin{cases} 1, & \alpha^{PD}_{name} = \alpha^{Q}_{name} \wedge \alpha^{PD}_{value} = \alpha^{Q}_{value} \\ 0, else \end{cases} \tag{5.2.6.2}$$

The operator " $\doteq_R$ " (left: strong, right: weak) is defined as:

$$\alpha^{PD} \asymp_{\doteq_R} \alpha^{Q} \rightarrow f_{\doteq_R}(\alpha^{PD}, \alpha^{Q})$$

with

$$f_{\doteq_R}(\alpha^{PD}, \alpha^{Q}) = \begin{cases} 1, \alpha^{PD}_{name} = \alpha^{Q}_{name} \wedge \alpha^{PD}_{value} \doteq \alpha^{Q}_{value} \\ 0, else \end{cases} \tag{5.2.6.3}$$

The operator " $\doteq_L$ " (left: weak, right: strong) is defined as:

$$\alpha^{PD} \asymp_{\doteq_L} \alpha^{Q} \rightarrow f_{\doteq_L}(\alpha^{PD}, \alpha^{Q})$$

with

$$f_{\doteq_L}(\alpha^{PD}, \alpha^Q) = \begin{cases} 1, & \alpha_{name}^{PD} \doteq \alpha_{name}^Q \wedge \alpha_{value}^{PD} = \alpha_{value}^Q \\ & 0, else \end{cases} \tag{5.2.6.4}$$

The operator " $\doteq$ " (left: weak, right: weak) is defined as:

$$\alpha^{PD} \asymp_{\doteq} \alpha^Q \rightarrow f_{\doteq}(\alpha^{PD}, \alpha^Q)$$

with

$$f_{\doteq}(\alpha^{PD}, \alpha^Q) = \begin{cases} 1, & \alpha_{name}^{PD} \doteq \alpha_{name}^Q \wedge \alpha_{value}^{PD} \doteq \alpha_{value}^Q \\ & 0, else \end{cases} \tag{5.2.6.5}$$

The operator " $>$ " (left: weak, right: strong) is defined as:

$$\alpha^{PD} \asymp_{>} \alpha^Q \rightarrow f_{>}(\alpha^{PD}, \alpha^Q)$$

with

$$f_{>}(\alpha^{PD}, \alpha^Q) = \begin{cases} 1, & \alpha_{name}^{PD} \doteq \alpha_{name}^Q \wedge \alpha_{value}^{PD} < \alpha_{value}^Q \\ & 0, else \end{cases} \tag{5.2.6.6}$$

The operator " $\geqslant$ " (left: weak, right: strong) is defined as:

$$\alpha^{PD} \asymp_{\geqslant} \alpha^Q \rightarrow f_{\geqslant}(\alpha^{PD}, \alpha^Q)$$

with

$$f_{\geqslant}(\alpha^{PD}, \alpha^Q) = \begin{cases} 1, & \alpha_{name}^{PD} \doteq \alpha_{name}^Q \wedge \alpha_{value}^{PD} \leq \alpha_{value}^Q \\ & 0, else \end{cases} \tag{5.2.6.7}$$

The operator " $<$ " (left: weak, right: strong) is defined as:

$$\alpha^{PD} \asymp_{<} \alpha^Q \rightarrow f_{<}(\alpha^{PD}, \alpha^Q)$$

with

$$f_{<}(\alpha^{PD}, \alpha^Q) = \begin{cases} 1, & \alpha_{name}^{PD} \doteq \alpha_{name}^Q \wedge \alpha_{value}^{PD} > \alpha_{value}^Q \\ & 0, else \end{cases} \tag{5.2.6.8}$$

The operator " $\leqslant$ " (left: weak, right: strong) is defined as:

$$\alpha^{PD} \asymp_{\leqslant} \alpha^Q \rightarrow f_{\leqslant}(\alpha^{PD}, \alpha^Q)$$

with

$$f_{\leqslant}(\alpha^{PD}, \alpha^Q) = \begin{cases} 1, & \alpha_{name}^{PD} \doteq \alpha_{name}^Q \wedge \alpha_{value}^{PD} \geq \alpha_{value}^Q \\ & 0, else \end{cases} \tag{5.2.6.9}$$

The operator " >" (left: strong, right: strong) is defined as:

$$\alpha^{PD} \doteq_> \alpha^Q \rightarrow f_>(\alpha^{PD}, \alpha^Q)$$

with

$$f_>(\alpha^{PD}, \alpha^Q) = \begin{cases} 1, \alpha^{PD}_{name} = \alpha^Q_{name} \wedge \alpha^{PD}_{value} < \alpha^Q_{value} \\ 0, else \end{cases} \qquad (5.2.6.10)$$

The operator " ≥" (left: strong, right: strong) is defined as:

$$\alpha^{PD} \doteq_\geq \alpha^Q \rightarrow f_\geq(\alpha^{PD}, \alpha^Q)$$

with

$$f_\geq(\alpha^{PD}, \alpha^Q) = \begin{cases} 1, \alpha^{PD}_{name} = \alpha^Q_{name} \wedge \alpha^{PD}_{value} \leq \alpha^Q_{value} \\ 0, else \end{cases} \qquad (5.2.6.11)$$

The operator " <" (left: strong, right: strong) is defined as:

$$\alpha^{PD} \doteq_< \alpha^Q \rightarrow f_<(\alpha^{PD}, \alpha^Q)$$

with

$$f_<(\alpha^{PD}, \alpha^Q) = \begin{cases} 1, \ \alpha^{PD}_{name} = \alpha^Q_{name} \wedge \alpha^{PD}_{value} > \alpha^Q_{value} \\ 0, else \end{cases} \qquad (5.2.6.12)$$

The operator " ≤" (left: strong, right: strong) is defined as:

$$\alpha^{PD} \doteq_\leq \alpha^Q \rightarrow f_\leq(\alpha^{PD}, \alpha^Q)$$

with

$$f_\leq(\alpha^{PD}, \alpha^Q) = \begin{cases} 1, \ \alpha^{PD}_{name} = \alpha^Q_{name} \wedge \alpha^{PD}_{value} \geq \alpha^Q_{value} \\ 0, else \end{cases} \qquad (5.2.6.13)$$

Furthermore, there exist two order relations $\mathcal{R}_1$ and $\mathcal{R}_2$ between $=, \doteq_L, \doteq_R, \doteq$ and $>, \geq, <, \geq, >, \geqslant, <, \leqslant$ respectively, whereby $\omega > \omega'$ indicates that the equivalence of ω is stronger than the equivalence of ω'. For the sake of readability, the semantic operators were framed by a box.

$$\mathcal{R}_1: \boxed{=} \succ \boxed{\doteq_L}, \boxed{\doteq_R} \succ \boxed{\doteq}$$

$$\mathcal{R}_2: \boxed{\geq}, \boxed{\leq} \succ \boxed{>}, \boxed{<} \succ \boxed{\geqslant}, \boxed{\leqslant} \succ \boxed{>}, \boxed{<} \qquad (5.2.6.14)$$

The implementations of the above S-PDL operators are provided by an environment that is referred to as "Semantic Product Server (SPS)", which is covered throughout the next chapter. As mentioned earlier, the S-PDL can be extended by any other operator. Since in semantic search queries operators claim symbols for explicit usage and as a reserved keyword, it is to be taken care of that semantic search queries do not contain operator symbols for any other purpose than the execution of the intended operator itself. Besides operators, there exist other aspects, such as language localization and culture localization, which play into the mechanics of matching semantic search queries with semantic product descriptions.

5.2.7   Localization of Product Descriptions

Localization refers to the process of adapting internationalized software to a specific language or culture (e.g. translating texts, customizing units), based on language-specific locales. Locales uniquely identify a language and its specific culture. Locales exist for every language and culture. Table 12 contains a brief overview of some locales.

Table 12: Sample Locales.

Language	Culture	Locale
German	German	de-DE
German	Austrian	de-AT
English	Great Britain	en-GB
English	United States	en-US
Chinese	Simplified	zh_CN
Chinese	Traditional (Taiwanese)	zh_TW

In the context of semantic product descriptions, localization means matching the language of a semantic search query with the language of a semantic product description (denoted as "language localization") and transforming product units into query units (denoted as "culture localization"). Both require the identification of the locale L as part of the semantic search query.

5.2.7.1 Language Localization

When matching product descriptions with queries, it is necessary to align the language of the query with the language of the product descriptions stored inside the catalog. This is done based on the locale contained within the search query. In section 5.2.4, it was shown how "translation sets" $TranslSet \in Ob(A_{Transl})$ are formed out of language-biased product descriptions $PD \in Ob(A_{Po})$. Localizing the language of a product description in order to align it with the query's locale L is achieved through two special morphisms $LangResolve^L$ and $LangConstruct^L$.

$LangResolve^L$ is defined as $f: Ob(A_{PoTransl})(L) \rightarrow TranslSet_{PD}(L)$. It resolves the objects of $Ob(A_{PoTransl})$ for a translation set $TranslSet_{PD}(L)$, which contains the attribute translations according to the locale L.

After the translation set was resolved, $LangConstruct^L$ constructs a localized product description PD_L by linking both $TranslSet_{PD}(L)$ and PD together. PD thereby stands for the internationalized product description. $LangConstruct^L$ is defined as $g: TranslSet_{PD}(L) \rightarrow PD_L$.

As far as textual elements, such as the name of an attribute or non-quantitative attribute values, are concerned, semantic search queries that were defined in a specific language can now be matched with PD_L, based on their locale L. Regarding quantitative elements (e.g., numerical attribute values), a second localization step, referred to as "culture localization", needs to be performed.

5.2.7.2 Culture Localization

When the operators defined in section 5.2.6 are applied to a query, the values in the product description stored within the catalog might have to be transformed to match the units of the query elements. If, for example, a query contains an attribute $price \leq USD30,000$ and the catalog contains a product with an attribute $price = EUR20,000$, both the query and the product attributes have to be converted into a common unit before they can be matched with another. In above example, this could happen by applying the exchange rate between Euro and Dollar to the product attribute. Two attribute values can only be transformed into another, if there exists a mapping between their units. The category $Conv$ ("Convertible") has as objects units and as morphisms arrows $f: U \rightarrow V$, if there exists a mapping between two units $U, V \in Conv$.

Table 13: Translation Groups.

TransGroup	Examples
Distance	$f_{m,km}:[m] \rightarrow [km]$, $f_{km,m}:[km] \rightarrow [m]$, $f_{km,mi}:[km] \rightarrow [mi]$, $f_{mi,km}:[mi] \rightarrow [km]$, $f_{cm,yd}:[cm] \rightarrow [yd]$, $f_{yd,cm}:[yd] \rightarrow [cm]$
Mass	$f_{g,kg}:[g] \rightarrow [kg]$, $f_{kg,g}:[kg] \rightarrow [g]$, $f_{kg,lb}:[kg] \rightarrow [lb]$, $f_{lb,kg}:[lb] \rightarrow [kg]$, $f_{ev,g}:[eV] \rightarrow [g]$, $f_{g,ev}:[g] \rightarrow [eV]$
Time	$f_{h,min}:[h] \rightarrow [min]$, $f_{min,h}:[min] \rightarrow [h]$, $f_{min,s}:[min] \rightarrow [s]$, $f_{s,min}:[s] \rightarrow [min]$, $f_{h,s}:[h] \rightarrow [s]$, $f_{s,h}:[s] \rightarrow [h]$
Currency	$f_{EUR,USD}:[EUR] \rightarrow [USD]$, $f_{USD,EUR}:[USD] \rightarrow [EUR]$, $f_{EUR,JPY}:[EUR] \rightarrow [JPY]$, $f_{JPY,EUR}:[JPY] \rightarrow [EUR]$, $f_{JPY,USD}:[JPY] \rightarrow [USD]$, $f_{USD,JPY}:[USD] \rightarrow [JPY]$

$$Conv = (Ob(Conv), Mor_{Conv}(U,V), \circ_{Conv}, id_{Conv}) \qquad (5.2.7.2.1)$$

Other examples of $Conv$ include the conversion of distance measures based upon the metric system (e.g., [cm], [m], [km], etc.) into miles, feet, yards and inches, and vice versa. More generally, for all $U, V \in Conv$ with U, V being distance measures, there exist two morphisms $f: U \rightarrow V$ and $f^{-1}: V \rightarrow U$, which convert U into V and V into U, respectively.

If, for any arbitrary set of units $Units$, with $U, V, W \in Units$ there exist the morphisms $f: U \rightarrow V$, $f^{-1}: V \rightarrow U$, $g: V \rightarrow W$, $g^{-1}: W \rightarrow V$, and $h: U \rightarrow W$, $h^{-1}: W \rightarrow U$, $\forall U, V, W \in Units$, then the elements of $Units$ form a "transformation group", namely $TransGroup$; that is, there exists a transformation for each unit $U \in TransGroup$ into every other unit $V \in TransGroup$. Table 13 features a non-exclusive list of "transformation groups":

Each element within $Conv$ belongs to a "transformation group". Two different "transformation groups" $TG_1, TG_2 \subset Ob(Conv), TG_1 \neq TG_2$ are mutually exclusive, which means that $TG_1 \cap TG_2 = \emptyset, \forall TG_1 \in Ob(Conv), \forall TG_2 \in Ob(Conv)$.

With transformation groups, it is possible to run a semantic search query Q, which specifies an attribute α^Q with a unit U that is different from a unit V specified in an attribute α^{PD} of a product description PD, as long as both units U, V

are members of the same transformation group ($U \neq V \wedge U, V \in TG$). In this case, the value of α^{PD} is transformed into a new value of α'^{PD}, while V is transformed into $V' = f_{V,U}(V, U)$, with $f_{V,U}: V \rightarrow U$, so that $V' = U$.

In the S-PDL, "transformation groups" are implemented through a more general concept, which throughout the next section is referred to as "attribute handlers".

5.2.8 Attribute Handlers

Attribute handlers represent a concept of processing attributes at query-time, including their values and their units. The main intention behind attribute handlers is to provide attributes with an on-attribute level behavior that depends on the time the attribute is queried and on parameters provided together with the query (cp. [PM06] in section 4.2.3). As compared to other product description approaches, attribute values are not static any longer, but instead can be processed, just before the product is queried by and sent to a client.

It was already indicated in section 5.2.7.2 that culture localization is achieved through a special attribute handler, which uses the standard attribute handler interface (cp. section 6.5) to receive input and provide output. A reference implementation of an attribute handler is detailed in the next chapter as part of a Semantic Product Server. Table 14 provides an overview of some example attribute handlers.

Table 14: A sample list of attribute handlers.

Attribute Handler	Attribute	Description
GetPriceInCurrency	<price>	translates the price of a product provided in base currency into a target currency,
TranslateUnit	Every attribute that has a unit	transforms the base unit of an attribute into a target unit,
TranslateAttribute	Every attribute	translates an attribute defined in a base language into a target language,
GiveDiscount	<price>	gives a discount on the price.

In section 5.2.3, an attribute was defined as a quadruple consisting of the following elements:

$$\alpha = (name, value, base\_unit, handler) \tag{5.2.8.1}$$

Attribute handlers can process and modify the attribute $value$ and the $base\_unit$ of an attribute. Contrarily, attribute handlers can neither modify the attribute $name$ nor the attribute handler list.

Given any product poset A_{Po} of attributes, a new set $A_{Po\,Hand}(A_{Po})$ can be constructed, the category of all handled attribute sets of A_{Po}. This idea utilizes the notion that functors are constructions which build, from objects of one category, objects of another [Walters 1991]. It suggests that it may be possible to extend $A_{Po\,Hand}$ to a functor:

$$A_{Po\,Hand}: A_{Po} \rightarrow Set(A_{Po}) \tag{5.2.8.2}$$

To do this, it is necessary to define $A_{Po\,Hand}$ on morphisms; that is, to define $A_{Po\,Hand}(f): A_{Po\,Hand}(X) \rightarrow A_{Po\,Hand}(Y)$, for each morphism $f: X \rightarrow Y$. The definition of $A_{Po\,Hand}$ is:

$$A_{Po\,Hand}(f): A_{Po\,Hand}(X) \rightarrow A_{Po\,Hand}(Y)$$

$$^{\circ}A_{Po\,Hand} \xrightarrow{\rightarrow \circ} A_{Po\,Hand}$$

$$x_1, x_2, \ldots, x_n \rightarrow f(x_1), f(x_2), \ldots, f(x_n) \tag{5.2.8.3}$$

When product descriptions are requested by clients, just before the matching with the query is performed all attribute handlers of a product have to previously be executed. Requests for attributes can originate from search queries that are run against the catalog as well as from requests for products that are triggered when the catalog is queried for entire product descriptions by clients.

When attribute handlers are executed, all of the attributes $\alpha \in PD$ within a product description $PD \in A_{Po}$ are transformed into new and handled attributes $\alpha_{Hand} \in PD_{Hand}$, whereby $PD_{Hand} \in A_{Po\,Hand}$. By definition, every attribute handler can be bound to every attribute, regardless of the meaningfulness of the handling operation. It is subject to the implementation of the attribute handler to decide, whether it can generate a modified transformed attribute $\alpha_{Hand} \in PD_{Hand}$ from an $\alpha \in PD$. This decision depends on the attribute's value and the value's type, the base unit of the attribute value, the base locale U and the targeted locale V, as well as other dynamically bound parameters, which are provided to the handler. If the handler is not able to generate a transformed attribute $\alpha_{Hand} \in PD_{Hand}$ from an $\alpha \in PD$, it will generate an untransformed attribute $\alpha_{Hand} \in PD_{Hand}$ from $\alpha \in PD$ with $\alpha_{Hand} = \alpha$.

5.3 BNF of the S-PDL

The S-PDL represents a semantic product description language, which supports the features detailed in section 5.2. While so far the S-PDL was described exclusively in a mathematical model, this section introduces the Backus-Naur Form (BNF) of the S-PDL as it was described throughout the previous sections. The following section 5.4 details how the BNF of the S-PDL is used to develop an XML-based model of the S-PDL.

The BNF of the S-PDL stringently respects the fact that product descriptions represent hierarchies of attributes. That is why the BNF of the S-PDL heavily relies upon recursion of tags, indicated as "<tag></tag>". Listing 4 details the essential components of the S-PDL in BNF notation.

```
1.  <Literal> ::= a | b | c | d | e | f | g | h | i | j | k |
    l | m | n | o | p | q | r | s | t | u | v | w | x | y | z
    | 0 | 1 | 2 | 3 | 4 | 5 | 6 | 7 | 8 | 9
2.  <String> ::= <Literal> | <Literal> <String>
3.  <Pdl_Open> ::= '<PDL>'
4.  <Pdl_Close> ::= '</PDL>'
5.  <Attribute_Open> ::= '<attribute>'
6.  <Attribute_ Close> ::= '</attribute>'
7.  <Name_Open> ::= '<name>'
8.  <Name_Close> ::= '</name>'
9.  <Name> ::= <Name_Open> <String> <Name_Close>
10. <Id_Open> ::= '<id>'
11. <Id_Close> ::= '</id>'
12. <Id> ::= <Id_Open> <String> <Id_Close>
13. <Value_Open> ::= '<value>'
14. <Value_Close> ::= '</value>'
15. <Value> ::= <Value_Open> <String> <Value_Close>
16. <Unit_Open> ::= '<unit>'
17. <Unit_Close> ::= '</unit>'
18. <Unit> ::= <Unit_Open> <String> <Unit_Close>
19. <Ah_Open> ::= '<ah>'
```

```
20. <Ah_Close> ::= '</ah>'
21. <Ah> ::= <Ah_Open> <String> <Ah_Close>
22. <Attribute_Sequence> ::= <Attribute> | <Attribute> <At-
    tribute_Sequence>
23. <Attribute> ::=
24. <Attribute_Open> <Name> <Id> <Value> <Attribute_Close> |
25. <Attribute_Open> <Name> <Id> <Value> <Attribute_Sequence>
    <Attribute_Close> |
26. <Attribute_Open> <Name> <Id> <Value> <Attribute_Close>
    <Attribute_Sequence> |
27. <Attribute_Open> <Name> <Id> <Value> <Attribute_Sequence>
    <Attribute_Close> <Attribute_Sequence> |
28. <Attribute_Open> <Name> <Id> <Value> <Unit> <Attrib-
    ute_Close> |
29. <Attribute_Open> <Name> <Id> <Value> <Unit> <Attrib-
    ute_Sequence> <Attribute_Close> |
30. <Attribute_Open> <Name> <Id> <Value> <Unit> <Attrib-
    ute_Close> <Attribute_Sequence> |
31. <Attribute_Open> <Name> <Id> <Value> <Unit> <Attrib-
    ute_Sequence> <Attribute_Close> <Attribute_Sequence> |
32. <Attribute_Open> <Name> <Id> <Value> <Ah> <Attrib-
    ute_Close> |
33. <Attribute_Open> <Name> <Id> <Value> <Ah> <Attrib-
    ute_Sequence> <Attribute_Close> |
34. <Attribute_Open> <Name> <Id> <Value> <Ah> <Attrib-
    ute_Close> <Attribute_Sequence> |
35. <Attribute_Open> <Name> <Id> <Value> <Ah> <Attrib-
    ute_Sequence> <Attribute_Close> <Attribute_Sequence> |
36. <Attribute_Open> <Name> <Id> <Value> <Unit> <Ah> <Attrib-
    ute_Close> |
37. <Attribute_Open> <Name> <Id> <Value> <Unit> <Ah> <Attrib-
    ute_Sequence> <Attribute_Close> |
38. <Attribute_Open> <Name> <Id> <Value> <Unit> <Ah> <Attrib-
    ute_Close> <Attribute_Sequence> |
39. <Attribute_Open> <Name> <Id> <Value> <Unit> <Ah> <Attrib-
    ute_Sequence> <Attribute_Close> <Attribute_Sequence>
40. <Pdl> ::= <Pdl_Open> <Attribute_Sequence> <Pdl_Close>
```

Listing 4: BNF of the S-PDL.

Lines 1-2 define characters that are allowed for a string, which is later used as basis for the name (Name), id (Id), value (Value), unit (Unit) and the attribute handler (Ah) of an attribute. Lines 3-21 define the tags for the previously mentioned name (Name), id (Id), value (Value), unit (Unit) and the attribute handler (Ah). Lines 22 define a sequence of attributes (Attribute_Sequence). This sequence expresses that there can be multiple attributes next to another on the same level of the hierarchy. Attribute_Sequence is then used in lines 23-39 to define what a valid attribute can consist of. Since the unit (Unit) as well as the attribute handler (Ah) of an attribute are optional, four cases of attribute composition need to be distinguished (lines 24-27: attribute with value, lines 28-31: attribute with value and unit, lines 32-35: attribute with value and attribute handler, lines 36-39: attribute with value, unit, and attribute handler). As can be seen from lines 24-27, each of the four cases again distinguishes into attributes with a sequence of nested child attributes (on the next hierarchy level), attributes with a sequence of sibling attributes (on the same hierarchy level), as well as attributes with a sequence of nested child attributes and a sequence of sibling attributes. The entire attribute hierarchy is nested into a root tag (Pdl).

Any implementation of the S-PDL that respects the above BNF is formally capable of providing support for the eight characteristics of a semantic product description language, as outlined in section 5.2. The following section provides an XML-based sample implementation of the BNF of the S-PDL.

5.4 S-PDL Schema

A product description, whether semantic or not, must be general enough to describe every kind of good or service. This implies a highly general structure of the schema. Thereby, the schema cannot contain any product-specific information. Otherwise, the generality requirement would be violated. The only standardized information, which the schema can contain, is how it provides access to information. The schema, however, does not expose which information it provides access to. The "weight" of a product, for example, is a product characteristic that might be specified for one product A, but not for another product B. That is why the schema does not contain an element "weight", representing the weight characteristic of the product. Instead, the schema defines an element that is called "attribute", which itself can contain information about the product weight. The approach pursued in this thesis aims at developing a schema for product definition that –rather than prescribing a set of product characteristics that the schema can be queried for– provides an interface to an arbitrarily complex set of product characteristics, whereby the interface can be queried for the existence of any particular product characteristics, and finally also for the characteristic itself. The formal fundamentals for this were laid throughout previous sections and led to the BNF of the S-PDL.

For the sample implementation into an S-PDL schema, XML was chosen. Besides XML, any other notation with support for hierarchies, such as JSON, YAML, or even a relational schema, could be used instead. Section 7.1.1, however, provides empirical evidence for relational schemas being problematic from a performance point of view, as far as implementation-specific aspects are concerned. Listing 5 contains the XSD schema of the S-PDL in version 1.0 and besides minor adaptations fully complies with the BNF of the S-PDL.

```xml
<xs:schema xmlns="xsdPDL" targetNamespace="xsdPDL"
xmlns:xs="http://www.w3.org/2001/XMLSchema" element-
FormDefault="qualified">
  <xs:element name="PDL">
    <xs:complexType>
      <xs:sequence>
        <xs:element name="meta" maxOccurs="1">
          <xs:complexType>
            <xs:sequence>
              <xs:element name="attribute" maxOccurs="unbounded"
              type="pdl_attribute"></xs:element>
            </xs:sequence>
          </xs:complexType>
        </xs:element>
            <xs:element name="attribute" minOccurs="0" max-
            Occurs="unbounded" type="pdl_attribute"/>
      </xs:sequence>
      <xs:attribute name="id" type="xs:string"/>
    </xs:complexType>
  </xs:element>
  <xs:complexType name="pdl_attribute">
    <xs:sequence>
      <xs:element name="id" minOccurs="1" maxOccurs="1"
      type="xs:string"/>
      <xs:element name="value" minOccurs="1" maxOccurs="1"
      type="xs:string"/>
      <xs:element name="unit" minOccurs="0" maxOccurs="1"
      type="xs:string"/>
```

```
    <xs:element name="ah" minOccurs="0" maxOccurs="1"
    type="xs:string"/>
    <xs:element name="attribute" minOccurs="0" max-
    Occurs="unbounded" type="pdl_attribute"/>
  </xs:sequence>
 </xs:complexType>
</xs:schema>
```

Listing 5: S-PDL 1.0 schema in XSD.

One of the before mentioned adaptations is that the XSD defines an explicit attribute "meta". The "meta" attribute, however, is very implementation-specific, which in the reference implementation of the Semantic Product Server (SPS) is used for fast access to high-level data. It must furthermore be noted that –though for every attribute the id and the value are required exactly once– unit and ah are optional and can exist once at maximum. An attribute, on the other hand, can have an unlimited number of child as well as sibling attributes, which is indicated as maxOccurs="unbounded". Both points are reflected in the BNF of the S-PDL attribute sequence.

5.5 Chapter Summary

This chapter covered the development of a formal model for a semantic product description language (S-PDL), which provides support for the eight requirements generality, attribute-based schema, internationalization, interpretation through semantic operators, language localization, culture localization, dynamic binding of functionality through attribute handlers, as well as relevance.

The model of the S-PDL utilizes category theory in order to describe its components and thereby exploits the property of posets to natively support hierarchies, which is a fundamental building block of the S-PDL. It was shown how based upon the formal model of the S-PDL the Backus-Naur Form (BNF) of the S-PDL can be developed. Lastly, it was demonstrated how the BNF serves as basis for the translation of the S-PDL concepts into a technological schema, in this case XSD, which can be used in real-world applications. Figure 51 shows how the S-PDL adds to the Internet of Products.

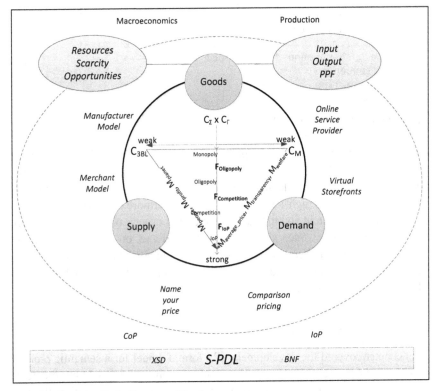

Figure 51: S-PDL in the Internet of Products.

The following chapter covers the development of an execution environment, namely the Semantic Product Server (SPS), which hosts S-PDL product descriptions in a catalog and provides the necessary infrastructure to allow for client interaction and product search.

6 Semantic Product Servers

*"The goal is to move from the current situation of complexity and frustra-
tion to one where technology serves the human needs invisibly, unobtrusive-
ly: the human-centered, customer-centered way." (Donald A. Norman)*

After the previous chapter covered the design and development of a formal model for the Semantic Product Description Language (S-PDL), this chapter details
the internals of the execution environment "SPS" that runs and interprets semantic product descriptions. It is shown how the functors of the category-based model of the S-PDL (Chapter 5) smoothly translate into software artifacts, and which
advantages so called "memoized" functors bear with respect to the runtime performance of the SPS. Furthermore, it is reviewed how different ways of SPS
deployment support the EC's vision of establishing a Single Market by creating
an integrated, highly scalable and transparent online market that spans across
cultural and lingual boundaries.

6.1 SPS Implementation

Chapter 5 introduced the Semantic Product Description Language (S-PDL). It
was mentioned that the S-PDL would need an environment in which product
descriptions authored in the S-PDL could be hosted and clients could be given
access to them. This environment is provided through the SPS. The SPS wraps
the concepts of the S-PDL into a piece of technology that –as it will be shown
later– can either be run on premise as a stand-alone server or in the Cloud as the
backbone of a product Cloud (cp. section 4.1.1.4).

Chapter 3 briefly mentioned that the SPS represents the core technology, which
the IoP would be based upon. The central tasks of the SPS are:

[SPS01]   Exposing client interfaces for accepting queries and returning results,

[SPS02]   Storing semantic product descriptions in a catalog,

[SPS03]   Providing the execution environment for attribute handlers, and

[SPS04]   Processing S-PDL queries and matching them with the catalog.

Throughout the remainder of this chapter, the above four points are further detailed.

6.2 SPS Client Interfaces

SPS client interfaces expose a gateway for clients to connect to the SPS, submit search queries, and obtain search results (cp. [SPS01]). The client interfaces are distinguished into "inbound" and "outbound". The inbound interface accepts queries from clients. The outbound interface outputs the result of search operations that were initiated by clients. As shown in

Figure 52, both inbound and outbound interfaces communicate with clients via a technology-independent and abstract format, which is referred to as "representational format" (RF).

Figure 52: Inbound and outbound interfaces of an SPS.

The RF of the inbound interface is denoted as RF-I. The RF of the outbound interface is denoted as RF-O. Both RF-I and RF-O are independent of particular technologies, such as XML, JSON, YAML, Web-QL, etc. The only restriction that underlies RF-I and RF-O is that they must be capable of expressing hierarchies, the fundamental pillar of the S-PDL (cp. section 5.1). Whether RF-I is based upon XML or a more advanced query language, such as Web-QL, is irrelevant, as long as hierarchies are fully respected. Analogously, whatever format is chosen for RF-O is an implementation-specific aspect and does not affect the validity of the concepts proposed in this chapter. Chapter seven shows how a prototypical implementation of an SPS, which is called "ArbiterOne" uses XML for both RF-I and RF-O. ArbiterOne, however, could as well have been based upon JSON, YAML, etc.

6.3 SPS Catalog

Product descriptions that were authored in the S-PDL need to be stored inside a catalog (cp. [SPS02]), from where they are exposed to clients. Regardless of the used technology, the catalog ensures the appropriate storage of product descriptions, so that they can later be efficiently queried and matched with search queries. The main functions of the catalog are to provide interfaces for adding, updating, and deleting product descriptions from it.

The SPS catalog might be based upon state-of-the art technology, such as a standard database management system. Since in essence the catalog addresses the question of how to store data, so that it can be efficiently retrieved again and since this problem has been sufficiently investigated by the research community, the remainder of this chapter will not pay closer attention to the internals of the catalog.

6.4 SPS Execution Environment and Reference Architecture

Chapter seven introduces the reference implementation of an SPS, called "ArbiterOne". Based on the experiences that were made with ArbiterOne, a reference architecture for an SPS was developed (cp. [SPS03]). The reference architecture in Figure 53 describes the necessary components of an SPS and how they interact with each other in a UML component diagram. The term component, thereby, was chosen in a broader sense and does not strictly refer to the component paradigm (cp. section 4.3.1). Instead, throughout this thesis the term component is used to refer to a logically encapsulated software artifact. In this sense, the components of the reference architecture can either be components in the narrower sense (e.g., Enterprise Java Beans, etc.) or web services, or even software agents (cp. Figure 47 ("Technology-based paradigm evolution") in section 4.3.3). Whatever paradigm is chosen for an implementation of the reference architecture is de facto irrelevant.

The components of the SPS reference architecture can adapt to all the three paradigms "components" (in the narrower sense), "services", and "agents". The ArbiterOne reference implementation, however, is based upon the service paradigm. This means that the components of the diagram in Figure 53 are actually implemented through web services. The decision for web services is backed by the many advantages of SOSE over CBSE ([CS01] – [CS08] in Table 6). The decision for services in favor of agents (SOSE vs. AOSE) is based upon the (current version of the) SPS not leveraging the peculiarities of software agents (e.g., mobility, autonomy, proactivity, etc.).

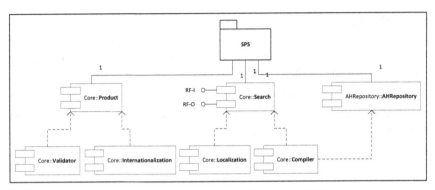

Figure 53: Reference architecture of a Semantic Product Server (SPS).

Table 15: SPS reference architecture components.

Component in Reference Architecture	Description
SPS	the package that comprises the Core and the AHRepository components,
Core::Product	the product component (a.k.a "catalog"), which allows the administration (e.g., add, edit, delete) of product descriptions,
Core::Validator	the validator, which is used by the product component to validate the formal correctness of product descriptions,
Core::Internationalization	the internationalization component, which performs the internationalization of product descriptions as explained in section 5.2.4,
Core::Search	the search component, which exposes inbound (RF-I) and outbound interfaces (RF-O) interfaces to clients and hosts the matching logic of product descriptions with queries,
Core::Localization	the localization component, which is used by the search component to localize internationalized product descriptions to fit the language and culture of the query (cp. section 5.2.7),
Core::Compiler	the compiler component, which is used by the search component to execute all attribute handlers contained within a product description upon matching (see section 5.2.8),
AHRepository::AHRepository	the attribute handler repository component, which is used by the compiler to host and execute attribute handlers in a runtime environment. It furthermore allows for the administration of attribute handlers, such as adding of new or deleting of existing attribute handlers.

In Table 15, the individual components of the SPS reference architecture are briefly explained. Components that are of particular importance are explained in detail throughout the remainder of this chapter.

6.5 Dynamic Binding

One core component of the SPS is the attribute handler repository, a runtime environment that hosts and executes attribute handlers. Attribute handlers are used to define and invoke dynamic behavior on product attributes and thus allow for product attributes that change their values over time. Attribute handlers were defined in section 5.2.8 as functors between two categories. Inside the SPS, they represent software artifacts that implement a certain interface, so that they can be hosted and accessed by the attribute handler repository via this interface. Attribute handlers cannot exist alone but require an execution environment. The attribute handler repository represents this execution environment that hosts and executes the attribute handlers. The attribute handler repository is part of the SPS. Figure 54 schematically characterizes the role of the attribute handler repository.

Figure 54: Tasks of the attribute handler repository.

According to Figure 54, the Attribute Handler Repository consists of two components, the Runtime and the Manager component. The Runtime instantiates, deletes, and provides access to attribute handlers stored within the Attribute Handler Repository. The Manager provides the means for uploading new attribute handlers to the system, registering them with the attribute handler repository, or sharing them among other repositories.

Attribute handlers can be developed outside the SPS by implementing an interface called "AH_Interface". Attribute handlers are compiled into a binary format and uploaded to the attribute handler repository. The interface that attribute handlers need to implement is depicted in Listing 6.

```csharp
public abstract class AH_Interface
{
        public    abstract    AH_ReturnType    Execute(object    _value,
        string _strBaseUnit, string _strLocale, Dictionary<int,
        object> _params);


        /*...*/

}
```

Listing 6: Attribute handler interface (in C# code).

Among others, the above interface contains one member function "Execute". "Execute" is called by the attribute handler repository, when an attribute handler is to be executed. The parameters of Execute are particularly important:

■ _value: the value of the attribute that is to be processed (S-PDL tag "<value>"),

■ _strBaseUnit: the unit of the attribute prior to processing (S-PDL tag "<unit>"),

■ _strLocale: the locale of the product description (is an attribute of the S-PDL tag "<PDL>"), and

■ _params: parameters the attribute handler might need for processing (is set by clients).

Based on above data, attribute handlers can start their processing. Thereby, they might require only a subset of the parameters that go into "Execute". In any case, upon completion attribute handlers have to return an object of the type "AH_ReturnType". This object provides the S-PDL compiler with important data on how to treat the attribute handler's result. "AH_ReturnType" consists of:

■ returnValue: the new value of the attribute after processing,

■ strTargetUnit: the new unit of the attribute after processing, and

■ volatile: indicates the S-PDL compiler, whether the result of the attribute handler execution is volatile or not and thus whether it can be cached or not.

After a new attribute handler was uploaded, the attribute handler repository manages the creation and tear-down of attribute handler instances and makes them accessible to product descriptions. The process of assigning an attribute handler to an attribute is referred to as "dynamic binding of attribute handlers".

When an attribute handler was bound to an attribute, the attribute handler is executed, whenever a product description is accessed, either by a direct request or via a search. The binding is dynamic, because the actual binding occurs only for the time when the attribute handler is being executed. The binding is established via an ID in a product attribute that uniquely identifies the attribute handler.

The instance that establishes the binding between an attribute handler and an attribute is the S-PDL compiler ("Core::Compiler" in Figure 53). Before a semantic product description can be delivered to a request or matched as part of a search operation, it needs to be parsed for the existence of dynamically bound attribute handlers. Every attribute handler ID contained in a semantic product description needs to be bound to the corresponding attribute handler in the attribute handler repository. The corresponding attribute handler then needs to be parameterized and executed. Finally, the result of the attribute handler execution is written back to the value of the attribute that bound the attribute handler. The above described process is referred to as "compilation of semantic product descriptions" (cp. [SPS04]).

Figure 55 demonstrates the S-PDL compilation process.

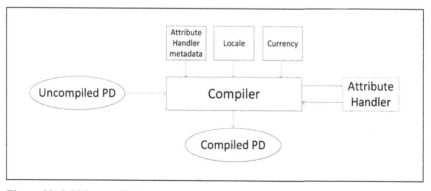

Figure 55: S-PDL compilation process.

According to Figure 55, an uncompiled product description ("uncompiled PD") is loaded from the catalog and transformed by the compiler into a compiled product description ("compiled PD"). The compilation occurs for every attribute handler that is contained within the uncompiled product description. The attribute handler metadata, the locale and the currency, which are necessary for the compilation, are submitted together with the query and can now be used to adjust the language and the unit system of the product description and the respective attribute handler to the query. In case of the attribute handler expecting parameters that are to be filled in by the client, the compiler receives these as "attribute handler metadata" and passes them on to the actual attribute handler.

Listing 7 samples an uncompiled product description as it is stored inside the catalog. The product description contains an attribute "bc83c253-8de7-4021-afd6-66dfb6f45c5d" ("price") that has as value "15000" and as unit "EUR". This attribute furthermore contains a reference to an attribute handler ("<ah></ah>" and "<ahid></ahid>"), which converts the price of the product to any arbitrary currency that might be specified within the query.

```
<PDL id="17b76499-16f3-43be-b600-66b928de4dc2"
xmlns="xsdPDL">
  <meta>
    <attribute>
      <id>bc83c253-8de7-4021-afd6-66dfb6f45c5d</id>
      <value>BMW X3</value>
    </attribute>
    <attribute>
      <id>7acd6013-a7c3-42e9-8a3f-1b4682b41c53</id>
      <value>15000</value>
      <unit>EUR</unit>
      <ah>
        <ahid>060df21e-678e-4848-b770-d0c987bae17b</ahid>
      </ah>
    </attribute>
  </meta>
  <attribute>
    <id>42bae485-d4af-4fed-b120-493b7c996717</id>
    <value>BMW</value>
  </attribute>
  <attribute>
    <id>c278931a-45e4-4c2e-bb68-f790af33023b</id>
    <value></value>
    <attribute>
      <id>8c3f7b26-a634-45fa-b09b-832c59c60608</id>
      <value>200</value>
      <unit>PS</unit>
    </attribute>
```

```
    </attribute>
    <attribute>
      <id>86cc2477-1130-4bee-85aa-dbbbf646c6db</id>
      <value>1000</value>
      <unit>kg</unit>
      <ah>
        <ahid>48ce3492-134b-4701-82a1-e5476922f126</ahid>
      </ah>
    </attribute>
  </PDL>
```

Listing 7: Sample of an uncompiled product description.

Listing 8 contains the metadata that corresponds to the above uncompiled product description and that is required for an attribute handler execution by the
compiler. The tag "<ahparamid>" indicates that this attribute handler has only
one parameter, the currency which the price is to be transformed into. The actual
value of this parameter (e.g., "USD", "JPY", "GBP", etc.) is inserted at query
time and submitted together with the query.

```
  <ahmeta id="17b76499-16f3-43be-b600-66b928de4dc2"
  xmlns="xsdAHMeta">
    <ah>
      <ahid>060df21e-678e-4848-b770-d0c987bae17b</ahid>
      <ahparams>
        <ahparam>
          <ahparamid>1</ahparamid>
        </ahparam>
      </ahparams>
    </ah>
    <ah>
      <ahid>48ce3492-134b-4701-82a1-e5476922f126</ahid>
      <ahparams>
        <ahparam>
          <ahparamid>1</ahparamid>
        </ahparam>
      </ahparams>
    </ah>
  </ahmeta>
```

Listing 8: Sample of an attribute handler metadata description.

6.5.1   Mapping Functors to Software

Functors in software allow for a technique that is called "memoization", and which is intensively used for the implementation of attribute handlers. The importance of memoization originates from it being a means for a unified way of writing well-performing code. To provide an illustrative example for functors in software, the Category of data structures and Algorithms (COA) can be considered (e.g., real numbers and any arbitrary function on them). The results of the functions on Ob(COA) depend on no hidden variables. They are non-memoized and might require a significant amount of time to execute. To speed-up performance, a memoized endofunctor $F: COA \rightarrow COA$, which takes objects to themselves and algorithms to their memoized versions, can be defined. The memoized algorithms use hidden variables to cache intermediate results and improve performance. The results, however, do not.

Non-memoized functors can be found in literally every modern programming language, either as functions or as function objects. In the C++ Standard Template Library (STL), for example, "a Function Object, or Functor (the two terms are used synonymously) is simply any object that can be called as if it was a function. An ordinary function is a function object, and so is a function pointer; more generally, so is an object of a class that defines operator()"[url14]. More specifically, the term "Function Object" was coined by James O. Coplien to describe objects that can be used like functions [Coplien 1992]. The basic concepts behind "Function Objects" are "Generator", "Unary Function", and "Binary Function" [url14]. "Generators" describe objects that can be called as f(). "Unary Functions" describe objects that can be called as f(x). "Binary Functions" describe objects that can be called as f(x,y). Functions with more than two parameters (e.g., ternary functions) are generalizations of the previously mentioned three functions.

Functors, or Functor Objects, are used to parameterize so called Higher-order functions, which take as parameters other functions, to then parameterize and call them. A very similar but yet different concept to Functor Objects are Function Pointers. In C++, for example, Function Pointers represent pointers (in address space) to functions that are defined "static" or "global". Function Pointers are dereferenced and called similarly to normal functions by adding "()" to their names and passing in the parameters the referenced function expects.

The Java programming language does not know the concept of function pointers. Nevertheless, Function Objects exist in Java as objects that implement a certain interface method surrogating "operator()", whereby the interface is used as a parameter type of the higher-order function.

In C#, the concept of Function Pointers is incorporated through delegates, which represent managed references to functions (comparable to managed pointers to functions). As C# programs are entirely managed by their runtime, the term function pointer does not apply any longer; that is, because delegates do not represent address space pointers to functions, but references to functions that are managed by the .Net runtime.

While both delegates and Function Pointers are very close concepts, the difference to Functional Objects is that the latter one is capable of preserving state ("memoization"). Other than Function Pointers, Functional Objects can track configurable references to input/output variables that might or might not be modified during execution through their higher-order function. Moreover, these input/output variables can be used to transition state during multiple calls with a non-constant effect on the calculation of the final result, every time the Functor is called. Function objects can also maintain their own member variables and read or write to them during execution. Changes to the value of member variables, however, are not persisted among multiple calls through the higher-order function. This is because the higher-order function, every time it is called, creates a new instance of the Functor Object, thereby initializing the member variables with the values they were assigned before the higher-order function call occurred. The capability to maintain its own context before and after invocation by streaming in and streaming out data is what distinguishes Function Objects from Function Pointers or Functions.

6.5.2   Memoized Functors

In the C++ Standard Template Library (STL), Functional Objects can be used to parameterize higher-order functions, such as std::sort (Listing 9). The template for std::sort contained in "algorithm" defines two versions [url$_{15}$]:

```
<algorithm>

template <class RandomAccessIterator>

void sort (RandomAccessIterator first, RandomAccessItera-
tor last );

template <class RandomAccessIterator, class Compare>

void sort (RandomAccessIterator first, RandomAccessItera-
tor last, Compare comp );
```

Listing 9: Functional objects in the C++ Standard Template Library.

The first version of sort performs a comparison based on "operator<". The second version accepts a Comparison Functor Object "comp" that defines the rules of the comparison. In C++, the "comp" parameter also accepts plain Function Pointers, and not only Functor Objects. Listing 10 demonstrates how std::sort is used for both a "Comparison Functor Object" and a "Comparison Function Pointer".

The above example showcases how „SortByPriceFunction" is passed in to std::sort as a Functional Object that defines the comparison "i < j". "SortBy-PriceFunctor", in addition to the comparison defines a member variable "piStep-Count" that points to an external buffer that keeps track of the number of required sorting steps. Though Functions can –similarly to member variables in Functional Objects– define local variables that point to a buffer in memory and use this buffer to stream in and stream out data during execution, this reference is hard-coded and cannot be configured from outside the Function. Passing in the address to the buffer as a parameter of the function would alter the signature of the Function as well as the Function Pointer and thus break the interface to the Higher-order function that expects the Function Pointer. That is why this approach does not create a Functor out of a "Function Pointer".

```
#include <iostream>
#include <algorithm>
#include <vector>
using namespace std;

bool SortByPriceFunction (int i, int j)
{
        return (i < j);
```

```
}

class SortByPriceFunctor
{
public:

        int* piStepCount;

        bool operator() (int i, int j)
        {
                ++*piStepCount;
                return (i < j);
        }
};

int main ()
{
        int numbers[] = {16, 5, 24, 26, 13, 90, 34, 22,
41};

        vector<int> vec (numbers, numbers + 8);

        // default comparison for first 4 numbers
        sort (vec.begin(), vec.begin() + 4);

        // sort function pointer for next 4 numbers
        sort (vec.begin() + 4, vec.end(), SortByPrice-
Function);

        // sort functor object that outputs required
sorting steps
        SortByPriceFunctor func = SortByPriceFunctor();
        int iStepCount = 0;
        func.piStepCount = &iStepCount;

        sort (vec.begin(), vec.end(), func);

        // print out sort steps:
        cout << "Required sorting steps: " << iStepCount;

        return 0;
}
```

Listing 10: Function vs. Function Object.

6.5.3   Memoization and Memory Utilization

In section 5.2.8, attribute handlers were modeled as functors that construct the category of handled attributes from the category of attributes. Furthermore, the previous section demonstrated how functors from category theory map to functors in software. Thereby, a special kind of functors, the Memoized Functors, were emphasized. Memoized Functors are of particular relevance to attribute handlers, if the execution of an attribute handler requires substantial processing. It was said earlier that memoization is used to speed up computer algorithms by storing or caching intermediate results. Since attribute handlers might very often also communicate with external systems (in order to fetch data that is relevant for their processing) a large amount of their processing time might be spent on comparably slow inter-system communication. The attribute handler "GetPrice-InCurrency", for example, which was first mentioned in section 5.2.8 needs to fetch the exchange rate between the currencies that are to be converted from an external system, in order to calculate the correct price. Listing 11 contains a naive implementation of "GetPriceInCurrency", which –every time it is called– fetches the current exchange rates from a web service provided through the European Central Bank (ECB), even though the ECB refreshes the exchanges rates only once a day.

Since attribute handlers might be invoked throughout the search process and for every individual product description that is involved in the search, they must, however, quickly execute and return their results. Regarding "GetPriceInCurrency", in most cases it might be sufficient, if the exchange rate is refreshed once a day. That is why for the sake of performance, "GetPriceInCurrency" must be capable of "caching" the exchange rates between the global currencies and refreshing them once per day. One solution to this problem could lie in the attribute handler repository instantiating all attribute handlers at the time it is booting up and refreshing the instances on a regular basis. This, however, would mean a significant zero-load utilization of memory of the web server, which the SPS is running on, as all attribute handlers would need to be loaded and kept in memory. Moreover, the web server's memory is a precious resource and needed for serving as many parallel client requests as possible.

```
public class AH_GetPriceInCurrency : AH_Interface
{
        public   override   AH_ReturnType   Execute(object   _value,
        string  _strBaseUnit,  string  _strLocale,  Dictionary<int,
        object> _params)
        {
        string strCurrency = (string) _params[1];
        double dValue = double.Parse((string)_value);

                GetPriceInCurrencyImpl converter = new GetPriceIn-
                Curren-
                cyImpl("http://www.ecb.europa.eu/stats/eurofxref/eu
                rofxref-daily.xml");

                double  dReturnValue  =  converter.ConvertCurrency
                (_strBaseUnit, dValue, strCurrency);
                if (double.IsInfinity(dReturnValue))
                        throw new Exception("Currency conversion \""
                        + _strBaseUnit + " => "+ strCurrency + "\"
                        is not supported.");

                return new AH_ReturnType() { returnValue = dReturn-
                Value, strTargetUnit = strCurrency, Volatile = true
                };
        }

        /*…*/
}
```

Listing 11: Naive implementation of GetPriceInCurrency.

An alternative solution aims at implementing "GetPriceInCurrency" as a Memoized Functor that "remembers" the exchange rates beyond instantiation and tear-down of the underlying Function Object. This way, the attribute handler repository instantiates an attribute handler object at the time the attribute handler is to be executed and it tears down the object immediately after the attribute handler execution has finished. Though memoization requires memory (the memorized data has to be stored somewhere), in many cases the difference between the size of the memorized data and the size of the entire object might be significant. In other cases, however, the amount of memorized data might be relatively high, compared to the size of the entire object. If so, memoization might still be useful, if the memorized data is written to a persistent storage (e.g., database, file system), so that the web server's memory is still kept free of permanent utilization through attribute handlers. Despite memory utilization, data that comes from time-intensive inter-system communication is now cacheable, which results in a speed-up of attribute handler execution. Listing 12 lists the memoized version of "GetPriceInCurrency" that promises a significant gain in performance as well as less utilization of web server memory.

```
public class AH_GetPriceInCurrency : AH_Interface
{
        public override EBF_AH_ReturnType Execute(object _value,
        string _strBaseUnit, string _strLocale, Dictionary<int,
        object> _params)
        {
        string strCurrency = (string) _params[1];
        double dValue = double.Parse((string)_value);

        GetPriceInCurrencyImpl converter = TryGetPriceInCurren-
cyFromCache();

                if(converter == null)
                        converter    =    new    GetPriceInCurren-
                        cyImpl("http://www.ecb.europa.eu/stats/eurof
                        xref/eurofxref-daily.xml");

                double        dReturnValue        =        convert-
                er.ConvertCurrency(_strBaseUnit, dValue, strCurren-
                cy);

                if (double.IsInfinity(dReturnValue))
                        throw new Exception("Currency conversion \""
                        + _strBaseUnit + " => "+ strCurrency + "\"
                        is not supported.");

                return new AH_ReturnType() { returnValue = dReturn-
                Value, strTargetUnit = strCurrency, Volatile =
                false };
        }

        /*…*/
}
```

Listing 12: Memoized version of GetPriceInCurrency.

It can be seen from the above Listing 12 that the memoized version of GetPrice-InCurrency sets the "volatile" flag of the AH_ReturnType instance to false. This property of the attribute handlers' return value is used to indicate whether or not the results of attribute handlers can be buffered by a caching system, in order to yield gains in system performance. Quality-related aspects of SPS's in general and performance in particular are covered throughout chapter the next chapter.

6.6 Query Matching

As it was mentioned earlier, the matching of a query with the product descriptions within the catalog is performed after all attribute handlers specified in the product descriptions were executed. The Core::Search component of the SPS performs this task (cp. [SPS04]). The matching is performed on attribute-level, which means that every attribute contained within the query is matched with every attribute of every product description within the catalog. During matching, the matcher needs to consider operators that might potentially be contained in the query. The general syntax of the matcher is very simple:

```
input: query, catalog


foreach pd in catalog
{
        Match_PD(pd, query)
}
```

Listing 13: Simple Matching algorithm.

The actual matching is done inside "Match_PD". It is subject to the particular implementation of "Match_PD" to decide how a query is matched with a product description. In general, matching should occur on attribute-level. One simple way of on-attribute-level matching aims at comparing every attribute in the query with every attribute in the product description:

```
input: pd, query


foreach a_query in query

{

        Foreach a_pd in pd

        {

                Match_attributes(a_pd, a_query)

        }

}
```

Listing 14: Attribute-based matching.

The above approach, however, does neither respect the hierarchies of the query nor the product description. While for many cases simple on-attribute-level matching might work just fine, there might be other cases when respecting the hierarchy might be of particular importance. An example for how simple on-attribute-level matching can lead to confusion is given below in Figure 56:

In Figure 56, both PD1 and PD2 describe neckties, yet with a subtle difference. While PD1 is described as a necktie with a blue, dotted pattern, PD2 is described as a blue necktie with dotted pattern. In case of simple on-attribute-level matching, the query q1 as sampled in Figure 56 is ambiguous, since the information about what is blue (the pattern or the necktie) got lost. Both PD1 and PD2 would be a match to the query. In case of hierarchical on-attribute-level matching, however, the result for q2 would be unambiguously PD1. The hierarchy in q2 is thereby depicted as nested curly brackets.

Listing 14 contained a "Match_attributes", which performs the operator-based matching of one query attribute with one product description attribute. The formal basics for "Match_attributes" and operator-based attribute matching were laid in section 5.2.5. The implementation of operator-based attribute matching occurs by implementing the operator morphisms in section 5.2.5 in software algorithms. For reasons of clarity and comprehensibility, the particular operator implementations are not going to be detailed any further.

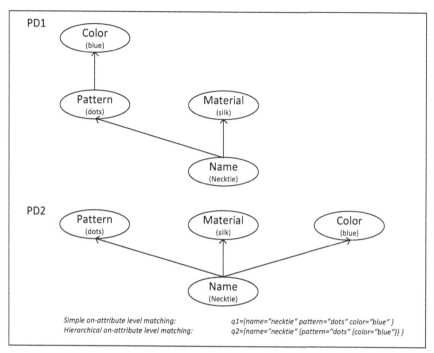

Figure 56: Example for the necessity of hierarchical on-attribute level matching.

6.7 SPS Deployment

Semantic Product Servers consist of a number of components that are grouped together by a namespace (cp. Figure 53 "reference architecture"). On their very basis, SPSs are hosted by a web server, which provides the platform and infrastructure to operate upon. SPSs can be hosted on premise and on a single web server as one-instance deployment (Figure 57).

Furthermore, SPSs can be hosted on premise and in a cluster. This aspect is independent of the SPS reference architecture, but requires certain specific features of the hosting platform. Generally, any arbitrary platform is capable of providing support for clustering Semantic Product Servers. Clustered deployments of SPSs were initially mentioned in section 4.1.1.2 as "Clouds of Things" (category CoT) and address high-load scenarios with many concurrent users. With respect to the

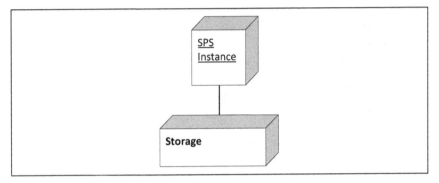

Figure 57: Single instance on-premise deployment of an SPS.

Internet of Products, where multiple SPSs integrate into a network to form a common product information system, clustered deployments of SPSs are an absolute necessity.

Hosting either a single SPS or a cluster of SPSs on premise requires the installation and maintenance of computing hardware. Since this kind of deployment has always been very capital-intensive, throughout recent years another business model, where computing power is offered as a centralized resource, has started gaining wide acceptance. Cloud Computing describes an approach to offering computing resources as a service (cp. section 4.3.4). According to [Cloud01] – [Cloud15] (section 4.3.4), this commoditization of computing resources facilitates the deployment of additional computing instances in times when the number of users is high as well as the reduction of instance count in times when less computing power is needed. The main argument for a real-time adaptation to different load levels lies in avoiding over provisioning and hence in saving cost (cp. [CloudEco01] – [CloudEco03] in section 4.3.4).

Cloud-based Semantic Product Servers were first mentioned in [Neumann 2010b] and [Neumann 2010c], and represent the implementation of "Clouds of Products" (cp. CoP category in 4.1.1.4). The following Figure 58 demonstrates the conceptual architecture of an SPS Cloud deployment, as it was established as the ArbiterOne reference implementation of an SPS. It features a pool of SPS instances whose number might –in correspondence with the actual load– scale up or down. A load balancer implements an algorithm to distribute load among the

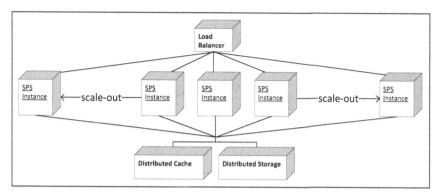

Figure 58: Cloud deployment of an SPS.

SPS instances. The load balancer also reacts to fault scenarios by failing over to new instances. The instances fetch/store data from/to a distributed Cloud storage system. In case of ArbiterOne, the SPS instances operate upon a non-relational Cloud storage system, which is especially beneficial, when many concurrent transactions are run. ArbiterOne could as well have been based upon a relational Cloud storage system, which might, however, perform weaker in high-load scenarios. In order to enhance response time, a distributed Cloud caching system is used to buffer frequently reoccurring queries. ArbiterOne was developed for and hosted on the Microsoft Windows Azure Cloud platform.

The architecture for an on-premise SPS cluster would conceptually be identical to Figure 58. The only difference would lie in the number of potential instances being limited to the available hardware. Contrarily, Cloud Computing promises, at least hypothetically, unlimited computing resources.

6.8 Chapter Summary

At its very basis, the Internet of Products relies upon a Semantic Product Server that implements the S-PDL and provides interfaces to clients for product search and retrieval. The SPS reference architecture that was introduced throughout this chapter is completely independent of any particular technology. The "ArbiterOne" reference implementation, however, which is covered throughout the next chapter, is based upon the service paradigm, since it provides the most obvious benefits for this particular problem.

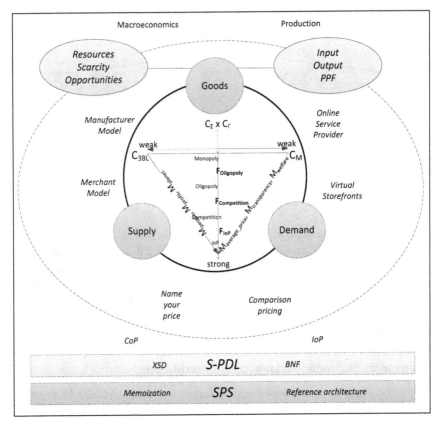

Figure 59: SPS in the Internet of Products.

The SPS reference architecture details the components necessary for providing semantic product search capabilities. Two particularly important components are the Attribute Handler Repository (AHRepository::AHRepository) and the S-PDL Compiler (Core::Compiler). Both together equip semantic product descriptions with the capability of dynamically altering their attribute values, depending on the time, the language, and the culture of the client. It was shown how the abstract concept of functors, which dominated the design of the S-PDL in chapter 5, easily translates into functors in code (so called "Functional Objects"). One particular kind of Functional Objects are the memoized functors, which are used within the SPS reference implementation for performance improvements.

Semantic Product Servers can be hosted on-premise or in the Cloud. While on-premise installations might be useful in scenarios with moderate traffic requirements or for private organizations, Cloud deployments are easier to maintain and allow for a dynamic adaptation of computing power to system load. Figure 59 adds the SPS to the running overview graphic.

The following chapter describes the insights that were gained from prototypes and projects, which are based upon the Semantic Product Server technology. In particular, empirical data that was gathered from test deployments and performance measurements is analyzed and evaluated. Based upon the findings, certain architectural decisions that were made throughout this chapter can be better comprehended.

7 Validation and Applications

"If you cannot measure it you cannot control it."(H. James Harrington)

This chapter provides an overview of the four prototypical systems that either implement the SPS reference architecture or were built on top of the SPS reference architecture. All four systems, namely ArbiterOne, eVoces, EscapeMisery, and SpotCrowd have a very different application domain, which provides strong evidence for the SPS and the S-PDL being truly applicable across a vast variety of domains. The second part of this chapter provides insights into system quality-related aspects. Thereby, the focus is put upon the assurance of real-time performance of semantic search query processing. Based on the formal measurement process definition in section 4.4, the results of two measurements projects, which were carried out on the ArbiterOne system, are presented and interpreted.

7.1 SPS Prototypes and Applications

Four prototypes, namely ArbiterOne, eVoces, EscapeMisery, and SpotCrowd were developed, based on the SPS technology. This section gives an overview of the domain and field of application of the prototypical systems as well as how the SPS supported their development.

7.1.1   ArbiterOne

Based on the reference architecture as introduced in section 6.4, a reference implementation of a Semantic Product Server, namely ArbiterOne, was developed. In addition to the components contained within the reference architecture, ArbiterOne features a web-based user interface for product authors to maintain product descriptions and for clients to search and retrieve product information. ArbiterOne was developed based on the Microsoft Windows Communication Foundation (WCF) and the Microsoft .Net Stack (version 4.0). Earlier versions of ArbiterOne, as mentioned in [Neumann 2010b] and [Neumann 2010c] were named "Goliath". ArbiterOne exposes a WebService API that can be consumed by client applications to implement their own frontend.

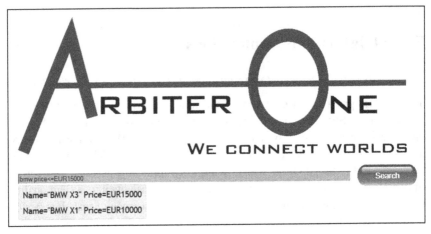

Figure 60: Attribute-based search query in ArbiterOne.

ArbiterOne provides full support for semantic search queries that span across multiple languages and cultures (cp. section 5.2.6 & 5.2.7). As of today, the ArbiterOne system provides cross-language support for 38 languages. Figure 60 shows how in ArbiterOne products can be searched, based on their attributes. The two products that are found by the system in Figure 60 were authored in German language and with "EUR" as the currency unit. The query language, however, is English.

Figure 61: Automatic currency translation in ArbiterOne.

Figure 61 demonstrates how the same product is being discovered, but with a different currency (USD). The product descriptions for the two discovered products, however, exist only once. The transformation into the currency of the search query is performed at query time through attribute handlers (cp. section 5.2.8). ArbiterOne was deployed as a 4-node cluster to Microsoft's Windows Azure Cloud platform. The 4-node ArbiterOne cluster is supported by another 4-node Membase cluster, a distributed caching system whose purpose is detailed later on in this section.

The storage backend of ArbiterOne consists of non-relational, tabular storage. Reasons for this design decision were elaborated upon in [Neumann 2012a]. Generally, tabular storage –especially in scenarios with many concurrent transactions that are run against the storage system– ensure high throughput of data by scaling out their load to an increasing number of storage nodes. Tabular storage on the Windows Azure Cloud Platform is called "Table Storage". The relational alternative to Table Storage is called "SQL Azure", a SQL server in the Cloud. In [Neumann 2011d], two methods of persisting S-PDL documents in a relational database were analyzed:

■ Using the XML data type of SQL Server and accessing the document via XPath, or

■ Breaking down the hierarchy of the XML contained in the S-PDL document to store every node together with its parent node [Neumann 2011d].

The measurements in [Neumann 2011d] showed that option (1) clearly dominated option (2) from a performance standpoint. In the ArbiterOne storage backend, S-PDL documents, similarly to the method employed in [Neumann 2011d], are stored as single properties of Table Storage entities. For a detailed overview of available storage types on the Windows Azure Cloud Platform, it is referred to [Neumann 2012a].

Though the non-relational property of Table Storage allows for many parallel transactions, other implications of the non-relational paradigm, such as non-relational secondary indices, complicate system development. Section 7.2.2 of this chapter contains measurement data that was collected from measurements of the Windows Azure Table Storage system. It was observed that there exist certain peaks in response times, when querying Table Storage for certain entities. To address this problem and flatten out the before mentioned peaks as well as to generally improve the performance of the ArbiterOne storage subsystem, Section

7.2.2 proposes a Hybrid Storage Framework (HCSF) that tries to keep frequently queried entities in a fast distributed cache, as compared to fetching them from Table Storage, every time the entity is requested. The core principles of the HCSF as well as a benchmark of the framework, which compares it with Table Storage, are covered later in section 7.2.2.

7.1.2   eVoces

A second prototype called eVoces was developed in 2010 and uses the ArbiterOne backend for product data storage and retrieval. eVoces is an online language learning platform, where individuals who offer courses can earn credit. Individuals can redeem their earned credit for other courses offered on eVoces by other individuals. Figure 62 samples a screenshot of the current iteration of the eVoces platform. The search experience as shown in Figure 62 is identical to the ArbiterOne search experience.

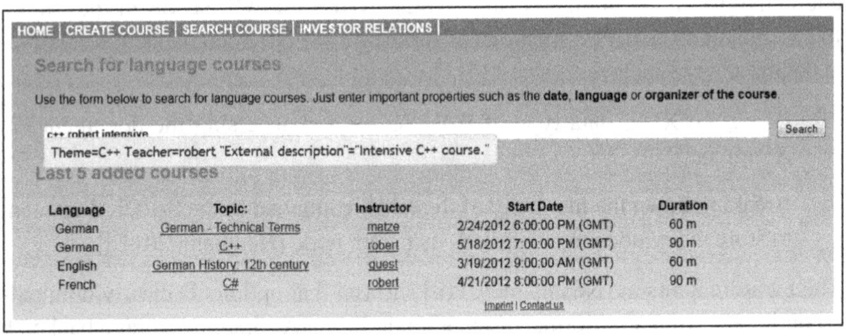

Figure 62: The eVoces platform with ArbiterOne search capabilities.

Courses on eVoces are maintained as semantic product descriptions and authored in the S-PDL. The eVoces frontend integrates the ArbiteOne services for product data maintenance and retrieval. Every search or browse transaction on eVoces that was triggered by a user is routed through the ArbiterOne service backend. Hence, ArbiterOne and with this the Semantic Product Server Concept serve as technological backbone for eVoces. The eVoces platform adds a voice server where online learning lessons can be conducted. In 2012, the eVoces platform developed into an "Open Network University" project, a joint venture between the University of Magdeburg (Germany) and the University of Wisconsin in Stevens Point (USA) that aims to provide an integrated online study platform, where professors can give live online lessons to students. The project is still under development.

7.1.3   EscapeMisery

When in March 2011 the tsunami hit the east coast of the Japanese main island Honshu and destroyed the nuclear power plant Fukushima I, thousands of Japanese who lost their homes due to the catastrophe were accommodated in temporary shelters. The online platform escapemisery.com was developed within only a few days to allow for an act of solidarity, where Japanese people who were not affected by the tsunami could offer a temporary shelter to their fellow-countrymen who lost their homes.

Technologically, EscapeMisery used a customized ArbiterOne frontend that routed search requests through to the ArbiterOne backend services. Those users on EscapeMisery who wanted to offer accommodation could enter their data via a web form. The data in the web form was then compiled into an S-PDL document and sent to the ArbiterOne backend services. EscapeMisery thereby enormously benefitted from the cross-language capabilities of ArbiterOne's Semantic Product Server.

Though there were some offers on EscapeMisery, even from Europe and from the United States, due to a lack in public awareness the success of EscapeMisery was rather moderate. Nevertheless, EscapeMisery has proven that based on ArbiterOne's SPS technology, building and setting up new electronic markets has become a matter of just a few days.

7.1.4   SpotCrowd

The fourth and last project that was developed based on ArbiterOne and the SPS aimed at providing a spot market for crowd-sourced computing resources. Cloud spot markets thereby represent markets where computing resources are traded for immediate delivery [Muhss 2011]. Amazon was one of the pioneers of Cloud spot markets, offering spare computing resources in an auction-based system. The SpotCrowd projects generalized Amazon's approach and not only allowed private organizations but also individuals to offer their spare computing resources to the public. Prices could be set by the sellers themselves. Service level agreements were standardized and had to be chosen by sellers from a list that was provided through the platform.

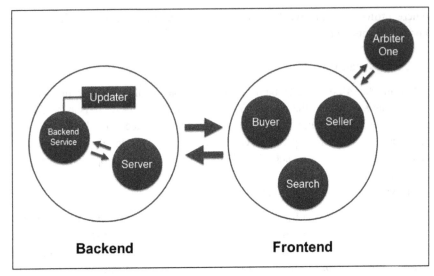

Figure 63: SpotCrowd architecture.

Technologically, SpotCrowd was distinguished into a frontend and a backend (see Figure 63). The frontend provided the market where sellers were able to create offers and buyers were able to search for offers. The SpotCrowd frontend was completely based upon ArbiterOne's SPS services. The backend consisted of a modified Debian image, namely "SpotCrowd Server", which could be downloaded by sellers and booted up on their hardware. The image would then automatically register with the SpotCrowd frontend and wait for new jobs. Jobs would be assigned, when buyers rented a given resource from a seller. In this case, the seller was asked to provide a Virtual Machine image to the SpotCrowd frontend. The frontend would then upload the Virtual Machine image to the seller's SpotCrowd Server. After the upload completed, the SpotCrowd Server would load the image into its VMWare-based hypervisor and boot it up. From thereon, buyers could start interacting with their SpotCrowd Virtual Machine. Technologically, the SpotCrowd Virtual machine did not underlie any constraints and could be used for whatever purpose.

7.2 System Performance and Caching

This section summarizes certain quality-related topics of Semantic Product Servers. In particular, performance-related aspects are examined. The performance improvement strategies that are developed throughout the following two sections are based on empirical data, which was gathered from multiple measurement beds in [Neumann 2011a], [Neumann 2010c], and [Neumann 2011d].

Section 4.4.1 defined the business software measurement process as:

$$BMP: (G \times A \times M)_{T,P} \rightarrow (V)_{T,P} \rightarrow (E' \times A')_{T,P} \qquad (7.2.1)$$

with G being the measurement goals, A being the measurement artifacts, M being the measurement methods, V being the measurement values, E' being the extended experiences, and A' being the extended artifacts. T and P represent the measurement tools and the personnel, respectively (cp. section 4.4).

With respect to the performance measurement and improvement of ArbiterOne and the SPS, the components of the measurement process can be characterized in a simplified way as:

- G: performance profiling/enhancement,

- A: "ArbiterOne",

- M: improvement,

- V: performance values,

- E': extended academic,

- A': improved "ArbiterOne",

- T: Visual Studio 2010, and

- P: researchers.

The goal of the measurement is to profile the "ArbiterOne" system for performance bottlenecks and fix them. The collected quantities are mainly aggregations of single measurement values. The experience is mainly based upon academic experience. Results that are generated by the measurement process are performance values. Extended experiences that were made during the measurement complement the initial experience. The extended artifact is an enhanced "ArbiterOne" system (at least from a performance point of view). Among the employed tools is Visual Studio 2010. The personnel that conducted the measurement consisted of researchers.

Analogous to 4.4.7, emphasizing the individual components through an instantiation of BMP leads to:

$$quality Assurance \atop scheduled} BMP^{aspect-oriented}_{research} :$$

$$\left({externalGoal \atop market} G^{improvement}_{evaluation} \times {ArbiterOne \atop integrated} A^{original}_{referred} \times \right.$$

$$\left. {inhouse \atop improvement} M^{webService}_{measurement} \right) automated_T {integrated \atop internal^I} researcher_P^{experienced}_{self-motivated} \rightarrow$$

$$\left({ratioScale \atop visualization} V^{executionTime}_{ITProject} \right) automated_T {integrated \atop internal^I} researcher_P^{experienced}_{self-motivated} \rightarrow$$

$$\left({formula \atop threshold} E'^{practice}_{extension} \times \right.$$

$$\left. {ArbiterOne \atop integrated} A'^{original}_{improved} \right) automated_T {integrated \atop internal^I} researcher_P^{experienced}_{self-motivated} \qquad (7.2.2)$$

The attributes of every single component in 7.2.2 briefly characterize the complexity of the software measurement process and its many aspects, as it is conducted throughout sections 7.2.1 and 7.2.2.

The following two sections detail the results of two independently run performance measurement processes.

7.2.1   Optimal Query Caching

All four prototypes mentioned above provide evidence for the hypothesis stated in chapter 5 that query processing in Semantic Product Servers might consume significantly more computing resources as compared to standard text-based search engines. The reason for that lies in semantic search queries being interpreted at runtime by the SPS, in order to resolve languages, cultures, as well as references to attribute handlers (see sections 5.2.5, 5.2.6, 5.2.7, and 5.2.8).

To enhance the system responsiveness, intermediate as well as previous search results can be buffered in a cache, so that reoccurring queries or reoccurring parts of queries can be looked up directly from the cache. At the same time, this approach takes load from service instances and database nodes, which without cache would have to recalculate the same queries over and over again. A detailed discussion of the measurement results and the possibilities for enhancing the response time of Cloud-based Semantic Product Servers through a distributed cache can be found in [Neumann 2011a]. The following paragraphs contain a summary of the findings in [Neumann 2011a].

7.2.1.1   Measurement Bed Description

The possibilities, which a cache opens up regarding the enhancement of system responsiveness, were analyzed through measurements that were conducted on the research system "ArbiterOne". Without cache, the system's response time for a semantic search query lied at around 460ms in average (Figure 64). This includes the transportation of the search data to the Azure-based ArbiterOne Cloud instance, the calculation of the results, and the transportation of the response back to the client. According to the measurement results, the major portion of response time is spent on calculating the query result.

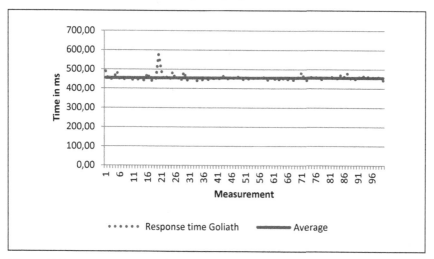

Figure 64: Response time without cache.

Due to reasons of simplicity, for the measurement in Figure 64 semantic search queries with an identical number of attributes were employed. In case of a measurement bed with a varying number of attributes in the semantic search queries, the measurement results in Figure 64 would substantially differ. In general, the relation between the execution time and the number of attributes in a semantic search query can be characterized as linear, with a constant growth in processing time per additional attribute.

By adding a distributed cache to the ArbierOne Cloud deployment, the time necessary to process a semantic search query could be reduced to merely a few

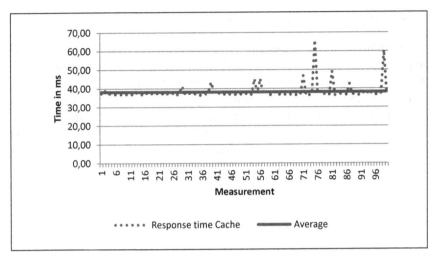

Figure 65: Response time with caching.

milliseconds. The employed caching infrastructure consisted of a distributed 4-node Membase cluster, which was ported to a Windows Azure Worker Role. Both the ArbiterOne service and the Membase cache cluster were hosted within the same collocation center in Dublin/Ireland. With Membase, the average response time of the ArbiterOne research system dropped to 38ms (Figure 65).

The second measurement results in Figure 65 imply an overall improvement in performance by factor 12. This performance gain results from the cache being able to directly serve the search queries without performing expensive calculations in the service and data backend of the "ArbiterOne" system. Instead, the distributed cache tries to lookup the current search query in its list of previously processed search queries and –if an entry exists– directly returns the cached result to the client.

In case of a partial match of cached search queries with the current search query, for those attributes of the current search query that do not have a corresponding entry in the distributed cache a partial search needs to be performed. The partial search only searches the catalog for those attributes that do not yet have an entry in the distributed cache. The result of the partial search is finally merged with the attributes stored within the cache and returned to the client.

7.2.1.2 Cache Economies

The ArbiterOne research system has shown that by employing a distributed cache, Cloud applications can significantly improve their performance in terms of responsiveness. With respect to the ArbiterOne system, the average response time could be lowered by factor 12, given a hit rate of 1. In reality, however, hit rates of 1 are hard to achieve as certain search queries might appear much more frequently than others. In this case, caching so called long-tail search attributes might not be economical as they are simply not entered frequently enough by the users. In order to better align the cache size with the hit rate, it is necessary to understand the frequency of the queries and their attributes, which are sent to the system.

To better visualize the relationship between hit rate and cache size, Table 16 samples the data that was included in the measurement bed. It can be seen that there exist a few search strings that come up for a relatively large portion of the hit rate. Doubling the number of cached attributes from 10,000 to 20,000 increases the hit rate from 37% to 63%. Adding another 10,000 search strings from 20,000 to 30,000, however, only yields an increase in hit rate by 14%. Adding once again 10,000 search strings to the cache increases the hit rate by merely 7%. While in Table 16 the number of search strings grows constantly, the hit rate grows under-proportionally until it reaches 100%.

Table 16: Search strings and hit rate.

Number of cached attributes	Hit rate in %
10,000	37
20,000	63
30,000	77
40,000	84
50,000	89
60,000	93
70,000	96
80,000	98
90,000	99
100,000	99,6
110,000	100

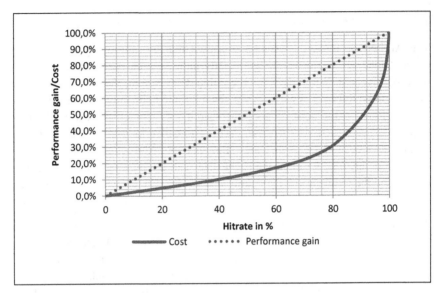

Figure 66: Performance gains vs. cost.

Figure 66 projects the cost curve onto the performance gain curve of a cache, using the data from the above table. It is clearly observable that an increase in hit rate for smaller values is relatively more cost-effective than for larger values. The marginal cost for every gained percent of hit rate, however, is getting higher and higher. To reach a hit rate of 37%, it is sufficient to store the 10,000 most frequent queries in cache. Doubling the cache size from 10,000 attributes to 20,000 attributes yields only a hit rate of 63% and not of 74%.

Though the size of the cache has doubled and with it the cost, the gain in hit rate developed under-proportionally. Moreover, the higher the hit rate, the more cost-intensive the gains will become. That is because the marginal gain in hit rate develops regressively. Doubling the cache size again from 20,000 attributes 40,000 attributes increases the cache-related cost by 100%, but only increases the hit rate by 21% (from 63% to 84%). The regressive marginal gain in hit rate raises the question for an optimal cache size that balances the hit rate with cache-related cost. The following section introduces an approach that aims to identify the optimal cache size, based on the distribution of the search attribute frequency and the cost per cache size.

7.2.1.3 Optimal Cache Size

Figure 67 depicts three search attribute distributions in a diagram, which were extracted from the measurements. It is observable that in case of the search attribute distribution being relatively scattered, the cache-related cost increases faster than it would be the case with a relatively cohesive search attribute distribution. If a few search attributes show a relatively high frequency, the slope of the cost curve increases comparably slowly. In order to be able to provide a quantitative statement about the optimal hit rate, it is necessary to take a closer look at the graph of the cost curve depicted in Figure 67.

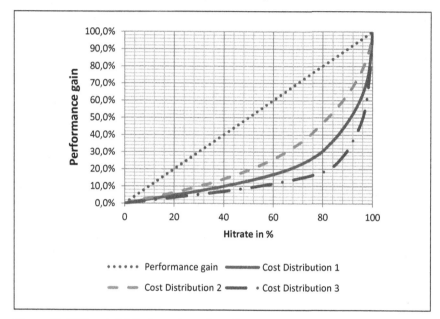

Figure 67: Different distributions of search attributes.

From a TCO (Total Cost of Ownership) perspective, it is desirable to increase the size of the cache, as long as the gain in hit rate and with this the gain in performance is higher than the cost of the gain. That is because the performance increases over-proportionally to the cost. There exists, however, a hit rate from where on every additional marginal hit rate gain will become more and more expensive. The break-even is characterized by the point where the slope of the performance curve equals the slope of the cost curve. All points to the left of the break-even stand for a hit rate or performance gain bigger than one per every additionally spent monetary unit. All points to the right of the break-even represent a hit rate gain smaller than one per every additionally spent monetary unit.

$$m' = \frac{dCost}{dHitRate} = \tan\gamma \qquad (7.2.1.3.1)$$

As mentioned earlier, the performance gain is directly proportional (in fact it is identical) to the hit rate, which results in the slope of the performance curve always being 1. In the above diagram, this means that 50% of the overall performance gain can be achieved at a hit rate of 50%. The same holds true for all other performance gain values. This reduces the problem of finding the optimal hit rate in terms of cost-effectiveness to determining the point on the cost curve, where the slope equals 1 (45°). In Figure 66, the optimal hit rate lies at around 80%.

$$m' = \frac{dCost}{dHitRate} = 1 \qquad (7.2.1.3.2)$$

With the above formula, it is possible to determine the most cost-effective cache size, measured by the gain in hit rate per monetary unit.

7.2.2   Hybrid Cloud Storage Framework

When caching search queries, another problem arises from keeping the cache and the storage backend synchronized. Some aspects of cache synchronization were covered in [Neumann 2011a]. This section introduces a Hybrid Cloud Storage Framework (HCSF) [Neumann 2012b] that was developed to mitigate the problem of cache/storage synchronization while providing performance gains of about 3x for Semantic Product Servers, but also for other Cloud applications.

In addition to the non-relational, tabular storage system that was used as a storage backend for ArbiterOne, the Azure Services platform offers a distributed caching system. Though Table Storage provides for data integrity, consistency, and endurance, it is comparably slow. The distributed cache, on the other hand, provides for significantly faster data access, but data stored within the cache is highly volatile.

The so called HCSF provides for faster read access than Table Storage, but –due to the additional synchronization logic– performs slower than Azure's distributed cache. At the same time, the HCSF ensures data consistency and endurance by mirroring the data stored within the cache to Table Storage.

7.2.2.1 Solution Modeling

The HCSF is optimized for read access. For Cloud applications, where the number of write operations significantly outweighs the number of read operations, the HCSF might have a negative impact on the overall system responsiveness. Since ArbiterOne, however, shows significantly more read operations than write operations, it was possible to enhance its overall system performance by more than 3x.

The HCSF provides service methods to clients for reading, writing, and deleting entities. The write and delete operations, however, are of minor relevance, since it is the declared goal of the HCSF to enhance read performance. Upon a read, denoted as RHCSF, the HCSF will try to first fetch the entity from the distributed cache. There exist, however, three possibilities (RHCSF1, RHCSF2, and RHCSF3), which the HCSF might choose, in order to generate the query result, with a minimum of one and a maximum of three steps (Table 17).

Table 17: HCSF read options.

Step	RHCSF1	RHCSF2	RHCSF3
1	ReadFromCache	ReadFromCache	ReadFromCache
2	-	ReadFromStorage	ReadFromStorage
3	-	WriteToCache	-

For the performance gain modeling of the HCSF, the following acronyms are introduced:

- RFC: ReadFromCache,

- WTC: WriteToCache,

- DFC: DeleteFromCache, and

- RFS: ReadFromStorage.

If, as in RHCSF1, the entity can immediately be located in the cache, it is returned to the caller and the process ends. In this case, $t(RHCSF) < t(RFS)$, as long as $t(RFC) < t(RFS)$.

In case of RHCSF2, the lookup of the entity from Table Storage compromises the potential performance gain of RHCSF. In RHCSF2, the entity cannot immediately be located in the cache and the HCSF therefore attempts to locate the entity in Table Storage (RFS). If the entity was found in Table Storage, it needs to be written to the cache (WTC), so that it can be served out of cache the next time it is requested via the HCSF. RHCSF2 performs significantly slower than RHCSF1 and RFS, since t(RFC) + t(RFS) + t(WTC) > t(RFS). However, the next time the same entity is requested via the HCSF, it can be served out of cache through RHCSF1.

In RHCSF3, the entity can again not immediately be located in the cache and the HCSF therefore again attempts to locate the entity in Table Storage (RFS). However, the entity can also not be found in Table Storage and RHCSF returns without result. RHCSF3, similarly to RHCSF2, performs slower than RFS, since t(RFC) + t(RFS) > t(RFS).

Whether or not the HCSF can provide positive performance gains depends on the probability distribution of RHCSF1, RCHSF2, and RHCSF3 (cp. section 7.2.1). Generally, if entities are requested more often than once within a certain timeframe, RHCSF1 will have a higher probability than RHCSF2. One fundamental condition for the above statement, however, is that RFS needs to succeed. If RFS does not succeed, since the entity is not stored in Table Storage, reoccurring calls to RHCSF will result in reoccurring calls to RHCSF3, thereby compromising the performance of HCSF.

The probability distribution of RHCSF1, RHCSF2, and RHCSF3 fundamentally depends on the cache hit rate. The more likely the cache is to store a requested entity, the better the performance of RHCSF will be. The following theoretical framework provides an ex-ante estimation of the "HCSF Performance Factor" (HPF_{THE}), a metric for the factor at which RHCSF performs faster than RFS.

For simplicity, it is assumed that RFC and WTC require the same execution time.

$$t(RFC) = t(WTC) \tag{7.2.2.1.1}$$

Furthermore, it is assumed that in general RFC performs α times faster than RFS. The variable α thereby represents the theoretical read cache performance factor.

$$t(RFS) = \alpha t(RFC) \tag{7.2.2.1.2}$$

Since for the theoretical model, real values are not important, both t(RFS) and t(WTC) are set to a constant $\bar{c}$. The unit of $\bar{c}$ is thereby named [tu], which stands for time unit.

$$t(RFS) = t(WTC) = \bar{c} \qquad\qquad (7.2.2.1.3)$$

Based on Table 17 and formulas (7.2.2.1.2) and (7.2.2.1.3), the execution time of RHCSF1, RHCSF2, and RHCSF3 can be determined. Table 18 samples values for t(RHCSF1), t(RHCSF2), and t(RHCSF3), based on four different values for α.

Table 18: Expected operation execution times.

Operation (o)	Steps	t(o), $\alpha = 2$	t(o), $\alpha = 4$	t(o), $\alpha = 6$	t(o), $\alpha = 8$
RHCSF1	$t(RFC)$	1	1	1	1
RHCSF2	$t(RFC)$ $+ t(RFS)$ $+ t(WTC)$	4	6	8	10
RHCSF3	$t(RFC)$ $+ t(RFS)$	3	5	7	9

For the purpose of illustrating the potential performance gains of RHCSF, it is assumed a theoretical 100,000 read requests on HCSF (count(RHCSF) = 100,000), whereby 80,000 requests are answered via RHCSF1 (count(RHCSF1) = 80,000), 10,000 requests are answered via RHCSF2 (count(RHCSF2) = 10,000), and another 10,000 requests are answered via RHCSF3 (count(RHCSF3) = 10,000). The implied cache hit rate would thus be 80% (ignoring negative caching). Let lastly the read cache performance factor be 4 ($\alpha = 4$). This data results in the following table:

Table 19: Sample case with a hit rate of 80% and $\alpha = 4$.

Operation (o)	$t(o)$ in [tu]	Count	Product	Total in [tu]
RHCSF1	1	80,000	80,000	
RHCSF2	6	10,000	60,000	190,000
RHCSF3	5	10,000	50,000	
RFS	4	100,000	400,000	400,000

The above table shows that –with a hit rate of 0.8– RHCSF would consume 190,000[tu], as compared to 400,000[tu] for RFS. This implies that RHCSF performs more than twice as fast as RFS ($HPF_{THE} \sim 0.5$). Base on the above example, it seems possible to determine HPF$_{THE}$ ex-ante with only a given value for α. The resulting formula is shown in (4):

$$HPF_{THE} = \frac{\begin{array}{c} count(RHCSF1)*t(RFC)+ \\ count(RHCSF2)*(t(RFC)+t(RFS)+t(WTC))+ \\ count(RHCSF3)*(t(RFC)+t(RFS)) \end{array}}{\begin{array}{c} (count(RHCSF1)+count(RHCSF2)+count(RHCSF3)) \\ *t(RFS) \end{array}} \qquad (7.2.2.1.4)$$

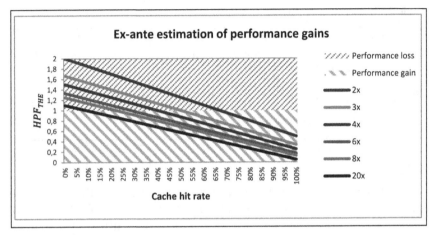

Figure 68: Estimation of performance gains.

The diagram in Figure 68 depicts HPF$_{THE}$ (on the vertical axis) for α values of 2, 3, 4, 5, and 20, based on a given cache hit rate (horizontal axis). Thereby, an HPF$_{THE}$ value of 1 functions as break-even, from where on the performance gain of HCSF turns into a performance loss. The diagram can be used to quickly estimate the minimum cache hit rate that is required to yield a performance improvement, when HCSF is used.

7.2.2.2   HCSF Benchmark

The benchmark of the HCSF was performed based upon the measurement bed in Table 20.

Table 20 contains three different measurement configurations with different entity sizes. The "Entity count" parameter indicates how many entities are que-

Table 20: Measurement configurations.

Conf	CID	byte[] count	Array size	Sum of bytes	Object size in bytes	Entity count	Session count	Measure-ment value count
1	A	3	125	375	869	33	10	330
	B	6	125	750	1,417			
	C	9	125	1,125	1,964			
3	A	3	2,000	6,000	6,494	33	10	330
	B	6	2,000	12,000	12,667			
	C	9	2,000	18,000	18,839			
4	A	3	8,000	24,000	24,494	34	10	340
	B	6	8,000	48,000	48,667			
	C	9	8,000	72,000	72,839			

ried per run. The total number of entities sum up to 100. Figures 69–71 and Tables 21–23 contain the results of the performance measurements for configuration 1, configuration 3, and configuration 4.

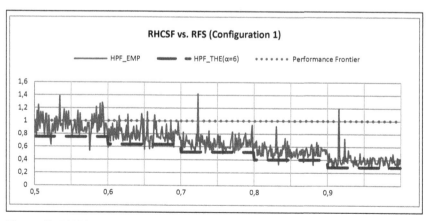

Figure 69: RHCSF vs. RFS (Configuration 1).

Table 21: HCSF Benchmark (Configuration 1).

Configuration 1					
Cache hit rate (%)	50	60	70	80	90
Sum RFS (ms)	117,894	117,896	119,986	113,542	120,415
Sum HPF_{EMP}(ms)	109,462	92,028	77,988	59,254	46,781
Savings	8,432	25,868	41,998	54,288	73,634
HPF (%)	92.85	78.06	65.00	52.19	38.85

Other configurations also existed but due to limitations in space, configurations 2 and 5 were excluded from this summary. The dashed line represents the development of the theoretically determined HCSF Performance Factor (HPF$_{THE}$). Since HPF$_{THE}$ depends on the cache hit rate and α, and both remain constant for a configuration, the HPF$_{THE}$ also remains constant for one configuration. The spiky curve represents the empirical values for the HCSF Performance Factor (HPF$_{EMP}$), which were gained from the benchmark. The dotted horizontal line represents the Performance Frontier (PF). All values on the spiky curve that lie above PF indicate that in this case RFS performs faster than RHCSF. Table 21 - Table 23 contain the data that underlies Figure 69 - Figure 71.

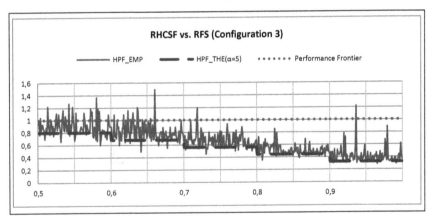

Figure 70: RHCSF vs. RFS (Configuration 3).

Table 22: HCSF Benchmark (Configuration 3).

Configuration 3					
Cache hit rate (%)	50	60	70	80	90
Sum RFS (ms)	124,790	119,063	115,931	120,726	119,007
Sum HPF_{EMP}(ms)	109,503	94,378	75,753	60,624	47,907
Savings	15,206	24,685	40,178	60,102	71,100
HPF (%)	87.81	79.27	65.34	50.22	40.26

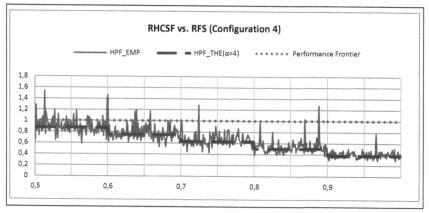

Figure 71: RHCSF vs. RFS (Configuration 4).

Table 23: HCSF Benchmark (Configuration 4).

Configuration 4					
Cache hit rate (%)	50	60	70	80	90
Sum RFS (ms)	119,329	125,059	120,600	118,114	115,309
Sum HPF_{EMP}(ms)	105,311	945,833	78,337	61,823	44,948
Savings	14,018	29,226	42,263	56,291	70,361
HPF (%)	88.25	76.63	64.96	52.34	38.98

What can furthermore be observed from Figure 69 is that almost all values of the spiky curve lie above HPF$_{THE}$. The interpretation of this would be that for configuration 1 the theoretical estimate for HPF$_{THE}$ was too optimistic. Nevertheless, it is clearly observable that HPF$_{EMP}$ (spiky curve) follows HPF$_{THE}$ (dashed curve) in its trend. HPF$_{THE}$, however, appears to be shifted upwards. This shift upwards suggests that there must be a scaling factor that was not included in the theoretical model in section 7.2.2.1.

Another interesting observation that can be made from all three examined configurations is that the amplitude of HPF_{EMP} decreases with an increasing hit rate. The more requests against the HCSF can be served directly out of the cache, the more stable the performance gain will be. The measurement data suggests that the before mentioned phenomenon is due to the relatively high standard deviation of read operations that are performed on Table Storage. Since for lower hit rates the HCSF needs to access Table Storage more frequently, the RFS operation promotes its high standard deviation as well to the HCSF. Based on the observations that were made in Figure 69 - Figure 71, it is concluded that RCPF is not the only parameter of the HCSF Performance Factor. In fact, the cache hit rate weighs even stronger.

7.3 Chapter Summary

This chapter introduced ArbiterOne as an implementation of the SPS reference architecture, as well as the three applications eVoces, EscapeMisery, and SpotCrowd as clients of ArbiterOne, with three very different problem domains. Based on these three systems, certain performance-related aspects of Semantic Product Servers were analyzed and ways of mitigating compute-intensive semantic search query processing were proposed. It was shown how the measurement process in section 4.4 can be instantiated and how the components of the measurement process map to real artifacts. The Hybrid Cloud Storage Framework (HCSF) furthermore introduced a means that combines the benefits of tabular storage with a fast distributed cache into a Cloud storage intermediary. Based on the HCSF, a performance gain of about 3x could be achieved, while ensuring that storage backend and distributed cached were permanently kept in sync.

With the introduction of the HCSF, the query performance of the ArbiterOne system reached real-time quality. Figure 72 complements the running illustration and shows how the technologies that were developed throughout his thesis interrelate with the economic aspects outlined in chapters 2 and 3.

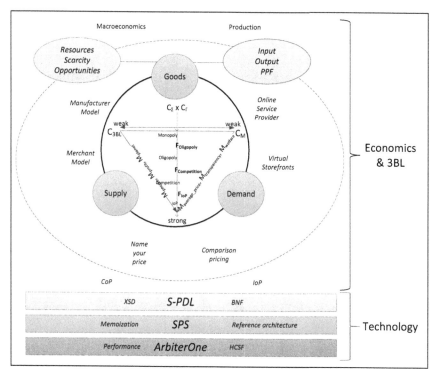

Figure 72: ArbiterOne in the Internet of Products.

8 Conclusion

"My interest is in the future because I am going to spend the rest of my life there." (Charles F. Kettering)

In April 2011, the intentions and motivations of this thesis gained additional momentum, when the European Commission (EC) released a document that demands for more inner-European electronic commerce, the so called Single Market Act. It might well be that the welfare argument and with this the desire for economic growth is also what led the EC to formulate its goal: to double the portion of inner-European electronic commerce (measured by the totality of inner-European trade) from 3.4% to 6.8%, until the year 2015. Though the development of this thesis and with this the framing of the IoP idea started about three years ago, the recognition of the problem through the EC might equip the IoP with the necessary strength to potentially turn from a vision into reality.

8.1 Summary

This thesis introduced the idea of an openly accessible Internet of Products (IoP). Chapter 2 expressed the economic gains of the IoP in terms of welfare through a formal model and showed that dropping prices –as a consequence of reduced transaction cost– result in an increase in welfare (cp. [RQ1]). Chapter 3 extended the welfare-centered gains analysis of the IoP by two additional dimensions and jointly expressed them as the Triple Bottom Line, a unified measure for public sector full cost accounting (cp. [RQ2], [RQ3]).

This thesis approached the IoP (and also the core of the Single Market Act) from a product information accessibility perspective. Chapter 4 reduced the problem of efficient access to language and culture-independent openly accessible product information to an information systems problem (cp. [RQ4]). To counter the insufficient support for semantic product search capabilities of contemporary online marketplaces and search engines (cp. benchmark in chapter 3), a new and semantic product description language, the S-PDL, was developed in chapter 5 (cp. [RQ5], [RQ6]). Chapter 6 contained the design of an execution environment for the S-PDL that hosts and maintains semantic product descriptions, the SPS [RQ7]. The main capabilities of the S-PDL and the SPS are summarized as:

- Translingual and transcultural product search,

- Semantic operators that are executed at query time,

- Dynamic product descriptions whose behavior is implemented through attribute handlers,

- Standard- based implementation of the S-PDL (in XML),

- Self-assessment of the quality of search results,

- Customizability and extensibility of attribute handlers through an SDK,

- On-premise or Cloud deployment of the SPS, and

- Real-time performance of semantic search queries.

The concepts of the S-PDL and the SPS were validated in chapter 7 through a reference implementation, named "ArbiterOne". Other applications, which were based on ArbiterOne's SPS, include an online language learning platform (eVoces), a platform for the victims of the tsunami that hit the Japanese east coast in 2011 (EscapeMisery), and a spot market for computing resources (SpotCrowd). Tests revealed that especially the query-time execution of attribute handlers (for currency conversion, language conversion, etc.) negatively influence the real-time capability of the SPS reference architecture (cp. [RQ8]). A solution to ensure real-time support of the SPS and ArbiterOne for semantic query operations was proposed in the form of a Hybrid Cloud Storage Framework (HCSF).

8.2 Future Work

The vision of the Internet of Products involves that suppliers use the S-PDL to author their product descriptions and make them accessible to consumers through either on-premise or Cloud-based SPS instances. Consumers could then conduct product search among all SPS instances. Therefore, SPS instances would need to register with a Product Name Server (PNS), which would route search queries that were initiated by a consumer to all registered SPS instances and return the combined search result to the client.

The procedure described above is similar to online price comparison engines, but bases upon a standard format for product descriptions and semantic product search. Contrary to price comparison engines, the end-user's search experience in the IoP would potentially benefit from significant improvements in the quality of search results. No in-depth research and analysis of the PNS concept has been done yet and might be subject to future work of the author's working group.

Other points of future interest might address the automatic extraction of similar product descriptions from all product descriptions available in the IoP. Though with the S-PDL suppliers are given a tool to model their products and equip them with semantic search capabilities, search quality and product comparability might be hindered, if many suppliers authored different product descriptions, which are conceptually describing the same product. Different words for the names or the values of product attributes might result into consumers potentially not being able to discover all products that are relevant to their search query. [Baumann 2012] suggested a template generation algorithm for semantic product descriptions that were authored in the S-PDL. The algorithm comprises steps for a complexity analysis, a structural analysis, a semantic analysis, the forming of similarity groups, as well as the generation of product templates. After product descriptions were clustered into similarity groups, a matroid-based greedy search algorithm resolves the similarity groups for similar product descriptions. Details on automated product template generation can be found in Appendix A.

From an information technology point of view, the vision of highly transparent online markets, based on openly accessible product information in the Internet of Products, seems to be truly realizable. Efficient access to product information, however, is only one aspect of the IoP. The Triple Bottom Line demands that –in addition to profit– economic activities need as well be evaluated based on their ecological and environmental impact.

In 2009 and 2011, the author together with two students and the Institute of Logistics and Material Handlings Systems of the University of Magdeburg conducted an analysis on how the IoP and in particular the distribution of online orders through an agile Logistics Service Provider (LSP) could potentially reduce CO_2 emissions (cp. [Sakautzky 2009] and [Hu 2011]). Consumers would benefit from savings in gasoline, since they would not need to drive to the store and pick up their orders. All in all, the prices for goods, including their transportation cost, could potentially drop.

[Hu 2011] suggested three models for quantifying the routes that need to be traveled by either every individual consumer to pick up the goods or by a shared LSP to distribute the orders:

- A triangle inequality-based model,

- An ellipse-based model, and

- A segments-based model.

The triangle-based model works very well for simple setups with only a few suppliers and a few consumers, but its complexity increases very fast. The ellipse-based model is also only applicable to simple setups with very few suppliers and consumers, but yields the highest accuracy out of all three. The complexity of the segments-based model remains simple, even in setups where there are many suppliers and many consumers. Its accuracy, however, is the least of the three models, since it is based upon the average route length or all possible routes consumers and LSPs could travel. The segments-based model counts the segments that are required for either the consumers or the LSP to deliver the order.

The detailed models can be found in Appendix B. The general outcomes of the segments-based model include:

- If at least three consumers procure from the same supplier, the LSP's travel distance is less than the consumers' aggregated travel distance,

- If all consumers procure from different shops, the LSP's travel distance is always longer than the aggregated travel distance of the consumers,

- If there are N consumers and M suppliers involved in a setup, then LSP's travel distance is definitely not better than the aggregated consumers' travel distance, until at least one of the suppliers received orders by more than 3 consumers, or at least one consumer procures from more than three suppliers. The impact of the shared LSP will be even more significant, the more often the same supplier received orders from different consumers.

Even though none of the three models presented above produce an entirely correct answer toward the question of how the IoP affects the emission of CO_2, they at least provide strong indicators for an enhanced eco-balance in combination with the fact that consumers spend less time on travelling in order to pick up their purchases. Research in this field, especially with respect to novel business models for shared logistics providers, might be an indispensable part of future work.

In the end, the success of the Internet of Products to a vast extent depends on as many suppliers as possible contributing to it. An open product data movement might not be in the interest of large online suppliers (e.g., Amazon) who have manifested their position in the market. The hope, however, is that smaller suppliers –as they are participating in the IoP– start realizing certain competitive advantages, especially in terms of market visibility and transparency. These advantages might attract additional suppliers to participate in the IoP, until their joined standing in a transparent online market has gained sufficient momentum to even lead large suppliers to reconsider their attitude with respect to the IoP.

Until then, another major core problem will lie in sensitizing especially micro and small businesses to start online exposing their products and services with a technology, which they have not had yet any interaction with. This might involve a long-lasting and tedious process, since quite a substantial number of micro and small businesses rarely make use of e-commerce as a distribution channel for their products and services. An analysis that was conducted in 2011 by the author's team in two medium-sized German cities revealed that only about 12% of all businesses are able to accept online orders [Neumann 2011b]. Considering only micro, small, and medium enterprises, merely 6.9% of all analyzed businesses were able to accept online orders. In order for micro, small, and medium enterprises to assess their e-commerce maturity, [Neumann 2011b] proposed the KULI model of e-commerce maturity. Appendix C contains the detailed analysis results and provides details for the KULI model.

9 Appendix

9.1 Appendix A: Transport Efficiency Analysis

(appeared as a Master's Thesis at the Department of Distributed Systems/University of Magdeburg [Hu 2011])

9.1.1   Triangle Inequality-based Model

This model assumes that there are two consumers who want to procure from one supplier. Thus, an LSP could pick up both orders from the supplier and deliver them to the consumers or both consumers travel themselves to the stores to pick up their orders.

Assumption: C_1 (consumer 1), C_2 (consumer 1) and R (supplier) are not collinear, which means that, they are not on the same line, but they form a triangle $\Delta C_1 C_2 R$.

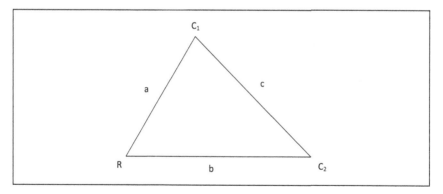

Figure 73: Two consumers, one supplier, and one LSP.

Without LSP, the consumers have to pick up their goods from the supplier individually. C_1's route is $\overline{C_1 R} + \overline{RC_1}$. C_2's route is $\overline{C_2 R} + \overline{RC_2}$. Their aggregated route is:

$$R_C = 2a + 2b \tag{A1.1.1}$$

If an LSP delivered the orders, the LSP would first have to pick up the goods and then deliver them to C_1 and C_2 (on the shortest route). If C_1, C_2, and R are considered as a triangle $\Delta C_1 C_2 R$, there are several possibilities for the position of the LSP's depot (G).

Assumption: G is located inside $\Delta C_1 C_2 R$:

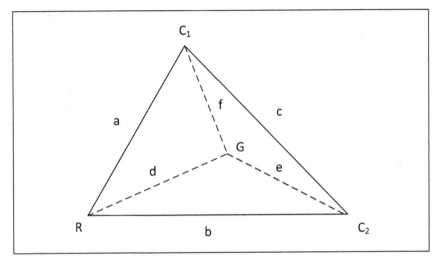

Figure 74: Routes inside the triangle $\Delta C_1 C_2 R$.

The route of the LSP to pick up the goods and deliver them to the consumers is:

■   The LSP drives to the supplier $(\overline{GR})$ to pick up the goods,

■   The LSP delivers the goods to C_1 $(\overline{RC_1})$,

■   From C_1, the LSP drives to C_2 $(\overline{C_1 C_2})$,

■   After the deliveries, the LSP will return to the depot $(\overline{C_2 G})$.

The total length of the LSP's route is:

$$R_{LSP} = d + a + c + e \tag{A1.1.2}$$

Now, it is to be shown that $R_{LSP} < R_C$:

$$d + a + c + e < 2a + 2b \tag{A1.1.3}$$

Transformation yields:

$$d + e < a + 2b - c \qquad (A1.1.4)$$

Since G is inside $\Delta C_1 C_2 R$, there exists a second triangle $\Delta G C_2 R$ that is inside $\Delta C_1 C_2 R$. Both triangles share side b with another. The sum of the two sides of the inner triangle (that are not shared with the outer triangle) is always smaller than the sum of the sides of the outer triangle:

$$d + e < a + c \qquad (A1.1.5)$$

Due to the transmission of inequality, it is possible to replace $d + e$ with $a + c$, so that:

$$a + c + c < a + b + b$$

or

$$c < b \qquad (A1.1.6)$$

Consequentially, it depends on the relative position of the consumers to the supplier, whether an LSP would travel less distance, if the LSP delivered the goods, as compared to both consumers separately picking up their goods from the supplier.

[Hu 2011] expands on this model and includes more suppliers and more consumers, which results in a dramatically increasing complexity. In order to be able to quantify the area around the triangle, a second, ellipse-based model was proposed:

9.1.2   Ellipse-based Model

Similarly to the triangle inequality-based methods, C_1, C_2, R, and LSP are nodes in a 2-dimensional space. Geographical factors, such as the altitude or detours are again not considered. The routes between C_1, C_2, R, and LSP are straight lines.

C_1, C_2, and R again form a triangle $\Delta C_1 C_2 R$. Now, the following simplifications are carried out: by shifting the origin of the coordinate system, R can be transformed into $(0,0)$. After the rotation, C_1 will lie on the vertical axis. A subsequent scaling transformation moves C_1 into $(0,1)$. Another shearing transformation moves C_2 into $(1,1)$. The transformations affect the lengths of the sides and the angles, but not the topology. Therefore, every transformation is revertible, which means that all the statements that can now be made maintain their validity, when retransforming to the original image.

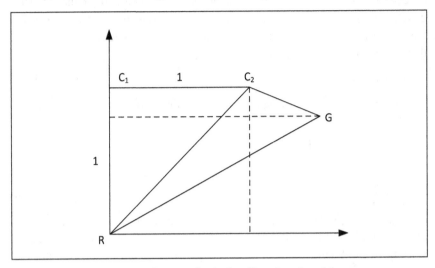

Figure 75: Two customers and one retailer in the ellipse-based model.

If both C_1 and C_1 travelled individually to R to pick up their orders, their aggregated travel distance would be:

$$R_C = 2 + 2\sqrt{2} \qquad (A1.2.1)$$

It is assumed that G is located somewhere in the coordinate system, and its coordinates are (x, y). Then the LSP's route to pick up and deliver the goods would be (based on the Euclidean distance):

$$R_{LSP} = d\big((x,y),(0,0)\big) + d\big((0,0),(0,1)\big) + d\big((0,1),(1,1)\big) +$$
$$d\big((1,1),(x,y)\big) = \sqrt{x^2 + y^2} + 1 + 1 + \sqrt{(x-1)^2 + (y-1)^2} \qquad (A1.2.2)$$

Now, both equations are used to form an ellipse around C_1, C_2, and R, inside which G would travel less distance than C_1 and C_2 together, in order to pick up and deliver C_1's and C_2's orders:

$$R_{LSP} = R_C$$
$$\sqrt{x^2 + y^2} + 1 + 1 + \sqrt{(x-1)^2 + (y-1)^2} = 2 + 2\sqrt{2} \qquad (A1.2.3)$$

Transformation yields:

$$\sqrt{x^2 + y^2} + \sqrt{(x-1)^2 + (y-1)^2} - 2\sqrt{2} = 0 \qquad (A1.2.4)$$

This defines an ellipse with the foci $(0,0)$ and $(1,1)$.

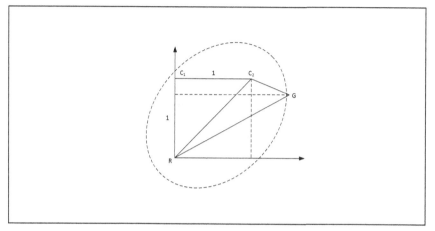

Figure 76: Ellipse defined through A1.2.4.

In particular, the ellipse surrounds the entire triangle $\Delta C_1 C_2 R$. This statement is true, even for the original image in Figure 75, since the transformations that were applied do not alter topological properties.

An evolution of the ellipse-based model can be reviewed in [Hu 2011]. Similarly to the triangle inequality-based method, the major disadvantage of the ellipse-based model is that its complexity increases very fast.

9.1.3   Segments-based Model

Compared to the previous two models, which aimed to exactly describe the travel distances, the segments-based model can be considered as a heuristic that assumes that the lengths of the routes between $C_1, C_2, ..., C_n, R$ and G are constant. The underlying idea is that there might be situations when the LSP has to travel long distances and that there might as well be situation, when the LSP only travels very short distances to deliver an order. This model only considers the average distance an LSP travels and refers to this average as a "segment". Consequentially, the segments-based model focuses upon counting the segments that need to be traveled by the LSP and C_1 and C_2.

Table 24 considers two consumers and two suppliers, and counts the segments both the LSP and C_1 and C_2 would have to travel.

Table 24: Segments for two consumers and two suppliers.

No. of con- sumers Cn (n = 2)	No. of suppliers visited by each consumer Sm		Route		No. of nodes	No. of Seg- ments
2	C1	1 (S1)	RC	C1S1+S1C1+C2S1+ S1C2	3	4
	C2	1 (S1)	RLSP	GS1+S1C1+C1C2+C2G	3+1	4
2	C1	1 (S1)	RC	C1S1+S1C1+C2S2+ S2C2	4	4
	C2	1 (S2)	RLSP	GS1+S1S2+S2C1+C1C2 +C2G	4+1	5
2	C1	2 (S1, S2)	RC	C1S1+S1S2+S2C1+ C2S1+S1C2	5	5
	C2	1 (S2)	RLSP	GS1+S1S2 +S2C1+C1C2+C2G	4+1	5
2	C1	2 (S1, S2)	RC	C1S1+S1S2+S2C1+ C2S1+S1S2+S2C2	6	6
	C2	2 (S1, S2)	RLSP	GS1+S1S2 +S2C1+ C1C2+C2G	4+1	5
...						

The number of nodes represents the total number of retailers that are visited by the consumers/LSP. If two different consumers order from the same supplier, then it will be counted twice for R_C, but only once for R_{LSP}.

Table 25 considers three consumers and three suppliers. Table 24 and Table 25 contain the allocations, when the LSP travels less segments than all consumers together, in order to pick up the ordered goods.

Table 25: Segments for three consumers and three suppliers.

No. of consumers Cn (n = 3)	No. of suppliers visited by each consumer Sm		Route		No. of nodes	No. of Segments
3	C_1	1 (S_1)	R_C	$C_1S_1+S_1C_1+C_2S_1+S_1C_2+C_3S_1+$ S_1C_3	6	6
	C_2	1 (S_1)	R_{LSP}	$GS_1+S_1C_1+C_1C_2+C_2C_3+C_3G$	4+1	5
	C_3	1 (S_1)				
3	C_1	1 (S_1)	R_C	$C_1S_1+S_1C_1+C_2S_2+S_2C_2+C_3S_3+$ S_3C_3	6	6
	C_2	1 (S_2)				
	C_3	1 (S_3)	R_{LSP}	$GS_1+S_1S_2+S_2S_3+S_3C_1$ $+C_1C_2+C_2C_3+C_3G$	6+1	7
3	C_1	1 (S_1)	R_C	$C_1S_1+S_1C_1+C_2S_1+S_1C_2+C_3S_2+$ S_2C_3	6	6
	C_2	1 (S_1)	R_{LSP}	$GS_1+S_1S_2$ $+S_2C_1+C_1C_2+C_2C_3+C_3G$	5+1	6
	C_3	1 (S_2)				
3	C_1	2 (S_1, S_2)	R_C	$C_1S_1+S_1S_2+S_2C_1+C_2S_1+S_1S_2$ $+S_2C_2+C_3S_2+S_2S_3+S_3C_3$	9	9
	C_2	2 (S_1, S_2)	R_{LSP}	$GS_1+S_1S_2+S_2S_3+S_3C_1$ $+C_1C_2+C_2C_3+C_3G$	6+1	7
	C_3	2 (S_2, S_3)				
...						

It is desirable to find a formula for when the LSP travels less distance than the individual consumers. To count the segments means to count the number of nodes. Each consumer counts as one node. The totality of consumer nodes is represented by N_C. The number of suppliers that is visited by every consumer is represented by the variable S_m.

Consequently, R_c consist of:

$$R_C = N_C + S_{m_1} + S_{m_2} + \cdots + S_{m_{NC}} \qquad (A1.3.1)$$

Transformation yields:

$$R_C = N_C + \sum_{i=1}^{N_C} S_{m_i} \tag{A1.3.2}$$

In case of the LSP delivering the online orders, N_C again represents the number of nodes of consumers. N_S is the number of supplier nodes, which the LSP hast to travel to in order to pick up the goods. Another node that has to be considered is the LSP's depot (G).

The resulting formula is:

$$R_{LSP} = N_C + N_S + 1 \tag{A1.3.3}$$

The goal is to find out when $R_{LSP} < R_C$:

$$N_C + N_S + 1 < N_C + \sum_{i=1}^{N_C} S_{m_i} \tag{A1.3.4}$$

Transformation yields:

$$N_S < \sum_{i=1}^{N_C} S_{m_i} - 1 \tag{A1.3.5}$$

The big advantage of the segments-based model is that it remains simple, even when the number of suppliers and consumers increases. It is, however, to be considered as a heuristic.

9.2 Appendix B: S-PDL Template Generation

(appeared as a Bachelor's Thesis at the Department of Distributed Systems/University of Magdeburg [Baumann 2012])

The single steps for the generation of S-PDL templates are described in Figure 77.

The objective function for template generation is based upon a metric that is referred to as Weighted PDL Template Distance (WPTD): WPTD depends on the attributes of the product description (A) and the template attributes (T).

$$WPTD(A, T) = \sum_{i=1}^{|A|} w_{PDL}(a_i, t_i) \tag{A2.1}$$

The metric considers all attributes that together occur in an S-PDL product description and a template, and sums up the values for its weighted function $w_{PDL}(a,t)$. If an attribute is only contained in either the product description or the

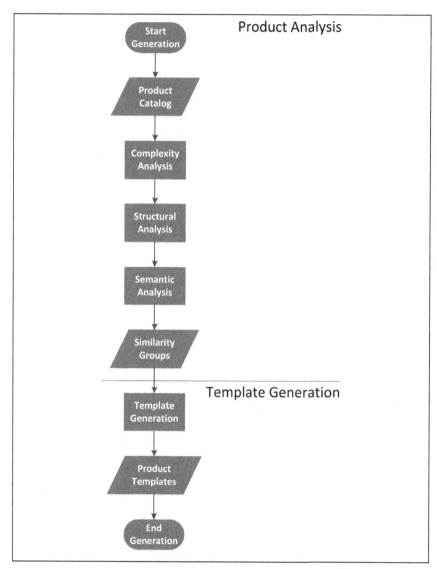

Figure 77: Template generation process.

template, the missing one that musses the attribute is filled up with an empty attribute. This means that every attribute, which does not exactly match all sub tags of a template attribute, is considered as not matching. The weighting function $w_{PDL}(a,t)$ is defined as:

$$w_{PDL}(a,t) =$$
$$\begin{cases} \frac{|T|}{l_i} \,, if \ t \notin T \wedge a \in A \\ \frac{1}{l_a} * S_{N_a} \,, if \ N_a \neq N_t \wedge N_a \in sub(a) \\ S_{N_a} \,, if \ V_a \neq V_t \wedge U_a \notin sub(a) \wedge V_a \in sub(a) \\ \frac{S}{2*l_a} \,, if \ V_a \neq V_t \wedge U_a \neq U_t \ \wedge AH_a \notin sub(a) \wedge U_a \in sub(a) \\ 0 \ otherwise \end{cases}$$

(A2.2)

whereby

t ... the corresponding attribute in the $S - PDL$ template

a ... the $S - PDL$ attribute

N_a ... name tag of the $S - PDL$ attribute

V_a ... value tag of the $S - PDL$ attribute

AH_a ... attribute handler of the $S - PDL$ attribute

U_a ... unit of the $S - PDL$ attribute

$sub(a)$ ... set of sub tags of the $S - PDL$ attribute a

l_a ... hierachy level of the $S - PDL$ attribute

S ... semantic weight

In the following, the weighting function is briefly explained:

- The corresponding S-PDL attribute has no equivalent attribute in the template and therefore is weighted with a relative value that depends on the size of the template ,

- A non-matching name-tag does not allow the attribute to be compared any further and therefore is weighted with a relatively high weight that depends on the level in the hierarchy,

- If the values of both the S-PDL and the template do not match and the value is not a number, the attribute is weighted with the semantic importance of the name-tag,

■   For numeric values that cannot be converted, the weight is relative to the semantic weight and the level in the hierarchy. The weight for wrong numeric values is less than the weight for text values, since the variety of possible numeric values is larger.

The metric introduced above only measures the distance between an S-PDL product description and a template. The scenario, however, requires forming a template from a group of S-PDL product descriptions. Hence, a metric that describes the distance between a group of S-PDL product descriptions (G), and the template is necessary. The formula below introduces the Weighted Average PDL Template Distance (WPTD):

$$\overline{WPTD(G,T)} = \frac{\Sigma_{g \in G} WPTD(g,T)}{|G|} \qquad (A2.3)$$

The quality of the template can be measured as the smallest possible distance. Therefore the goal of the template generation process is to minimize the Weighted Average PDL Template Distance.

$$g : \overline{WPTD(G,T)} \ \to \ \min(\overline{WPTD(G,T)}) \qquad (A2.4)$$

To find an optimal solution to the above problem, [Baumann 2012] proposes a greedy algorithm that is based on so called matroids. A matroid M is an ordered pair (E, I) that consists of a finite set E and a collection I of subsets of E and satisfies the following three conditions [Oxley 2006]:

■ $\emptyset \in I$,

■   If $i \in I$ and $i' \subseteq i$, then $i' \in I$,

■   If I_1 and I_2 are in I and $|I_1| < |I_2|$ then there is an element e of I_2 - I_1 such that $I_1 \cup e \in I$.

Based on [Oxley 1992] and [Baumann 2012], the algorithm for finding the optimal template contains the following steps:

$A \leftarrow \emptyset;$

while A is not a base of M **do**

$\qquad X \leftarrow \{x \in S \setminus A \,|\, A \cup x \in I\,\};$

$\qquad$ choose x_0 so that $\Delta\overline{WPTD(x)} = \ min_{x \in X} \Delta\overline{WPTD(x)};$

$$if\ x_0 = name(x) \vee name(x)\ \in A$$

$$A \leftarrow A\ \cup \{x_0\};$$

else

$$A \leftarrow A\ \cup name(x) \qquad (A2.5)$$

$$(A2.4)$$

9.3 Appendix C: The KULI Model of E-Commerce Maturity

(appeared as a publication in [Neumann 2011b])

KULI stands for knowledge, unawareness, logistics and investment. KULI tries to raise attention for the problems and difficulties MSMEs (micro, small, and medium enterprises) might face with respect to a possible adoption of e-commerce.

■ Knowledge: in order to setup, run and maintain an online shop, a variety of technical skills is required. Starting with the creation of a database and the setup of a web server towards the installation of the online shop software and the deployment to the web server, the majority of MSMEs would already get lost before they have specified even their first online product. Enterprises could compensate their lack of technical expertise by purchasing service hours of specialized companies and consultants. This cost might, however, be too high.

■ Unawareness: many MSMEs might simply be unaware of the chances e-commerce could bring to their business. This might be due to the size and the limited revenue MSMEs operate upon, so that no or only limited resources exist within the organization that could deal with strategic questions and new technologies. To the author's opinion, it has always been and it will always remain a core problem of all e-business related research to communicate the many benefits of e-commerce to MSME decision makers in a way, so that they can access them and clearly identify where information system technology could add value to their organization.

■ Logistics: the third aspect the KULI model tries to point out is logistics. If enterprises depend on an own logistics facility in order to dispatch their online products, they will in most cases have to run their own fleet. Running

an own fleet, however, is expensive and thus most enterprise would immediately withdraw this option, if no positive ROI (Return on Investment) was
within sight. For certain businesses, however, it turned out to be an appeal-
ing extension of their business model to run e-commerce in addition to their
traditional distribution channel. Pizza deliveries, restaurants or even phar-
macies, for instance, offer to immediately dispatch their orders by using
their own fleet. Businesses that wanted to online expose their products to a
local market (as in the case of the pizza delivery) would also need to be able
to rely upon an own fleet, or at least a logistics service provider that is capable of rapidly dispatching orders to local customers. In this context, one
should also evaluate the feasibility of a shared logistics provider or fleet that
could be owned by a conglomerate of local businesses. This way, local
MSMEs could share the cost for a fleet, which might at the same time be a
solution for overcoming the cost barrier of an instantaneous dispatch handling. For many MSMEs, a shared logistics model could even represent the
enabler for a future e-commerce go-live.

▪ Investment: last but not least, the KULI model points out the role of the
initial investment that is to be brought up for introducing e-commerce in an
enterprise. Though several MSMEs might already have thought about adding e-commerce to their order handling, another significant number might
find the investment for software, hardware, administration and consulting
services to be out of proportion in the respective case of their business
Though critics might argue that nowadays there exists a variety of open
source online shop software that can be procured for free, it is important to
emphasize that MSMEs would still need to know how to set up the software
(refer to "KULI/Knowledge"). Though so called rental shops, which represent online shops that are deployed and hosted by specialized companies,
eliminate the procurement and installation of soft- and hardware on the
MSME's side, the majority of enterprises will still not know how to custom-
ize the shop to reflect their individual requirements or how to model products in their online shop. Again, the services of administrators or companies
specialized on content management would need to be purchased.

Figure 78 summarizes the four KULI factors, where one question is proposed for
each KULI factor. Only if all four questions are answered with "Yes", an MSME
is mature enough to start running an online shop or engage in e-commerce.

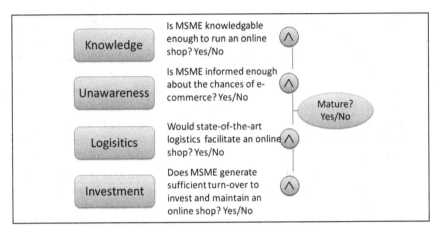

Figure 78: KULI model of e-commerce maturity.

With the questionnaire above, MSMEs are given a tool to evaluate and review their KULI maturity. Enterprises with a positive KULI maturity (overall "Yes") should seriously start considering an introduction of e-commerce to their business. Enterprises with a negative KULI maturity (overall "No") should start with analyzing how to increase their maturity, by for example, increasing their knowledge or awareness. Furthermore, MSMEs with a negative KULI maturity should evaluate how to deal with "logistics" or how to bring up the funds necessary for the initial investment.

10 Bibliography

[Abadi 2009] D.J. Abadi, "Data Management in the Cloud: Limitations and Opportunities," In: IEEE Bulletin, Volume 32, Issue 1, pp. 3-12, March, 2009.

[Abran 2006] A. Abran, M. Bundschuh, G. Büren, and R. Dumke, "Applied Software Measurement," Shaker Publishers, Aachen, Germany, 2006.

[Agapi 2011] A. Agapi, K. Birman, R.M. Broberg, C. Cotton, T. Kielmann, M. Millnert, R. Payne, R. Surton, and R. van Renesse, "Routers for the Cloud: Can the Internet Achieve 5-Nines Availability?" In: IEEE Internet Computing, Volume 15, Issue 5, pp. 72-77, September-October, 2011.

[Albani 2003] A. Albani, A. Keiblinger, K. Turowski and C. Winnewisser, "Domain Based Identification and Modelling of Business Component Applications," In: Proceedings of the 7th East European Conference Advances in Databases and Information Systems (ADBIS'03), Dresden, Germany, pp. 30-45, September, 2003.

[Alonso 2004] G. Alonso, F. Casati, H. Kuno, and V. Machiraju, "Web Services: Concepts, Architectures and Applications," Springer Publishers, Berlin-Heidelberg, Germany, 2004.

[Armbrust 2009] M. Armbrust, A. Fox, R. Griffith, A.D. Joseph, R.H. Katz, A. Konwinski, G. Lee, D.A. Patterson, A. Rabkin, I. Stoica, and M. Zaharia, "Above the Clouds: A Berkeley View of Cloud Computing," Technical Report UCB/EECS-2009-28, University of California, Berkeley, USA, February, 2009.

[Ashton 2009] K. Ashton, "That 'Internet of Things' Thing," In: RFID Journal, June, 2009.

[Asikainen 2003] T. Asikainen, T. Soininen, and T. Männistö, "Towards Managing Variability using Software Product Family Architecture Models and Product Configurators," In: The Proceedings of the Software Variability Management Workshop 2003 (SVM'03), Groningen, Netherlands, February, 2003.

[Asikainen 2004] T. Asikainen, T. Männistö, and T. Soininen, "Using a Configurator for Modelling and Configuring Software Product Lines based on Feature Models," In: Proceedings of the Workshop on Software Variability Management for Product Derivation, Software Product Line Conference (SPLC), Boston, USA, August-September, 2004.

[Aßmann 2003] U. Aßmann, "Invasive Software Composition," Springer Publishers, Berlin-Heidelberg, Germany, 2003.

[Assunção 2009] M.D. de Assunção, A. di Costanzo, and R. Buyya, "Evaluating the Cost-Benefit of Using Cloud Computing to Extend the Capacity of Clusters," In: Proceedings of the 18th ACM international symposium on High Performance Distributed Computing (HPDC'09), Munich, Germany, June, 2009.

[Au 2003] R. Au, M. Yao, and M. Looi, "Agent-Based Privilege Negotiation for E-commerce on World Wide Web," In: J.M. Cueva Lovelle, B.M. González Rodríguez, L. Joyanes Aguilar, J.E. Labra Gayo, and M. del Puerto Paule Ruíz (Eds.), "Web Engineering," Proceedings of the 3rd International Conference Web Engineering (ICWE'03), LNCS 2722, pp. 68-71, Springer Publishers, Berlin-Heidelberg, Germany, 2003.

[Avetisyan 2010] A.I. Avetisyan, R. Campbell, I. Gupta, M.T. Heath, S.Y. Ko, G.R. Ganger, M.A. Kozuch, D. O'Hallaron, M. Kunze, T.T. Kwan, K. Lai, M. Lyons, D.S. Milojicic, H.Y. Lee, Y.C. Soh, N.K. Ming, J.-Y. Luke, and H. Namgoong, "Open Cirrus: A Global Cloud Computing Testbed," In: IEEE Computer, Volume 43, Issue 4, pp. 35-43, April, 2010.

[Awodey 2010] S. Awodey, "Category Theory," Oxford University Press, 2nd edition, Oxford, UK, 2010.

[Bader 2008] P. Bader, "Sustainability – From Principle To Practice," Goethe Institute, Germany, March, 2008.

[Bailey 1997] J. Bailey and Y. Bakos, "An exploratory study of the emerging role of electronic intermediaries," In: International Journal of Electronic Commerce, Volume 1, Issue 3, pp. 7-20, 1997.

[Bakos 1991] J. Bakos, "A Strategic Analysis of Electronic Marketplaces," In: MIS Quarterly, Volume 15, Issue 3, pp. 295-310, September, 1991.

[Banerjee 2011] P. Banerjee, R. Friedrich, C. Bash, P. Goldsack, B.A. Huberman, J. Manley, C.D. Patel, P. Ranganathan, A. Veitch, "Everything as a Service: Powering the New Information Economy," In: IEEE Computer, Volume 44, Issue 3, pp. 36-43, March, 2011.

[Basili 1986] V.R. Basili, R.W. Selby, and D.H. Hutchens, "Experimentation in Software Engineering," In: IEEE Transactions on Software Engineering, Volume 12, Issue 7, pp. 733-734, July, 1986.

[Basili 2007] V.R. Basili, H.D. Rombach, K. Schneider, B. Kitchenham, D. Pfahl, and R.W. Selby, "Empirical Software Engineering," LNCS 4336, Springer Publishers, Berlin-Heidelberg, 2007.

[Baumann 2012] M. Baumann, "Generation possibilities for semantic product templates within a structured product catalog," Bachelor's Thesis, Otto-von-Guericke University, Magdeburg, Germany, March, 2012.

[Becker 2010] W.S. Becker, J.A. Carbo, and I.M. Langella, "Beyond Self-Interest: Integrating Social Responsibility and Supply Chain Management With Human Resource Development," In: Human Resource Development Review, Volume 9, Issue 2, pp. 144-168, December, 2010.

[Benabou 1985] J. Benabou, "Fibered categories and the foundations of naive category theory," In: The Journal of Symbolic Logic, Volume 50, Issue 1, pp. 10-37, March, 1985.

[Benjamin 1987] R.I. Benjamin, T.W. Malone, and J. Yates, "Electronic Markets and Electronic Hierarchies: Effects of Information Technology on Market Structures and Corporate Strategies," In: Communications of the ACM, Volume 30, Issue 6, pp. 484-497, June, 1987.

[Benjamin 1995] I. Benjamin and R. Wigand, "Electronic Markets and Virtual Value Chains on the Information Superhighway," In: MIT Sloan Management Review, Volume 36, Issue 2, pp. 62-72, 1995.

[Bergamaschi 2002] S. Bergamaschi, F. Guerra, and M. Vincini, "A Data Integration Framework for e-Commerce Product Classification," In: Proceedings of the First International Semantic Web Conference on The Semantic Web (ISWC'02), pp. 379-393, Sardinia, Italy, June, 2002.

[Berners-Lee 2001] T. Berners-Lee, J. Hendler, and O. Lassila, "The Semantic Web: A New Form of Web Content That Is Meaningful to Computers Will Unleash a Revolution of New Possibilities," In: Scientific American, pp. 34-43, May, 2001.

[Bichler 2001] M. Bichler, "The Future of e-Markets: Multidimensional Market Mechanisms," Cambridge University Press, UK, 2001.

[Bijl 1975] A. Bijl and G. Shawcross, "Housing site layout system," In: Computer-Aided Design, Volume 7, Issue 1, pp. 2-10, January, 1975.

[Birman 2009] K. Birman, G. Chockler, and R. van Renesse, "Toward a Cloud Computing Research Agenda," In: ACM SIGACT News, Volume 40, Issue 2, pp. 68-80, 2009.

[Bjork 1995] B.-C. Bjork, "Requirements and information structures for building product models (Dissertation)," VTT Technical Research Centre of Finland, Helsinki University of Technology, Helsinki, Finland, December, 1995.

[Böhms 1993] H.M. Böhms and G. Storer, "Architecture, methodology and Tools for computer integrated LArge Scale engineering (ATLAS) - Methodology for Open Systems Integration," Technical report, TNO - Netherlands Organisation for Applied Scientific Research, Delft, The Netherlands, 1993.

[Böhms 2008] M. Böhms, D. Leal, and H. Graves, "Product modelling and the Semantic Web," In: Proceedings of the Poster and Demonstration Session at the 7th International Semantic Web Conference (ISWC'08), Karlsruhe, Germany, October, 2008.

[Böhms 2009] M. Böhms, D. Leal, H. Graves, and K. Clark, "Product Modelling using Semantic Web Technologies," W3C Incubator Group Report 08, October, 2009.

[Bohrer 1998] K. A. Bohrer, "Architecture of the San Francisco frameworks," In: IBM Systems Journal, Volume 37 Issue 2, Riverton, USA, April, 1998.

[Borenstein 2011] N. Borenstein and J. Blake, "Cloud Computing Standards: Where's the Beef?" In: IEEE Internet Computing, Volume 15, Issue 3, pp. 74-78, May-June, 2011.

[Borkin 1982] H.J. Borkin, "Geometric modeling relational database system: ARCH:MODEL, Version 1.3," Architectural Research Laboratory, College of Architecture and Urban Planning, University of Michigan, Ann Arbor, USA, 1982.

[Bottema 1992] A. Bottema and L. van der Tang, "A Product Configurator as Key Decision Support System," Integration in Production Management Systems, H.J. Pels and J.C. Wortmann (eds.), Elsevier Science Publishers, Amsterdam, IFIP, 1992.

[Brickley 2006] J.A. Brickley, C.W. Smith, and J.L. Zimmerman, "Managerial Economics and Organizational Architecture," McGraw-Hill Publishers, 5th edition, New York, USA, 2006.

[Brown 1998] A.W. Brown and K.C. Wallnau, "The Current State of CBSE," In: IEEE Software, Volume 15, Issue 5, pp. 37-46, September-October, 1998.

[Bundschuh 2008] M. Bundschuh and C. Dekkers, "The IT Measurement Compendium," Springer Publishers, Berlin-Heidelberg, 2008.

[Cellary 2009] W. Cellary and S. Strykowski, "E-Government Based on Cloud Computing and Servce-Oriented Architecture," In: Proceedings of the 3rd International Conference on Theory and Practice of Electronic Governance (ICEGOV 2009), Bogota, Colombia, pp. 5-10, November, 2009.

[Chappell 2002] D.A. Chappell and T. Jewell, "Java Web Services," O'Reilly Publishers, Sebastopol, Canada, 2002.

[Chappell 2010] D.A. Chappell, "Introducing Windows Azure," Microsoft Corporation, October, 2010.

[Chopra 2001] S. Chopra and P. Meindl, "Supply Chain Management: Strategy, Planning, and Operation," Upper Saddle River, USA, 2001.

[Ciancarini 2001] P. Ciancarini and M.J. Wooldridge, "Agent-Oriented Software Engineering: The State of Art," In: Lecture Notes in Computer Science, Volume 1957/2001, pp. 55-82, Springer Publishers, Berlin-Heidelberg, Germany, 2001.

[Climate Group 2008] Climate Group, "SMART 2020: Enabling the low carbon economy in the information age," The Climate Group Press, London, UK, 2008.

[Cooper 2010] B. Cooper, "The Prickly Side of Building Clouds," In: IEEE Internet Computing, Volume 14, Issue 6, pp. 64-67, November-December, 2010.

[Coplien 1992] J.O. Coplien, "Advanced C++: programming styles and idioms," Addison-Wesley Publishers, New York, USA, 1992.

[Cusumano 2010] M. Cusumano, "Technology Strategiy and Management: Cloud Computing an SaaS as New Computing Platforms," In: Communications of the ACM, Volume 53, Issue 4, pp. 27-29, April, 2010.

[Dao 2011] V. Dao, I. Langella, and J. Carbo, "From green to sustainability: Information Technology and an integrated sustainability framework" In: The Journal of Strategic Information Systems, Volume 20, Issue 1, pp. 63-79, March, 2011.

[Davis 1995] A.M. Davis, "201 Principles of Software Development," McGraw Hill Publishers, New York, USA, 1995.

[Denton 2009] W. Denton, "How to Make Faceted Classification and Put It on the Web," In: Miskatonic University Press, March, 2009.

[Dignum 2000] F. Dignum and M. Greaves, "Issues in Agent Communication," In: LNCS 1916, Springer Publishers, Berlin-Heidelberg, Germany, 2000.

[Ding 2002] Y. Ding, M. Korotkiy, B. Omelayenko, V. Kartseva, V. Zykov, M. Klein, E. Schulten, and D. Fensel, "GoldenBullet: Automated Classification of Product Data in E-commerce," In: Proceedings of the 5th International Conference on Business Information Systems (BIS'02), Poznan, Poland, April, 2002.

[Drake 2011] M.J. Drake, V.W. Gerde, and D.M. Wasieleski, "Socially responsible modeling: a stakeholder approach to the implementation of ethical modeling in operations research," In: OR Spectrum, Volume 33, Issue 1, pp. 1-26, 2011.

[Dumke 1990] R. Dumke, "CASE: CAD-Systeme für den Software-Ingenieur," Wiss. Zeitschrift der TU Magdeburg, Volume 34, Issue 8, pp. 7-10, 1990.

[Dumke 1997] R. Dumke and A. Winkler, "Managing the Component-Based Software Engineering with Metrics," In: Proceedings of the 5th International Symposium on Assessment of Software Tools, pp. 104-110, Pittsburgh, USA, June, 1997.

[Dumke 2006] R.R. Dumke, M. Blazey, H. Hegewald, D. Reitz, and K. Georgieva, "Causalities in Software Process Measurement and Improvement," In: Proceedings of the IWSM/MENSURA'06, Cádiz, Spain, pp.42-52, November, 2006.

[Dumke 2008] R.R. Dumke, R. Braungarten, G. Büren, A. Abran, J.J. Cuadrado-Gallego, "Software Process und Product Measurement," Springer Publishers, Berlin-Heidelberg, Germany, 2008.

[Dumke 2009] R. Dumke, S. Mencke, and C. Wille, "Quality Assurance of Agent-Based and Self-Managed Systems," CRC Press, Boca Raton, USA, 2009.

[Dustdar 2011] S. Dustdar, Y. Guo, B. Satzger, and H.-L. Truong, "Principles of Elastic Processes," In: IEEE Internet Computing, Volume 15, Issue 5, pp. 66-71, September-October, 2011.

[Eastman 1977] C.M. Eastman and M. Henrion, "GLIDE: a language for design information systems," In: ACM SIGGRAPH Computer Graphics, Volume 11, Issue 2, pp. 24-33, July, San Jose, U.S.A, 1977.

[Eastman 1998] C. Eastman and F. Augenbroe "Product modeling strategies for today and the future," In: Proceedings of the CIB W78 Conference, B.C. Bjork and A. Jagbecj (eds.), The life-cycle of construction IT innovations, Technology transfer from research to practice, Stockholm, Sweden, June, 1998.

[Ebert 2007] C. Ebert and R. Dumke, "Software Measurement – Establish, Extract, Evaluate, Execute," Springer Publishers, Berlin-Heidelberg, Germany, 2007.

[ECMT 2007] ECMT, "Cutting Transport CO2 Emissions. What Progress?" OECD Publishers, Paris, France, January, 2007.

[Ehrig 1999] H. Ehrig, B. Mahr, F. Cornelius, M. Große-Rohde, and P. Zeitz, "Mathematisch-Strukturelle Grundlagen der Informatik," Springer Publishers, Berlin-Heidelberg, Germany, 1999.

[Eilenberg 1945] S. Eilenberg and S. MacLane, "General Theory of Natural Equivalences," In: Transactions of the American Mathematical Society, Volume 58, Issue 2, pp. 231-294, September, 1945.

[Endres 2003] A. Endres and D. Rombach, "A Handbook of Software and System Engineering," Pearson Education Publishers, Upper Saddle River, USA, 2003.

[Erens 1995] F.J. Erens and J.C. Wortmann, "Generic Product Modeling for Mass Customization," In: Proceedings of the 1st World Congress on Intelligent Manufacturing Processes and Systems, Mayagüez, Puerto Rico, February, 1995.

[European Commission 2011] European Commission, "Single Market Act: Together for New Growth," Brussels, Netherlands, April, 2011.

[European Commission 2001] European Commission, "The Impact of the E-Economy on European Enterprises: Economics Analysis and Policy Implication," Brussels, Netherlands, November, 2001.

[Ezran 1998] M. Ezran, M. Morisio, and C. Tully, "Practical Software Reuse: the essential guide," Freelife Publishers, Paris, France, 1998.

[Fenton 1992] N.E. Fenton, "Systems Construction and Analysis: A Mathematical and Logical Framework," McGraw Hill Publishing, New York, USA 1992.

[Fenton 1997] N.E. Fenton and S.L. Pfleeger, "Software Metrics: A Rigorous and Practical Approach," Thomson Computer Press, London, UK, 1997.

[Ferber 1999] J. Ferber, "Multi-Agent Systems: An Introduction to Distributed Artificial Intelligence," Addison-Wesley, New York, USA, 1999.

[Fiadeiro 2005] J.L. Fiadeiro, "Categories of Software Engineering," Springer Publishers, Berlin-Heidelberg, Germany, 2005.

[Fielding 2000] T. Fielding, "Architectural Styles and the Design of Network-based Software Architectures," Dissertation, University of California, Irvine, USA, 2000.

[Fox 1997] A. Fox, S.D. Gribble, Y. Chawathe, E.A. Brewer, and P. Gauthier, "Cluster-Based Scalable Network Services," In: ACM SIGOPS Operating Systems Review, Volume 31, Issue 5, pp.78-91, December, 1997.

[Frank 2002] U. Frank, "Modeling Products for Versatile E-commerce Platforms - Essential Requirements and Generic Design Alternatives," In: H. Arisawa, Y. Kambayashi, V. Kumar, H.C. Mayr, I. Hunt, (Eds.): Conceptual Modeling for New Information System Technologies, Springer, Berlin, Heidelberg, New York, pp. 444-456, 2002.

[Frank 2008] R. Frank, "Microeconomics and Behavior," 7th edition, McGraw-Hill Publishers, New York, USA, 2008.

[Fraunhofer 2001] T. Pastoors, O. Kelkar, and V. Schmitz, "BMECat V1.2 für Einsteiger," (English: BMECat V1.2 for Beginners), Fraunhofer IAO, Stuttgart, Germany, 2001.

[Friesen 2011] J. Friesen, "Beginning Java 7," APRESS Publishers, New York, USA, 2011.

[Garshol 2004] L.M. Garshol, "Metadata? Thesauri? Taxonomies? Topic Maps! Making Sense of it all," In: Journal of Information Science, Volume 30, Issue 4, pp. 378-391, August, 2004.

[Georgieva 2009] K. Georgieva, R. Dumke, R. Neumann, and A. Farooq, "Software Measurement Modelling and Improvement," In: Proceedings of the International Conference on Software Engineering Research and Practice (SERP'09), Las Vegas, USA, pp. 396-402, July, 2009.

[Gielingh 1988] W. Gielingh, "General AEC Reference Model (GARM)," In: CIB Conference on The Conceptual Modeling of Buildings, TC5.2 and 7.8, Lund Sweden, October, 1988.

[Gielingh 1996] W. Gielingh, R. Los, B. Luijten, J. van Putten, and V. Velten, "The PISA project: A survey on STEP," Shaker Publishers, Aachen, Germany, 1996.

[Golder 2006] S.A. Golder and B.A. Huberman, "Using Patterns of Collaborative Tagging Systems," In: Journal of Information Science, Volume 32, Issue 2, pp. 198-208, April, 2006.

[Graves 2010] H. Graves, "Logic for Modeling Product Structure," In: Proceedings of the 23rd International Workshop on Description Logics (DL'10), Waterloo, Canada, May, 2010.

[Griffel 1998] F. Griffel, "Componentware – Konzepte und Techniken eines Softwareparadigmas, " dpunkt Publishers, Heidelberg, Germany, 1998.

[Grossman 2009] R.L. Grossman, "The Case for Cloud Computing," In: IT Professional, Volume 11, Issue 2, pp. 23-27, March-April, 2009.

[Gruber 1995] T.R. Gruber, "Toward Principles for the Design of Ontologies Used for Knowledge Sharing," In: International Journal of Human-Computer Studies, Special Issue: The Role of Formal Ontology in the Information Technology 43, pp. 907-928, December, 1995.

[Günter 2000] M. Günter and M. Gisler, "Intellectual Properties as Intangible Goods," In: IEEE Computer Society, Volume 8, p. 8062, Hawaii, USA, 2000.

[Hadzic 2004] T. Hadzic, S. Subbarayan, R.M. Jensen, H.R. Andersen, J. Møller, and H. Hulgaard, "Fast Backtrack-Free Product Configuration Using a Precompiled Solution Space Representation," In: Proceedings of the International Conference on

Economic, Technical and Organisational aspects of Product Configuration Systems, Copenhagen, Denmark, June, 2004.

[Halpin 2007] H. Halpin, V. Robu, and H. Shepherd, "The Complex Dynamics of Collaborative Tagging," In: Proceedings of the 16th International Conference on World Wide Web (WWW'07), pp. 211-220, Banff, Canada, May, 2007.

[Han 2009] S.-M. Han, M.M. Hassan, C.-W. Yoon, and E.-N. Huh, "Efficient Service Recommendation System for Cloud Computing Market," In: Proceedings of the 2nd International Conference on Interaction Sciences (ICIS 2009), pp. 201-207, Seoul, Korea, November, 2009.

[Hansen 2003] T. Hansen, C. Scheer and P. Loos, "Product Configurators in Electronic Commerce - Extension of the Configurator Concept towards Customer Recommendation," In: Proceedings of the 2nd Interdisciplinary World Congress on Mass Customization and Personalization (MCPC), Munich, Germany, October, 2003.

[Hanson 2003] J. Hanson, "Coarse-grained interfaces enable service composition in SOA," JavaOne, August, 2003.

[Hart 2002] M.L. Hart and H. Allison, "ERP adoption by medium-sized organisations in the Western Cape," Research report, University of Cape Town, South Africa, 2002.

[Herschley 2009] M. Herschley, "Managerial Economics," South-Western Publishers, Mason, USA, 2009.

[Hofmann 2010] P. Hofmann and D. Woods, "Cloud Computing: The Limits of Public Clouds for Business Applications," In: IEEE Internet Computing, Volume 14, Issue 6, pp. 90-93, November-December, 2010.

[Horrocks 2003] I. Horrocks, P.F. Patel-Schneider, F. van Harmelen, "From SHIQ and RDF to OWL: the making of a Web Ontology Language," In: Web Semantics: Science, Services, and Agents on the World Wide Web, Volume 1, Issue 1, pp. 7-26, December, 2003.

[Hoskins 1976] E.M. Hoskins, "Computer aids in system building," In: Computer-Aided Design, Volume 8, Issue 2, pp. 127-140, April, 1976.

[Hu 2011] X. Hu, "Development of a Formal Model for Estimating the Economic and Ecological Impact of the Goliath Approach," Master Thesis, Otto-von-Guericke University, Magdeburg, Germany, March, 2011.

[Huang 2007] Y.L. Huang, W.K. Ng, H. Liu, W.F. Lu, B. Song, and X. Li, "Semantic Modeling and Extraction for Cross-Family Product Configuration," International Conference on Service Systems and Service Management (ICSSSM), Chengdu, China, June, 2007.

[ISBSG 2003] P.R. Hill, "Software Project Estimation – A Workbook for Macro-Estimation of Software Development Effort and Duration," Kwik Kopy Printing, Melbourne, Australia, 2003.

[ISO 2001] International Organization for Standardization, "Information Technology – Software Measurement Process," In: Metrics News, Volume 6, Issue 2, pp. 11-46, December, 2001.

[ISO 1993] International Organization for Standardization, "Product Data Representation and Exchange," ISO 10303, Standard for the Exchange of Product, 1993.

[ISO 1994] International Organization for Standardization, "Industrial automation systems and integration-Product data representation and exchange," Paper ISO 10303-1:1994, December, 1994.

[ISO 2003] International Organization for Standardization, "Software Engineering – Product Quality," Paper ISO/IEC 9126-1:2001, 2003.

[ITF 2008] International Transport Forum, "Key Transport and Greenhouse Gas Indicators: Germany," 2008.

[Jaatun 2009] M.G. Jaatun, G. Zhao, and C. Rong, "Cloud Computing," LNCS 5931, Springer Publishers, Berlin-Heidelberg, Germany, 2009.

[Jacob 2003] E.K. Jacob, "Ontologies and the Semantic Web," In: Bulletin of the American Society for Information Science and Technology, Volume 29, Issue 4, pp. 19-22, May, 2003.

[Jaksch 2005] S. Jaksch and M. Rudy, "An Ontological Decision Support System for the Design of Structural Simulation Models," In: Proceedings of The 8th 3IA, pp. 189-196, Limoges, France, May, 2005.

[Jehle 2011] G.A. Jehle and P.J. Reny, "Advanced microeconomic theory," 3rd edition, Prentice Hall Publishers, Harlow, UK, 2011.

[Juristo 2001] N. Juristo and A.M. Moreno, "Basics of Software Engineering Experimentation," Kluwer Academic Publishers, Boston, USA, 2001.

[Kang 1998] K.C. Kang, "Feature-oriented development of applications for a domain," Proceedings of International Conference on Software Reuse, pp. 354-355, Victoria, Canada, June, 1998.

[Khalidi 2011] Y.A. Khalidi, "Building a Cloud Computing Platform for New Possibilities," In: IEEE Computer, Volume 44, Issue 3, pp. 29-34, March, 2011.

[Kim 2009] W. Kim, S.D. Kim, E. Lee, and S. Lee, "Adoption Issues for Cloud Computing," In: Proceedings of the The 11th International Conference on Information Integration and Web-based Applications & Services (iiWAS'09), Kuala Lumpur, Malaysia, pp. 3-6, December, 2009.

[Kitchenham 2007] B. Kitchenham, "Empirical Paradigm – The Role of Experiments," In: V.R. Basili, H.D. Rombach, K. Schneider, B. Kitchenham, D. Pfahl, and R.W. Selby, "Empirical Software Engineering," Springer Publishers, Berlin-Heidelberg, Germany, pp. 25-32, 2007.

[Knapik 1998] M. Knapik and J. Johnson, "Developing Intelligent Agents for Distributed Systems," McGraw-Hill, New York, USA, 1998.

[Krikke 2003] H. Krikke, J. Bloemhof-Ruwaard, and L.N. van Wassenhove, "Concurrent product design and closed-loop supply chain design with an application to refrigerators," In: International Journal of Production Research, Volume 41, Issue 16, pp. 3689–3719, August, 2003.

[Krishnan 2010] S. Krishnan, "Programming Windows Azure: programming the Microsoft Cloud," O'Reilly Publishers, Sebastopol, USA, 2010.

[Krugman 2011] P.R. Krugman, M. Obstfeld, and M.J. Melitz, "International Economics: Theory and Policy," 9th edition, Pearson Publishers, Harlow, UK, 2011.

[Kumar 2010] K. Kumar and Y.-H. Lu, "Cloud Computing for Mobile Users: Can Offloading Computation Save Energy?" In: IEEE Computer, Volume 43, Issue 4, pp. 51-56, April, 2010.

[Laird 2006] L.M. Laird and M.C. Brennan, "Software Measurement and Estimation: A Practical Approach," John Wiley & Sons Publishers, New York, USA, 2006.

[Langella 2011] I.M. Langella and S. Zanoni, "Eco-efficiency in logistics: a case study on distribution network design," In: International Journal of Sustainable Engineering, Volume 4, Issue 2, pp. 115-126, 2011.

[Laudon 2006] K.C. Laudon and J.P. Laudon, "Management Information Systems: Managing the Digital Firm," Prentice Hall Publishers, 9th Edition, Englewood Cliffs, USA, 2006.

[Leavitt 2009] N. Leavitt, "Is Cloud Computing Really Ready for Prime Time?" In: IEEE Computer, Volume 42, Issue 1, pp. 15-20, January, 2009.

[Lee 2007] G. Lee, C. M. Eastman, and R. Sacks, "Product Model schemas: Twelve Design Patterns for Integrating and Normalizing Product Model Schemas," In: Computer-Aided Civil and Infrastructure Engineering, Volume 22, Issue 3, pp. 163-181, 2007.

[Lee 2010] C.A. Lee, "A Perspective on Scientific Cloud Computing," In: Proceedings of the 19th International Symposium on High Performance Distributed Computing (HPDC'10), Chicago, USA, pp. 451-459, June, 2010.

[Leukel 2002] J. Leukel, V. Schmitz, and F.-D. Dorloff, "A modeling Approach for Product Classification Systems," In: Proceedings of the 13th International Workshop on Database and Expert Systems Applications (DEXA'02), Aix en Provence, France, pp. 868-874, September, 2002.

[Li 2007] M. Li and R. Shea, "Studying Business Models for E-Commerce from a Market Perspective," In: Journal of Technology and Business, pp. 151-165, October, 2007.

[Lim 2009] H.C. Lim, S. Babu, J.S. Chase, and S.S. Parekh, "Automated Control in Cloud Computing: Challenges and Opportunities," In: Proceedings of the Automatic Control for Datacenters and Clouds (ACDC'09), Barcelona, Spain, pp. 13-18, June, 2009.

[Litoiu 2010] M. Litoiu, M. Woodside, J. Ng, and G. Iszlai, "A Business Driven Cloud Optimizuation Architecture," In: Proceedings of the 2010 ACM Symposium on Applied Computing (SAC'10), Sierre, Switzerland, pp. 380-385, March, 2010.

[Liu 2001] J. Liu, N. Zhong, Y.Y. Tang, and P.S.P. Wang, "Agent Engineering," World Scientific Publishers, Singapore, 2001.

[Lynch 2002] N. Lynch and S. Gilbert, "Brewer's conjecture and the feasibility of consistent, available, partition-tolerant web services," In: ACM SIGACT News, Volume 33, Issue 2, pp. 51-59, June, 2002.

[Maes 1994] P. Maes, "Agents that Reduce Work and Information Overload," In: Communications of the ACM, Volume 37, Issue 7, pp. 31-40, July, 1994.

[Mankiw 2007] N.G. Mankiw, "Macroeconomics," Worth Publishers, 6th Edition, New York, USA, 2007.

[Mannistö 1998] T. Mannistö, H. Peltonen, A. Martio, and R. Sulonen, "Modeling generic product structures in STEP," In: Computer-Aided Design, Volume 30, Issue 14, pp. 1111-1118, December, 1998.

[Marquis 2011] J.-P. Marquis, "Category Theory", The Stanford Encyclopedia of Philosophy, 2011.

[Marlow 2006] C. Marlow, M. Naaman, D. Boyd, and M. Davis, "HT06, Tagging Paper, Taxonomy, Flickr, Academic Article, To Read," In Proceedings of the 17th Conference on Hypertext and Hypermedia (HYPERTEXT'06), pp. 31-40, New York, USA, 2006.

[Masak 2009] D. Masak, "Digitale Ökosysteme," Springer Publishers, Berlin-Heidelberg, Germany, 2009.

[Mankiw 2011] N.G. Mankiw, "Principles of Macroeconomics," 6th edition, South-Western Publishers, Mason, USA, 2011.

[Marte 2008] B. Marte, C.M. Steiner, J. Heller, and D. Albert, "Activity- and taxonomy-based knowledge representation framework," In: International Journal of Knowledge and Learning, Volume 4, Issue 2-3, pp. 189-202, 2008.

[Mathes 2004] A. Mathes, "Folksonomies - Cooperative Classification and Communication Through Shared Metadata," Technical Report LIS590CMC, University of Illinois, Urbana-Champaign, USA, December, 2004.

[McConnel 2006] S. McConnel, "Software Estimation – Demystifying the Black Art," Microsoft Press, Redmond, USA, 2006.

[McIlroy 1968] M.D. McIlroy, "Mass produced software components," In: In Proceedings of the 1st International Conference on Software Engineering, Garmisch, Germany, pp. 88-98, October, 1968.

[Meager 1973] M.A. Meager, "The Application of Computer Aids to Hospital Building," In: Computer-Aided design, J. Vlietstra and R. F. Wielinga, pp. 424-453, North-

Holland, 1973. In: Proceedings of the IFIP Working conference on Computer-Aided design, Eindhoven, The Netherlands, October, 1972.

[Menasce 2000] D.A. Menasce and V.A.F. Almeida, "Scaling for E-Business – Technologies, Models, Performance and Capacity Planning," Prentice Hall Publishers, Upper Saddle River, USA, 2000.

[Merz 1999] M. Merz, "Elektronische Dienstemärkte: Modelle und Mechanismen des electronic commerce," (English: Electronic Service Markets: Models and Mechanisms of electronic commerce), Springer Publishers, Berlin-Heidelberg, Germany, 1999.

[Milde 2011] C. Milde, "An Assistance System for Product Search and Insertion in Organic Product Catalogues," Diploma Thesis, Otto-von-Guericke University, Magdeburg, Germany, March, 2011.

[Mills 2004] J. Mills, "Faceted Classification and Logical Division in Information Retrieval," In: Library Trends, Volume 52, Issue 3, pp.541-570, March, 2004.

[Mohanty 2005] B.K. Mohanty and B. Bhasker, "Product classification in the Internet business - a fuzzy approach," In: Decision Support Systems, Elsevier, Volume 38, Issue 4, pp. 611-619, January, 2005.

[Monday 2000] P. Monday, J. Carey, and M. Dangler, "SanFrancisco Component Framework: An Introduction," Addison-Wesley, Amsterdam, Netherlands, 2000.

[Muhss 2011] F. Muhss, A. Schmietendorf, and R. Neumann, "Pricing Mechanisms for Cloud Services: Status Quo and Future Models," In: Proceedings of the 4th IEEE/ACM International Conference on Utility and Cloud Computing (UCC'11), Melbourne, Australia, December, 2011.

[Munson 2003] J.C. Munson, "Software Engineering Measurement," CRC Press, Boca Raton, USA, 2003.

[Narasimhan 2011] B. Narasimhan and R. Nichols, "State of Cloud Applications and Platforms: The Cloud Adopters' View," In: IEEE Computer, Volume 44, Issue 3, pp. 24-28, March, 2011.

[Neches 1991] R. Neches and G. Arango, "NSF Workshop on Information Capture and Access in Engineering Design Environments," Working Group Report: Design capture, Cornell University, USA, November, 1991.

[Negri 2006] A. Negri, A. Poggi, M. Tomaiuolo, and P. Turci, "Agents for e-Business Applications," In: Proceedings of the 5th International Joint Conference on Autonomous Agents and Multiagent Systems (AAMAS'06), Hakodate, Japan, pp. 907-913, May, 2006.

[Neumann 2010a] R. Neumann, "The EBF Application Foundation - An Approach towards the Design of an E-Commerce Framework for Small and Medium Enterprises," Lambert Academic Publishers, Saarbrücken, Germany, January, 2010.

[Neumann 2010b] R. Neumann, A. Schmietendorf, and R. Dumke, "Cloud-based Organic Product Catalogs - A Highly Pervasive E-Business Approach for Small and Medium Enterprises," In: Proceedings of The 2010 International Conference on e-Learning, e-Business, Enterprise Information Systems, and e-Government (EEE'10), pp. 123-129, Las Vegas, USA, July, 2010.

[Neumann 2010c] R. Neumann, A. Schmietendorf, and R. Dumke, "Organic Product Catalogs - Towards an Architecture for Cloud-based Micro Enterprise E-Commerce," In: Proceedings of The 3rd International Conference on Cloud Computing (IEEE Cloud'10), pp. 530-531, Miami, USA, July, 2010.

[Neumann 2011a] R. Neumann, E. Göltzer, R. Dumke, and A. Schmietendorf, "Caching Highly Compute-Intensive Cloud Applications: An Approach to Balancing Cost with Performance," In: Proceedings of The Joint Conference of the 21st International Workshop on Software Measurement and the 6th International Conference on Software Process and Product Measurement, pp. 96-105, Nara, Japan, November, 2011.

[Neumann 2011b] R. Neumann, K. Georgieva, A. Schmietendorf, and R. Dumke, "Moving E-Commerce towards E-Commodity: A Consequence of Cloud Computing," In: Proceedings of The 5th International Conference on Digital Society (ICDS'11), pp. 32-38, Gosier, Guadeloupe (French Caribbean), February, 2011.

[Neumann 2011c] R. Neumann, K. Georgieva, A. Schmietendorf, and R. Dumke, "Reverse Commerce: Adding Information System Support for Customer-centric Market Coordination," In: Proceedings of The 5th International Conference on Digital Society (ICDS'11), pp. 24-31, Gosier, Guadeloupe (French Caribbean), February, 2011.

[Neumann 2011d] R. Neumann, M. Baumann, A. Schmietendorf, and R. Dumke, "Managing Semi-formal Product Data in E-Commerce Applications: A Performance Case Study of Relational vs. XML Databases," In: Proceedings of the 27th Annual UK Performance Engineering Workshop (UKPEW'11), pp. 174-182, Bradford, UK, July, 2011.

[Neumann 2012a] R. Neumann, M. Baumann, R. Dumke, and A. Schmietendorf, "Data Partitioning for Massively Scalable Cloud Applications," In L. Chao: Cloud Computing for Teaching and Learning: Strategies for Design and Implementation, pp. 251-268, IGI Global, Pennsylvania, USA, April, 2012.

[Neumann 2012b] R. Neumann, S. Taggeselle, R. Dumke, A. Schmietendorf, F. Muhss, and A. Fiegler, "Combining Query Performance with Data Integrity in the Cloud - A Hybrid Cloud Storage Framework to Enhance Data Access on the Windows Azure Platform," In: Proceedings of the 5th IEEE International Conference on Cloud Computing (Cloud 2012), Honolulu, USA, June, 2012.

[Niles 2001] I. Niles and A. Pease, "Towards a Standard Upper Ontology", In: Proceedings of The International Conference on Formal Ontology in Information Systems (FOIS'01), pp. 2-9, Ogunquit, USA, October, 2001.

[Noh 2009] T.-G. Noh, S.-B. Park, H.-G. Yoon, S.-J. Lee, and S.-Y. Park, "An Automatic Translation of Tags for Multimedia Contents Using Folksonomy Networks," In: Proceedings of the 32nd International ACM Conference on Research and Development in Information Retrieval (SIGIR'09), pp. 492-499, Boston, USA, July, 2009.

[Nwana 1998] H.S. Nwana and D.T. Ndumu, "A Brief Introduction to Software Agent Technology," In: N.R. Jennings and M. Wooldridge (Eds.), "Agent technology: Foundations, Applications, and Markets," pp. 29-47, Springer Publishers, New York, USA, 1998.

[OECD 1997] OECD, "Measuring electronic commerce," Paris, France, 1997. http://www.oecd.org/dataoecd/13/23/2093249.pdf

[Ojala 2011] A. Ojala and P. Tyrväinen, "Developing Cloud Business Models: A Case Study on Cloud Gaming," In: IEEE Software, Volume 28, Issue 4, pp. 42-47, July-August, 2011.

[Olden 2011] E. Olden, "Architecting a Cloud-Scale Identity Fabric," In: IEEE Computer, Volume 44, Issue 3, pp. 44-51, March, 2011.

[Ortiz 2011] S. Ortiz, "The Problem with Cloud-Computing Standardization," In: IEEE Computer, Volume 44, Issue 7, pp. 13-16, July, 2011.

[Owen 2008] M. Owen and J. Raj, "BPMN and Business Process Management Introduction to the New Business Process Modeling Standard," Springer Publishers, Berlin-Heidelberg, Germany, 2008.

[Oxley 1992] J.G. Oxley, "Matroid Theory," Oxford University Press, Oxford, UK, 1992.

[Pandian 2003] C.R. Pandian, "Software Metrics: A Guide to Planning, Analysis, and Application," CRC Press, Boca Raton, USA, 2003.

[Papadopoulos 2001] G.A. Papadopoulos, "Models and Technologies for the Coordination of Internet Agents: A Survey," In: A. Omicini, F. Zambonelli, M. Klusch, and R. Tolksdorf (Eds.), "Coordination of Internet Agents," pp. 25-56, Springer Publishers, Berlin-Heidelberg, Germany, 2001.

[Papazoglou 2008] M.P. Papazoglou, "Web Services: Principles and Technology," Pearson Education Publishers, Harlow, 2008.

[Papazoglou 2011] M.P. Papazoglou, V. Andrikopoulos, and S. Benbernou, "Managing Evolving Services," In: IEEE Software, Volume 28, Issue 3, pp. 49-55, May-June, 2011.

[Parrow 2001] J. Parrow, "The π calculus: An introduction," In: T. Hoare, M. Broy, and R. Steinbrüggen, "Engineering Theories of Software Construction," IOS Press, Amsterdam, Netherlands, 2001.

[Pels 2006] H.J. Pels, "Classification hierarchies for product data modeling", In: Production Planning and Control, Volume 17, Issue 4, pp. 367-377, June, 2006.

[Pfleeger 1998] S.L. Pfleeger, "Software Engineering – Theory and Practice," Prentice Hall Publishers, Englewood Cliffs, USA, 1998.

[Pham 2010] T.V. Pham, H. Jamjoom, and K. Jordan, "A Service Composition Framework for Market-Oriented High Performance Computing Cloud," In: Proceedings of The 19th International Symposium on High Performance Distributed Computing (HPDC'10), Chicago, USA, pp. 284-287, June, 2010.

[Picot 1996] A. Picot, C. Bortenländer, and H. Röhr, "Börsen im Wandel," Knapp Publishers, Frankfurt, Germany, 1996.

[Pokharel 2009] M. Pokharel and J.S. Park, "Cloud Computing: Future Solution for e-Governance," In: Proceedings of the 3rd International Conference on Theory and Practice of Electronic Governance (ICEGOV'09), Bogota, Colombia, pp. 409-410, November, 2009.

[Porter 1998] M.E. Porter, "Competitive Strategy: Techniques for Analyzing Industries and Competitors," The Free Press, 2nd edition, New York, USA, 1998.

[Poulin 1993] J.S. Poulin and K.P. Yglesias, "Experiences with a Faceted Classification Scheme in a Large Reusable Software Library (RSL)," In: Proceedings of The 7th Annual International Computer and Software Applications Conference, pp. 90-99, November, Phoenix, USA, 1993.

[Priebe 2005] T. Priebe, "Building integrative enterprise knowledge portals with Semantic Web technologies," In: M. Lytras and A. Naeve (eds.), "Intelligent Learning Infrastructure for Knowledge Intensive Organizations: A Semantic Web Perspective," pp. 146-188, IGI Global Publishing, Hershey, USA, 2005.

[PWC 2011] PricewaterhouseCoopers Private Limited, "Changing landscape and emerging trends," Indian IT/ITeS Industry Report, February, 2011.

[Rajput 2000] W.E. Rajput, "E-Commerce Systems Architecture and Applications," Artech House Publishers, London, UK, 2000.

[Ranabahu 2011] A. Ranabahu, P. Anderson, and A. Sheth, "The Cloud Agnostic e-Science Analysis Platform," In: IEEE Internet Computing, Volume 15, Issue 6, pp. 85-89, November-December, 2011.

[Randell 1996] B. Randell, "The 1968/69 NATO Software Engineering Reports," In: Dagstuhl-Seminar 9635: History of Software Engineering, Dagstuhl, Germany, August, 1996.

[Ranganathan 2006] S.R. Ranganathan, "Colon Classification 6th Edition," Ess Ess Publications, Delhi, India, April, 2006.

[Reed 2012] D.A. Reed, D.B. Gannon, and J.R. Larus, "Imagine the Future: Thoughts on Computing," In: IEEE Computer, Volume 45, Issue 1, pp. 25-30, January, 2012.

[Rensmann 2007] B. Rensmann, "Mediation Patterns in e³value," In: Workshop on Value Modeling, Tilburg, Netherlands, January, 2007.

[Rochwerger 2011] B. Rochwerger, D. Breitgand, A. Epstein, D. Hadas, I. Loy, K. Nagin, J. Tordsson, C. Ragusa, M. Villari, S. Clayman, E. Levy, A. Maraschini, P. Massonet, H. Muñoz, and G. Tofetti, "Reservoir – When One Cloud Is Not Enough," In: IEEE Computer, Volume 44, Issue 3, pp. 44-51, March, 2011.

[Saaty 2001] T.L. Saaty, "Decision Making for Leaders – The Analytic Hierarchy Process for Decisions in a Complex World," 3rd edition, RWS Publishers, Pittsburgh, USA, 2001.

[Sakautzky 2009] H. Sakautzky, "Development of a Logistics Concept for the E-Commerce Application 'Goliath'," Diploma Thesis, Otto-von-Guericke University, Magdeburg, Germany, December, 2009.

[Samuelson 2005] P.A. Samuelson and W.D. Nordhaus, "Economics," 18th Edition, McGraw-Hill Publishers, New York, USA, 2005.

[Sanchez-Alonso 2006] S. Sanchez-Alonso and E. Garcia-Barriocanal, "Making use of upper ontologies to foster interoperability between SKOS concept schemes," In: Online Information Review, Volume 30, Issue 3, pp. 263-277, May, 2006.

[Sarang 2001] P.G. Sarang, K. Gabhart, A. Tost, T. McAllister, R. Adatia, M. Juric, T. Osborne, F. Arni, J. Lott, V. Nagarajan, C.A. Berry, D. O'Connor, J. Griffin, A. Mulder, and D. Young, "Professional EJB – Enterprise Java Beans," Wiley India, New Delhi, 2001.

[Scharl 2000] A. Scharl, "Evolutionary Web Development," Springer Publishers, London, UK, 2000.

[Schmietendorf 2002a] A. Schmietendorf, E. Dimitrov, and R. Dumke, "Enterprise JavaBeans," MITP Publishers, Bonn, Germany, 2002.

[Schmietendorf 2002b] A. Schmietendorf, E. Dimitrov, J. Lezius, and R. Dumke, "Enterprise Application Integration Maturity, Architecture and Procedures," In: Proceedings of the 13th European Regional ITS Conference, Madrid, Spain, September, 2002.

[Schmietendorf 2007a] A. Schmietendorf, M. Mevius, and R.R. Dumke, "Bewertungsaspekte serviceorientierter Architekturen," (English: Evaluation aspects of service oriented architectures), Shaker Publishers, Aachen, Germany, 2007.

[Schmietendorf 2007b] A. Schmietendorf, "Eine strategische Vorgehensweise zur erfolgreichen Implementierung serviceorientierter Architekturen in großen IT-Organisationen," (Enlgish: A strategic approach to implementing service oriented architectures in large IT Organisations), Shaker Publishers, Aachen, Germany, 2007.

[Schrammel 2009] J. Schrammel, M. Leitner, and M. Tscheligi, "Semantically Structured Tag Clouds: An Empirical Evaluation of Clustered Presentation Approaches," In:

Proceedings of the 27th International Conference on Human Factors in Computing Systems (CHI'09), pp. 2037-2040, Boston, USA, April, 2009.

[Shull 2008] F. Shull, J. Singer, and D.I.K. Sjoberg, "Guide to Advanced Empirical Software Engineering," Springer Publishers, Berlin-Heidelberg, 2008.

[Siebert 1992] H. Siebert, "Einführung in die Volkswirtschaftslehre," Kohlhammer Publishers, Stuttgart, Germany, 1992.

[Silva 2002] F.S.C. da Silva, W.W. Vasconcelos, D.S. Robertson, V.V.B.B. Brilhante, A.C.V.D. Melo, M. Finger, and J. Agustí-Cullell, "On the insufficiency of ontologies: problems in knowledge sharing and alternative solutions," In: Knowledge Based Systems, Volume 15, Issue 3, pp.147-167, March, 2002.

[Skadron 2000] K. Skadron, M. Martonosi, and D.W. Clark, "A Taxonomy of Branch Mispredictions and alloyed Prediction as a Robust Solution to Wrong-History Mispredictions," In: Proceedings of The 2000 International Conference on Parallel Architectures and Compilation Techniques, pp. 199-206, Philadelphia, USA, October, 2000.

[Skyttner 2005] L. Skyttner, "General Systems Theory: Problems, Perspectives, Practice," World Scientific Publishers, 2nd Edition, Hackensack, USA, 2005.

[Slack 2011] N. Slack, R. Johnston, and A. Brandon-Jones, "Essentials of Operations Management with MyOMLab," Financial Times Press Publishers, New York, USA, 2011.

[Smith 1776] A. Smith, "An Inquiry into the Nature and Causes of the Wealth of Nations," March, 1776.

[Sodhi 1999] J. Sodhi and P. Sodhi, "Software Reuse – Domain Analysis and Design Process," McGraw-Hill, New York, USA, 1999.

[Sotomayor 2009] B. Sotomayor, R.S. Montero, I.M. Llorente, and I. Foster, "Virtual Infrastructure Management in Private and Hybrid Clouds," In: IEEE Internet Computing, Volume 13, Issue 5, pp. 14-22, September-October, 2009.

[Spulber 1999] D.F. Spulber, "Market Microstructure: Intermediaries and the Theory of the Firm," Cambridge Press, Cambridge, UK, 1999.

[Svátek 2004] V. Svátek, "Design Patterns for Semantic Web Ontologies: Motivation and Discussion," In: Proceedings of The 7th International Conference on Business Information Systems (BIS'04), pp. 437-446, Poznan, Poland, 2004.

[Taylor 2006] A.G. Taylor, "Introduction to Cataloging and Classification (Library and Information Science Text Series)," 10th Edition, Libraries Unlimited, Santa Barbara, USA, May, 2006.

[Turowski 2001] K. Turowski, "Fachkomponenten - Komponentenbasierte betriebliche Anwendungssysteme," (English: Business Components – Component-based business application systems), Habilitation, Magdeburg, Germany, 2001.

[Turowski 2002] K. Turowski, "Agent-based e-commerce in case of mass customization," In: International Journal of Production Economics, Volume 75, Issues 1–2, pp. 69-81, January, 2002.

[Uckelmann 2011] D. Uckelmann, M. Harrisson, and F. Michahelles, "An Architectural Approach Towards the Future Internet of Things," In: D. Uckelmann, M. Harrisson, and F. Michahelles (eds.), Architecting the Internet of Things, Springer, Berlin, Germany, 2011.

[Uschold 1996] M. Uschold and M. Grüninger, "Ontologies: Principles, Methods, and Applications," In: Knowledge Engineering Review, Volume 11, Issue 2, pp. 93-155, February, 1996.

[Vaquero 2011] L.M. Vaquero, L. Rodero-Merino, and R. Buyya, "Dynamically Scaling Applications in the Cloud," In: ACM SIGCOMM Computer Communication Review, Volume 41, Issue 1, pp. 45-52, January, 2011.

[Varian 1992] H.R. Varian, "Microeconomic Analysis," W. W. Norton Publishers, 3rd edition, New York, USA, 1992.

[Varian 1999] H.R. Varian, "Intermediate Microeconomics: a modern approach," Norton Publishers, 5th edition, New York, USA, 1999.

[Vasan 2011] R. Vasan, "A Venture Perspective on Cloud Computing," In: IEEE Computer, Volume 44, Issue 3, pp. 60-62, March, 2011.

[Vertica 2008] Vertica Systems Inc., "Transforming the economics of data warehousing with cloud computing," In: PC World Journal, White Paper 8143, December, 2008.

[Vogels 2008] W. Vogels, "Eventually Consistent," In: ACM Queue, Volume 6, Issue 6, pp. 14-19, October, 2008.

[Vollmann 2005] T. Vollmann, F.R. Jacobs, W.L. Berry, and D.C. Whybark, "Manufacturing Planning and Control for Supply Chain Management," McGraw Hill Publishers, New York, USA, 2005.

[Volz 2003] R. Volz, D. Oberle, and R. Studer, "Views for light-weight web ontologies," In: Proceedings of The 2003 ACM Symposium on Applied Computing (SAC'03), pp. 1168-1173, Melbourne, USA, March, 2003.

[Walker 2010] E. Walker, W. Brisken, and J. Romney, "To Lease or not to Lease From Storage Clouds," In: IEEE Computer, Volume 43, Issue 4, pp. 44-50, April, 2010.

[Walters 1991] R.F. Walters, "Categories and Computer Science," Cambridge University Press, New York, USA, 1991.

[Wang 2004] X.H. Wang, D.Q. Zhang, T. Gu, and H.K. Pung, "Ontology based Context Modeling and Reasoning using OWL," In: Proceedings of The Second IEEE Annual Conference on Pervasive Computing and Communications Workshop (PERCOM'04), pp. 18-22, Orlando, USA, March, 2004.

[Wei 2010] Y. Wei and M.B. Blake, "Service-Oriented Computing and Cloud Computing – Challenges and Opportunities," In: IEEE Internet Computing, Volume 14, Issue 6, pp. 72-75, November-December, 2010.

[Wetzker 2010] R. Wetzker, C. Zimmermann, C. Bauckhage, and S. Albayrak, "I Tag, You Tag: Translating Tags for Advanced User Models," In: Proceedings of the 3rd ACM International Conference on Web Search and Data Mining (WSDM'10), pp. 71-80, New York, USA, February, 2010.

[Whitmire 1997] S.A. Whitmire, "Object Oriented Design Measurement," John Wiley & Sons Publishers, New York, USA, 1997.

[Wille 2005] C. Wille, "Software Agent Measurement Framework," Shaker Publishers, Aachen, Germany, 2005.

[Wohlin 2000] C. Wohlin, P. Runeson, M. Höst, M. Ohlsson, B. Regnell, and A. Wesslén, "Experimentation in Software Engineering: An Introduction," Kluwer Academic Publishers, Boston, USA, 2000.

[Xing 2008] D. Xing, G.-R. X, Q. Yang, and Y. Yu, "Deep Classifier: Automatically Categorizing Search Results into Large-Scale Hierarchies," In: Proceedings of The International Conference on Web Search and Web Data Mining (WSDM'08), pp. 139-148, Palo Alto, USA, February, 2008.

[Xiong-Yi 2009] L. Xiong-Yi, "Research and Application of SOA in B2B Electronic Commerce," In: Proceedings of the International Conference on Computer Technology and Development, Kota Kinabalu, Malaysia, pp. 649-653, November, 2009.

[Yau 2011] S.S. Yau and H.G. An, "Software Engineering Meets Service and Cloud Computing," In: IEEE Computer, Volume 44, Issue 10, pp. 47-53, October, 2011.

[Yeo 2011] S. Yeo and H.-H.S. Lee, "Using Mathematical Modeling in Provisioning a Heterogeneous Cloud Computing Environment," In: IEEE Computer, Volume 44, Issue 8, pp. 55-62, August, 2011.

[Ziegler 2004] C.-N. Ziegler, G. Lausen, and L. Schmidt-Thieme, "Taxonomy driven Computation of Product Recommendations," In: Proceedings of the 2004 ACM International Conference on Information and Knowledge Management (CIKM'04), pp. 406-415, Washington D.C., USA, November, 2004.

[Zimmermann 2003] O. Zimmermann, M. Tomlinson, and S. Peuser, "Perspectives on Web Services – Applying SOAP, WSDL and UDDI to Real-World Projects," Springer Publishers, Berlin-Heidelberg, 2003.

[Zuse 1998] H. Zuse, "A Framework of Software Measurement," De Gruyter Publishers, Berlin, Germany, 1998.